MEMORY

Bernadette Mayer

NORTH ATLANTIC BOOKS

Memory

ISBN 0-913028-39-8

Publisher's Address:

North Atlantic Books
Route 2, Box 135
Creamery Road
Plainfield, Vermont 05667

Principal Distributor:

Book People
2940 Seventh Street
Berkeley, California 94710

Covers:
Front: the kitchen sink with my white pants in it; the Taconic
       Parkway; my self.
Center: the World Trade Center; Ridgewood.
Back: Ed, Kathleen, Tom.

Thanks to Holly Soloman

This project is partially supported by a grant from the National
Endowment for the Arts in Washington, D.C., a Federal agency.

This text was set in Aldine Roman, an adaptation of the typeface
designed for Aldus Manutius in the 15th Century. Composed on
the IBM Composer by Typographics, Plainfield, Vermont.

Introduction

This work is a new kind of autobiography. Adults do not normally remember that way in which they experienced as children. They remember events and incidents but they cannot recapture past ways of functioning and modes of experiencing. In the adults remembrances are brought into consciousness in a changed form. The past is represented in terms of present day ego structure, defenses, interests, needs and moral values.

In MEMORY, Bernadette Mayer not only provides us with data from the past, recent and remote, but she has somehow found the means to recreate archaic modes of representation of inner and outer sensory data, by reviving the quality of consciousness in which they occurred. Chronological ordering is replaced by shifts of consciousness, daytime logic by primary mechanism, and verbal thought by pictorial imagery.

With her opening line she puts us on notice that her "memory" is regulated by a constantly changing organization of consciousness, shifting from perceived external reality to internal images and from present to past as present. Various balances are struck between internal and external reality. In these altered states of consciousness internal stimuli are experienced as external reality, as in a dream. In such states, differentiation between internal and external perception, that is, between sensation, thought and feelings on the one hand, and perception of external reality on the other, is not fixed and rigid, but fluid and dynamic. Even fragmentary revival of such ancient ways of functioning usually requires either the deliberate alteration of consciousness as in hypnotic age regression, or spontaneously in dreams.

Bernadette Mayer has accomplished a much more impressive restoration in a waking state. How? Here is where my understanding fails. I know what she has done, but the "how" is the forever mystery of creative talent. Her writing is sensory prose poetry with immense evocative power. If the reader is able to suspend his usual waking daytime logic he will have a unique and stirring experience, and perhaps discover something important about himself.

If Bernadette Mayer has any progenitors they are most probably Proust and Joyce. But she is no mere epigone. Her writing is so original that it seems very much like her own invention. But I had better stop here since I realize suddenly that I am so envious that I am struggling with strongly competitive urges.

David Rubinfine, M.D.

July 1

& the main thing is we begin with a white sink a whole new language
is a temptation. Men on the wall in postures please take your foot
by your hand & think that this is pictures, picture book & letters to
everyone dash you tell what the story is once once when they were
nearly ready thursday july first was a thursday: back windows across
street I'm in sun out image windows & so on riverdale, did you know
that, concentrated dash was all there was mind nothing sink . . . with
my white pants in it. I dont remember this dont remember thinking
one on one white & whiter the word pictures, sing on the wall in
pictures did you get it right thought: yellow slat on the left side
where are you? first on the roll comes first but what is growing back-
wards, motion growing backwards rocking back & forth or still one
in a chair one lies in bed the tv is on out of boredom nothing soaking
the clothes were still in the sink from the night before water & soap
in the morning it's blue around & out the back windows of the blue
room there's light of course light & the number six waking up with
us crooked . . . under the windows other end under the street i look
at myself in the mirror a painter in the side window that brings in
the before noon light it was before that & so was i remembering what
was somebody saying, tea, that this person was old could be a hun-
dred years old that i could be a hundred years old my hair's back
chin on knee, see, you drop a hair on the floor a long one it'll be
there a long time floor as big as this we dont clean it too often like
the parking lot near west broadway you crack walnuts one by one
the one by the fire pump it was a hot day feel those people out, we
are an image speed we are an image sound & by now i think it's
speed sound by subway punched in the breast a drug bust ed dials
the phone:

1. Ed.

he leans against the machine a fortune in tom's shirt he isnt talking
he leans against the machine a fortune in t's shirt
wasnt anyone home some song sing being sun we are reminding you:
he isnt talking wasnt anyone home some song sing being sun
we are now in an image, sound, his hair was pulled back mind too
they're sons we are reminding you
but now he leans against the machine, reels, & while it's on i've turned
we are now in an image sound his hair was
off the light a powerful light that was on it's off & outside

pulled back
they've turned the people working have turned the saw drill scooper off
mine too but now he leans against the machine
& it's lights off & ed rests in bed but i'm already dressed in a rubber
reels & while it's on i've turned off the light a powerful light
coat waiting to go out to the bookstore & now their machine is a drill
that was on is off & outside they've turned the people working
it starts up again to drive down. heroine-strychnine. will our teeth
into rest
start to hurt & rear window in the rain did i hear it : hurricane
have turned the saw drill or scooper off & it's
Erica Attica state prison & demands free
lights off ed rests in bed but i'm already dressed in a
image in the window sound reels half. there's a bag with a
rubber coat waiting to go out to the bookstore & now their
container of coffee we drank it. i was sitting on my legs making phone
machine a drill starts up again to drive down
calls someone patted my head with shining eyes with eyes was working
        in
downtown heroine & strychnine will our teeth start
a room with a piano, in & out the door, i went to two record stores
to hurt & rear window in the rain did i hear it:
to get . . . we looked through catalogues of sounds i dont know but
        there
hurricane Erica Attica state prison & demands free
were always alot of papers around if i had started coming over there
image in & out the window sound reels half
all the time i would have flunked out of school, why didnt he?
there's a bag with a container of coffee
for paper full of sounds on record, the index file with a girl
we drank it. i was sitting on my legs making calls
on a beach in color on it the calendar behind it big breasts plugged in
someone pats you on the head with shining eyes with eyes
what view i've also seen from eddie's window two e.b.'s
was working in a room with a piano, in & out the door
he was here tonight you can always tell the time, the view was
I went to two record stores to get
coronet vsq brandy & yellow yellow taxis down broadway, myself as
we looked through catalogues of sounds but there

a whore, the circus theater climax i was bored that day listening to
were always alot of papers lying around working being done
sounds, i was looking at our notebook more lists of sounds a bakery
if i had started coming over there all the time i would
a restaurant a bar a plane taking off cars going by the 20th century
have flunked out of school
fox fanfare many songs & musics a sign saying vertically howard
and on for papers full of sounds on record
that view again higher it looked threatening like rain & clock
the index file with a girl on a beach in color on it
reads 12:10 we were up early we did the light on me was morning
    light
calendar behind it big breasts plugged in
where i look old saying vertically sony this is the part of
what view i've also seen from eddie's window two e.b.'s
sky that cleared first blue an earlier blue a blue under people
he was here tonight you can tell the time, the view was
under people across crossing the street we were in a car we had
corn yellow taxis taxi down broadway myself as a whore of some
met a guy that lives in vito's building we had talked about sounds
nationality the circus theater
hitched a ride from a guy from colorado or wyoming figured he
    couldn't
climax
refuse us down fifth avenue under blue no turns n.y. public library
i was bored sounds a bakery a restaurant a bar
want to go in no because the story goes
a plane taking off cars going by by the 20th century fox
tom met us at image tom & i went to hers to pick up
fantasy fanfare many songs 7 musics a sign says vertically howard
dope for the trip we had picked up money from his cashed it
that view again
at a first nation city skunks and, had alot of cash on us, hitched
& higher it's threatening like rain & clock reads
ride to the right street in colorado i had a camera we stopped for
12:10 we were up early we did the light on me was morning light
ice yellow & green ice the sun in the sun melting & smelting together
where i look older saying vertically sign sony
money melting in our pockets bought an ounce of grass for forty

dollars
this is the part of the sky that cleared first blue
got two tabs of sunshine then we still have them frozen later
an earlier blue a blue under people under people across crossing
his check bounced but ours didnt that is till much later but not that
    one
the street saying horizontally we are in a car we are
the image sound went out on the streets a completely blue face
moving we had met a guy we meet him he lives in v's bldg.
continuing on he was living in the country where we . . .
we talk about sounds hitch a ride from colorado or
on some corner on another corner i mailed the letter we went
wyoming figure he cant refuse us down fifth under blue no turns
back & skipping all the dishes we're in riverdale looking out the window
ny public library lions want to go in no because the
at two red cars with black tops was tom still with us no change that
story goes
to t. how did we get there?
tom met us at image we went to hers to pick up
out all the windows we go wishing we could go out the windows
dope for the trip we had money a check cash it at a first nation
i explained, wonder under are are looking the whole story stop
city skunk it's back it's cash
a third red car passes under next to 2 red black-tops we eat
hitch to the right hitch to the left of colorado on
& grey rain windows in the same place placed in the same
some map i have a camera we stop for ice yellow & green ice
where we had working & moving we had lived here ed had all
in the sun melting & smelting together the money melting
his left almost later we worked on windows i thought of stan brakhage
in our pockets buy an ounce of grass for forty dollars get
never had a baby here was pregnant in this room
two icy tabs of sunshine freeze them
back windows threatening but rain makes green or under brings
later one check bounced but the other didnt
a shady window & tom at the stove nikita kruschev dies
the image sound went out on the streets
elisha cook jr
a completely blue face continuing on he was living in the

i thought he had died how many times have you died in films
country where we
in humphrey bogart's suit?
on some corner on another corner i mail the letters we go
we think that t begrudges us fixes us cheeseburgers with a top
back & skipping all the dishes we're in riverdale north
on the pan his method we hasnt come to dinner i ate leftover chicken
looking diagonally out across the window opening at two
with gravy & a tomato with a saltshaker, t in the yellow curtain light
red cars with black tops
turns violet where does it come from i was resting on the top of the
out all the windows let me explain wonder under are are looking
refrigerator & white white hospital light on ed white rows of light
the whole story a 3rd red car passes under next to
rain makes green to purple come fluorescence i guess in the kitchen at
2 red black-tops we eat dinner
least ed was watching tv
& grey rain windows in the same place placed in the same
inside the refrigerators lots of soda beer & invisible violet
we had worked on moving here & windows back out the back is
food more food hot & damp tracing my steps through the house
threatening but rain makes green or brings it under
looking around the hallway focus on dark chair & telephone table
& a shady window with tom at the stove violet
clear yellow light of the white door what looks so square in design
nikita kruschev dies elisha cook jr says how many times
is everyone working involved no relation to anyone else's
he had died in humphrey bogart's suit
idea of projection image sound had come up with us a yellow & blue
      that
we think that t. fixes cheeseburgers with a top
isnt there & two paler blues, it got darker night thunderstorms with
on the pan his method is careful we hadnt come for dinner
parents are swell they bring back old times when protected life fell
i eat chicken & a tomato with saltshaker, t in the yellow curtain
evenly over us at night if a thunderstorm ever breaks out again
light turns violet where does it come from i am resting on
(atomic bombs) someone's parents be there
the top of the refrigerator light & white white hospital on ed white rows

there's a new apartment across the way blocking view with only
of light rain makes green to purple
one light on i had guesses people meeting an encounter group the
    blinds
what comes out of fluorescence i guess in the kitchen
are up i sit up someone hunches his shoulders someone is erect
at least ed was watching tv
did you ever play football me? it was tennis someone reaches forward
my cousin jane liked turquoise i hated jane things
& out extends arms for soda a glass on the table a scotch grant's
exactly as they are sure she would say when she was ten
scotch, someone is leaning forward we go downtown on the west side
i fall asleep as soon as my head hits the pillow her mother
highway we are slightly over green lights are blue red whites out
said the same thing birth control
rain majorska we get closer red stripes & i missed the moment of
he played the piano by ear i felt thick a long distance
red stripes at the moment of the flashing yellow signal's out
stayed away in
18th st. or canal east on grand st. travels coming brighter over
haze suns toward little italy rudolf bass reads
brighter than it is red green & violet sky coffee shop coca cola
grand & broadway flooded with rain or turquoise light
green light red light out the back was smoke rising or cars
passing or numbers letters lathes on scoops drill down
my cousin jane liked turquoise I hated jane things exactly as they
are she would say when she was ten i fall asleep as soon as
machines in front of lathes official lathes you have it printed
on glass DBH 14 scoop & a hole it makes in the ground
my head hits the pillow her mother said the same thing they practiced
birth control played the piano by ear i felt thick a long distance
they've taken the pipes away & chain saw
same construction crew they're on the outside now
away
haze suns toward little italy rudolf bass reads green light red light
they're gone tortured street & all its friends weeks & i'm
the agent up in a normal room pretending 2 b a normal person
out the back was smoke rising or cars passing or numbers letters
lathes on scoops drill down machines in front of lathes official

i spend my time looking at projections of weeks ago
on the wall what was downstairs were they the same which are the
lathes you have it printed on glass DBH 14 scoop & a hole in the
    ground
they've just taken the pipes away and chain saw
ones are the ones on the wall the same ones is the wall moving
are the cracks moving is the earth rising is the tidal
same construction crew they're outside now they're gone
tortured street & all its friends weeks & i'm the FBI agent up in a
    normal
wave coming or just an earthquake rising of violence coming right
in my door what is an edge
room pretending 2 b a normal person spending my time looking at
projections of weeks ago, what was downstairs, were they the same
they've found me out i'm in here i've exploded some
ed is on the fire escape looking down same ones
which are the ones are they the ones on the wall is the wall moving
are the cracks moving is the earth rising is the tidal wave coming or
same machines as before you start it all over this has happened before
list the years
just an earthquake of violence coming right in my door they've found
    me
out i've exploded some bomb or other
a whole you won a whole a continuous river running down the
street garbage & smells on the wheel of the tire flowing
ed is on the fire escape looking down, same ones same machines
you start it all over this has happened before list the years
pretty picture of memory noise technicolor sometimes memory
is noise just parallel to canal & we know it's the telephone
a whole, you won, a whole, a continuous river running down
the street garbage & smells on the wheel of the tire flowing
people a hundred fifty seven dollars worth though someone owes
us a turn around the street & down & across the street the buildings
(pretty picture of memory) noise, technicolor, sometimes memory is
just noise, parallel to canal & we know its the telephone people
flood in the rain incidentally how long is my assignment here
& the lights flicker on & off in both bldgs ours & theirs
a hundred fifty seven dollars though havent heard from the one
who owes us a turn around the street & down & across the street the

thunderstorms are parents including the first floor
you couldnt live there the plumbing's bad all brass pipes & brass
buildings flood when it rains incidentally how long is my assignment
    here
& the lights flicker on & off in both buildings ours & theirs
containers cooking pots for the stew always eat the
same thing with canned peas & carrots you became anemic thinking
    about
& thunderstorms are parents including the first floor you couldnt live
there the plumbing's bad all brass pipes & brass containers cooking pots
revolution come you went to the hospital are they fixing it
july too just any part of
no it's the phone co. resit residential they say or hurricane
one & two
flooding new jersey highways subways hurricanes in nova scotia
they say no to everything anything goes on on between two or between
say seventy foot waves in the bay of fundy according
nuns in habits make obsessions rage strange color wheel
to someone's father who likes geography & really likes rain
do you reach me
Fern in new york where are we no one can avoid distractions
i love you you are deer we dont hear images from you anymore
what else can you remember nothing something else
parents, come to the hurricane, it's on the first floor
wheel color color wheel i ate colors in a dream what do
bavaria & had to leave town was that us was that all
you say anymore to someone who's a person i'll wheel colors
tell me what you remember about the man who shot a deer in
you like to your new location if you'll tell me what
i'll wheel the colors you like to your new location if you'll
you know about the man who shot a deer in bavaria & had to
dream should i say anymore to someone who's a person
leave town was that was that us was that all
wheel color color wheel i ate colors in a dream what do you
parents, come to the hurricane, it's on the first floor
can you remember nothing something else
i love you you are deer we dont hear images from you
Fern in new york where are we no one can avoid distractions what else
anymore do you reach me

14

father who teaches geography & really likes rain
nuns in habits make obsessions strange color wheel
seventy foot waves in the bay of fundy according to someone's
they say no, to everything anything goes on on between two
flooding new jersey highways subways hurricanes in nova scotia
or between one & two
this month too just any part of

July 2
Lights. Lights all electric electric machines. This is an excuse. This
is a prescription. The f/stop is the ratio between the length of the
lens to the diameter of the opening it has less to do with you than
with light. No dreams. Typewriter tensor light slide projector tape
recorder holly in an electric red dress under electric light library
light electric coffee cups from china, we sense the presence of some-
thing from china real ice july too do you do you know what i mean
new ribbons roll into the library on ice to pick up film, daze fantasy
patron with one roll shot, i put one in from the bag of film & shoot
& still the ribbon with the hole in it talking to everything: will this
be something: earlier later top bottom in out gertrude stein & emily
dickinson on the stamp on heroin, ed working & going to toronto
tomorrow, something to put together & more memory into a
schedule of light: am i crazy & dont i want to fuck & manic's fucking
everybody, putting together the past of so much information the
same thing isnt it in numbers. Holly & portrait under electric light,
smoke on a dime: strike anywhere go to the theater we did, hair
still in knots since i was out of the state, street loft night lights i
put the two together & came out with, just more: i aimed at the
center of the bag & hit the rim none of that combs necessary: i
picked up the film & drove down second ave late for ann point out.
That's practical, parents, does it come with ego (parents) she would
never leave me alone, ashes spill: whistling outside it's saturday night
ed's gone out energy out of the room i'm misplaced. Letters to
everyone: H her maid calls her solomon & two of aquarius, larry
posing in a pink undershirt with breasts without them before a
garbage can & trees church brick iron & cobblestones graveyard ann
larry joan looking like me & ann is me, breasts larry arms up doesnt
have his breasts anymore, hair. We loaded up the car with worlds &

drove away. Ran out of gas. I ran over to 1st ave looking for a station,
it seems to me later this day we drove to massachusetts or some other
place, riverdale, I am sitting in the car saying to ed remind me to look
up the cab driver in the queens phone book: i had written his address
on the brown paper bag of film in the back of the car: no by this
time it was in my leather bag, stuffed in because I thought the breeze
of my running to look for gas would keep the film cool: the cab
driver trying to pick me up wouldnt take me for free finally: well
try to sit very close to me the hot seat & so that the meter wont
turn on well it didnt work, I told him everything I could fit into the
seat in the time we were together we had been drinking coffee. With
holly with ann to a station, gas can, he waited & took me back 47th
between park & lex, do you know where you are 57th between park
& lex I took the subway to work & hurrying they're waiting at the
barricade, lazy flesh, later anne took a shower we exchange identities
again, read each other book write talk look alike someone famous
said so. Jasper Johns his spoon the sonnets $8.50 a ruler, later 0 TO
9 early, late day, food. I think i am thinking the opportunity shop
is on 47th street under the gotham yes 47th street you tell them
you're making a delivery with commercial plates, I tried that later
they said mirrors, commercial plates fronts backs of cars which cars
should I go up to the theater to meet ed where is he now still parked
still on 47th street, how many times resting is the sky on 47th street
waiting always threatening & that one tall building on the right
bending over into the frame, we've stopped for that one we've
stopped for a light we've stopped for a storm i'm going to call ed &
go up to the theater i need glasses & the bel capri food company &
ice & red light one way construction a strange & stranger light comes
crashunging through the sky in beams in new york clouds make up
these dramas above bldgs nothing else. numbers. nos. At 6th ave
near the west 4th street subway stop guys come by with pocketbooks
tough guys shoe shine boy in front of the glass bank in sneakers a
red foot rest & one man in shorts lying on the ground feet towards
me shoes not shined write a mystery: anne's in the 5 & 10 getting
glue comes out with a big straw bag too big to pay for I look around
& motor on off the sun on the chrome of the bank disappears as-
suming anne talks to the guy in the phoenix & someone comes in to
autograph their part their part in a picture already filled with names
one is di prima, collection, the boys, michael mcclure is on the wall

so someone comes in a tall skinny guy, it was her & somebody &
him, he was looking for a thin yellow volume on cornelia street heres
the light on someone's federal savings & it's warm in here nine a's
nina's mother drank stout & went to afghanistan, that light on the
savings: gradually this strip a strip the color of old tarnished silver,
gradually it narrowed & seemed to recede, then it was converted
into an object that glistened like steel no bank, cheeseburgers &
coffee in the riviera a girl passes by we meet frances on the street, i
knew we would meet here converging irresistible, i'm on my way
home no we are: julie called to bring ed to work the sound church
bells tolled on the television pat pissed off, phone. I called the
theater the moviola's broken ed said not to bother to come up but
i didnt even talk to him talked to chris & john chris didnt show up
last night to shoot the new movie because he cant go on with it &
on west broadway in the late afternoon there's the truck full of
pieces of material packed in cardboard truck that always crosses the
street standing there on friday afternoon taking up most of the
whole street so that cars have to go around one way cause the street
goes two ways like going around driving crazy in the other lane &
they do it fast just in case. We went home to do the proofs down
on grand street under. I have, when I was about two or three years
old I was taught the words of a hebrew prayer. I didnt understand
them & what happened was that the words settled in my mind as
puffs of steam or splashes . . . even now I see these puffs or splashes
when I hear certain sounds: I was looking out the window around
at things anne took a shower lay down on the bed & made a phone
call the sky looked like this: profiles anne on the bed holding up a
piece of white paper the phone in her other hand, we worked, read
through the book aloud violet revolution & all all in hoarse men's
voices fast I massaged anne's neck. We decide to go to the movies,
ed tells us we may have a room in a sound studio in massachusetts
the next day we find out it's political, we are on contract, will take
the book to the printers ourselves, we drop off anne at prince street
& drive up 1st ave to see carnal knowledge ed took this, we waited
on a line to see it, we blended in to see it, when we saw how red the
screen of the theater was, when we saw how red ann-margret was, it
was worth it for ann-margret & a bank on lexington or park, we
must've passed union square & driving down bway where at the
time there were some extraordinary steam type construction sites,

caverns, men at work, steam behind, in front of lights turns green & tracks all around in the middle of the forest we light the interiors with generators we light the forest with generators, and to set it straight if everybody thinks life is shit but me then isnt this writing shit & old, gulliver's travels, lord jim, the secret sharer heart of darkness marble faun scarlet letter moby dick vanity fair old man & the sea sun also rises great gatsby the red pony daisy miller puddnhead wilson spiller: I am happy for the occasion to send a note your way, always pleasant memories are attached to your name, we heard here that sister irmengard was anointed is it true? sister m felician must be worried, tell her that her friends here are praying for her & sister irmengard, please direct this big news to your school paper & if possible send me the copy that carries it may god reward you, happy lent: when tom would not speak to her she finally told him of his identity. This is another example of her pride. When she learned of tom's method of repaying his debts, she condoned the thefts & even helped him for which he sold her down the river, this, in her opinion, was the worst possible fate to which anyone could be doomed. Yet when she escaped to st.louis she forgave tom easily, everything was put aside for him even to the extent of murder quotes: the experience of each new age requires a new confusion & the world seems always waiting to be waiting for its poet. A spill ed's back & joe colombo had been shot long before this, still hanging on, we went to the luna for dinner at about 3 am, we chose carnal knowledge over insects we wanted to see people in a movie, ann-margret 9 annes eat luna 1st time see moon in month fear murder roaming rampaging gangs of black men coming to kill the italian men but we had dinner anyway next: blacks in little italy a little sunny, food: after coffee that again iced, cheeseburger & leaf (2), kathleens rivers (naive) cheese pear beer burnt bread (luna: bread water wine priests of nyu having a discussion & crazy people horrible sarcasm of veal with peppers lasagna (lights) asparagus (iron) & thank you very much) i thought this was one of the days we recorded sound all day ed was exhausted in tom's green & white striped shirt. In front of the city where the silver moon always shines & someone's always up, like the late show replaced by stars coming in thru your window, do they want us to stay up volunteer or get jobs, which is it, deserted streets exhaustion food & to finish last night one movie one more movie for the play ending up with a shot of scotch & breakfast & two cups coffee

& drilling awake till 8 am thinking of crystal clear, what pill should
i take we get home two fluorescent lights are on & the door opens
to a yellow house with books a light my painting joe's piece ed's
picture: down the street green, up the street flags & eduardo a whole
floor lit where the man, nevermind, i need boxes, & thank the simple
art of murder: gas + can: $2.65 + 45c = $3.10 & a neat nozzle for
someone's dream: something that happened changed the lives of 10
people, a day you're not sure of there's no space for you:

July 3
So why dont you come over every saturday, why dont you teach us
every monday: more than 30 years have passed since that moment
when is anything permanently forgotten photograph: monday-a
window of a factory, tuesday-a small white handkerchief with 'a
merry christmas' embroidered in red across one corner, wednesday-
a man's black striped pants, thursday-a light brown earthenware jar,
friday-an earthenware jar like thursday but darker in color, saturday-
a saucer with a pattern of brown & gold squares round the edge,
sunday-a metal cream pitcher. No I know we didnt know yet no &
new: or: monday to friday-he described the fall of his native-at the
hands of the-after a ten year seige telling how the armed-had entered
the city in the belly of a great wooden horse & how the-had fled
from their burning city among them-& his father-& young-not long
afterward-had advised setting sail for distant lands blown by varying
winds we quickly-the next day-again on the shores-finally they
reached-again the-a hero-in a dream he-when-warned in a dream-
decreed that the body-led his band-of the-world & the question was
how to tell you in a way you'd remember: we still didnt know when
we were going to massachusetts, i think jacques & kathleen had left
already, yesterday with anne holly carnal knowledge & the day be-
fore collecting sound effects, so we got up early i think & went
straight to grand union with the nagra, the door just banged so i
locked it there was nobody there, ed put the nagra in a shopping
cart put on his earphones & went to work. there was no musak in
grand union because it was a holiday the day before fourth of july,
everybody in the city had gone away with the sounds & the store
was empty, cash registers sounded great & they were having a red
tag cookie sale, the door banged again, there were people buying

only a few things at the store, all the people in the store that day were buying only a few things, another thing, grand union used to sell cigarettes but now they've got a machine from joe colombo, what if i locked the door, then somebody came in thru the window, then when i rushed out the door, there was the original somebody standing there waiting, somebody's coming in's not that bad, grand union is right a cross the street from j&k's, i took a picture of the guys standing out in front of the drome social club on the first floor where j plays poker when he's in town, now the club's a bakery, we drive uptown to find a good department store, stop at macys & gimbels, no good. I thought a fire pump next to a coke bottle looked good but the coke was in shade. I saw alot of weird people hanging around 6th ave & 34th street on that holiday weekend paralyzed parked waiting for ed to get the sound out of the department store. Usually I wait for yellow cabs to pass by, one of them stopped & somebody got out. They catch the sun. Imagine spending the day on your bicycle, I was parked in front of a discount drug store sell- ing something called nodor or hodor no it was a furniture store a rip-off place but they had a 34 piece junior dinette. So I pulled up around the corner so ed could go to another store & a hot dog man was doing a big business & there was a sun tan ad that caught my eye: tan hawaiian. ed went into korvettes or sonic arts i think steel buildings catch the sun like taxi cabs. We parked on a downtown street to stop another store maybe 5th ave this time I cant remember, no, we were just around the corner on 7th near pennsylvania station & i was looking at windows again. no luck. just drifters so we went uptown to bloomingdale's to check that place out & record some street noise there it was a really clear day but there wasnt enough traffic to make the noise level boom & bloomingdale's noise was fine except they didnt have & neither did any of the other stores, they didnt have those bells you remember hearing, the bells called floorbells ringing like the bell at the end of the line but more reso- nant, so we stopped where we were at 3rd & 60th for quite some time recording cars passing with a long boom sometime goes by in car, some guy thinks our booms a geiger counter & we're at niagara falls waiting for the traffic to build up at the lights there's a big schlitz ad, it reads reach for the gusto in life & all the familiar pan- cake buildings, i wonder how carol that fainted is she was nervous when i saw her & what the fuck somebody starts playing the drums so loud across the street it sounds like trashing & i see more people on bicycles & while i'm looking ed's answering questions about his machine, is it a three or a four, this guy really knows what he's talking about, it aint no geiger counter, the nagra is made in switzerland, yes, so we did all we could with department stores & traffic & then we went to daly's & daly's aint there anymore either to record some bar noise but they serve too much food & it's always crowded, turned out we couldn't use their noise at all cause you could hear the sound of frying in the background & the tv was on i think but we had a good beer & so & then went to a horn & hardart's lunch counter to see if we could get good restaurant noise musak & all, now this horn & hardart's noise turned out pretty well except, again, for the intermittent frying & sizzle noise but the musak was great & so was the clinking & I had iced coffee & ed had a coke & we shared a grilled cheese or maybe I ate the cheese sandwich & ed had a piece of pie. Anyway they treated us pretty well in there & didn't complain about the tape recorder & there were alot of people eating dinner, a sort of dinner, including one priest who sat right down next to us, he aint afraid of no geiger counter & these people eating dinner again looked like the people in the market & seemed to me they must have had a regular schedule to live on which in-cluded dinner at horn & hardart's a place with an old reputation every day or at least every saturday or at least every July 3 & after that we came home & I went up on the roof to take some pictures. It was still a clear day. I took six or eight pictures looking out in every possible direction from the roof where the moon was already up, just a sliver still or approaching half & i didnt change exposures except when i shot directly at the sun & when i shot my own shadow. The house was a mess of machines that day tapes & cords lying all over doing nothing, we had been working so we cleaned up a little & ed used vito's tape recorder, the one he left there, v in toronto i think, to listen to the tapes we had gotten. I asked ed to take a pic-ture of me from the back by the fluorescent light & i looked at the light itself which always comes out green on film & ed's desk, we had just set it up & tore down some shelves so he could have that corner, the desk was covered with tapes & lists of sounds, catalogs of equipment, tape cleaner & de-gauzer, if i'm remembering it right a de-gauzer is a machine that de-magnetizes tape so you can re-record on it clean. We did the dishes too. I think we had been drinking alot of espresso around that time, alot of coffee of all kinds. I looked at all the lights in the room & the lights across the street, you can see them from the fire escape, they're always on twenty-four hours a day: impossible to take make pictures of this scene's not dull of white it down, we are recording sound listen supermarket department store bells no bells we move to a different turn spot tune gimbels to corn at macys looking 4 bells this is a girl who must take make pictures, she, not postpone, smoothly into focus comes foods notes sounds taken in the car taken while every one & every thing goes on moving in some experiment with isolation, is that what it is. Look around new spot small shirt white pants i'm inside not outside & cars & stares, to record, machines? stare? notes? stare? you? stare? where was i at that point - W34THST&7THAVE park double park park expose, goes on click, man in shades turns around he's a convict, joe colombo, go about observing & checking with a set of rules a certain set of rules in marked cars & uniforms the cops are too obvious in their observation & they these scraps are out of a need, this stuff is out of a need, i need a book two books, one for ed that's three, where are you a room & cereal - W35THST&7THAVE. Observation honk observation bleep there's always more there, traffic unit B unit B goes away, as long as I dont set up a 2546621 tripod on the streets they wont arrest me & I am the one taking notes mr. man & cars, a new yellow scrap, line the street. Colors & colors they're yellow blue brick grey white green pink words taxi lights my things tag $2.19 people radio balloon baby chair bright blue car l'escargot the chimes the boardwalk 3rd ave el baronet & coronet king movies can move backwards diamond ice cubes co. maneuvering not able to maneuver true sea & ski & rheingold beer the woman drive defensively from the canadian rockies up on the roof violins horn & hardarts black white up down shoes clothes rear view mirror love a guy gets out of his car, looks around a kid gets out he gets back in he parked in the middle of the street, flashers, all the way to texas if you want, stirring up dust, if any. Light blue delivery truck slams the door woman in yellow with a dress says take care & woman in a cadillac waiting & a guy in a suit on a bicycle & it's saturday & a guy in a cadillac going backwards from michigan the great lake state, glory boy bananas and a guy in an apron who is the poet. A woman talking to ed ed is not a woman, he doesnt wear sunglasses where is he & what's he looking for?

22

Sound. Sound & carfare & gas & then the rest of the story goes: out
in the open here & hot, trying to bite down trying to bite it down
that's the trouble, we had a beer the bar was no good, reasons were
frying, air conditioning, read about food poisoning in the new york
post & put it down in case we die tomatoes from italy are good. I
have no way of remembering a day. Rosemary calls & I talk her ear
off we listen to tapes call tom not home call vito put scattered ap-
plause the appaloosa on to him & ed talks his ear off so we got rid
of them, there's a house in maine for ten thousand dollars, we'll get
a grant, we'll think of the mystery of the renovated barn, a house is
for, a, protection and, b, insulation & we'll think of boys in the
puglia, boys walking walking boys puglia walking edward & kathleen
b b b bernadette mayer christophe cauchoix on a matchbook comma
we'll think of this & this is even older:

> rte. nine east between keene & brattleboro
> cinema theater motel, you watch thru the window
> of your room, drive in dont drive in & then
> nathaniel hawthorne college, antrim, new hampshire
> & stewartstown, new hampshire it's halfway
> between north pole & equator, the 200th anniversary
> of this.
> asbestos canada asbestos cinema
> back in the ussr by chubby checker played
> on a jukebox in canada, well
> where have you been? all over.
> where have you been? all over.
> have you been to alaska?
> where do you want to go for xmas?
> have you been to greece?
> have you been to the bahamas?
> where do you want to go for christmas?
> the paname bistro
> make up ed for photo
> in sillery in racetrack in tv
> ed says, behind the scenes
> busride & a list of corporate injustices
> made up by a child
> if you indians are from china
> if you indians are from china

why dont you call yourselves chinese?
& something upside down
& a cover & pictures & paint
& something crossed out
& something crossed out, it was done
& an idea about transcription, off to the side
& some numbers, a theater & service equipment
& some long division
& some copying
& a face a tree a girl with her head down
the sun, marks, a head an ax an ax-flag
& food & a photo of M & a note:
the negative's in the trunk, the key is mailed,
will arrive at 33 tomorrow,
signed.

We'll think of talking backwards, i'm talking backwards, i'm working
more the way strudents in science are working in a lab, a movie is
only the result of two to three months exploration of something, i
tried to find a picture of karl marx when he was young but i found
it only afterwards, he was very beautiful young just like warren
beatty today everytime you see a picture of marx you see him with
a big beard & he was just like james dean when he was 20 years old,
i used to like disney documentaries on animals, if john wayne played
an animal perhaps i would like him too, there is image & there is
sound & i see no difference between a face being interviewed & just
a picture of a word for example, they are just two shots, it doesnt
bother me at all actually every time i see a film i sleep fifteen
minutes there are two reproductions a matisse & a rembrandt & i
very often sleep while looking at them, i can look like a business
person or i can look like somebody in love, in love with that person
for whom this piece is a personal message, from 19 to 20 i went to
college & took easily about 150 examinations, then i got my degree
which qualifies me to teach language & literature, i am talking back-
wards, but while i was going to college i was editing a literary maga-
zine where we published the first translations of - the first dreams by
- some - some - his experience with mescaline, the first - the first -
& so on, we also published the works of our own group, some of the
things were really good, at the same time i made a series of porno-
graphic . . . i'd give a years wages for that gun/i'd give my left hand/

to some unintelligible/i guess so/gunshots/this is july 3rd/you re-
member that dont you?/is that jacques & kathleens?/yes/what's
that?/that's the door to the roof/one dollar/doesnt look like the
roof does it?/dont worry joe'll be delighted to see you, he will, well
of course he will, now where's your luggage, oh dont worry about
me i'm gonna stay at the hotel, you're doing nothing of the sort
you're staying right here with us, now you come along with me &
we'll fix up the spare room, nice little place you got here, i've got a
great idea, let's you & i be honest with each other this isnt a nice
little place & you know it, well it is kinda, yeah it is, why's he live
in a place like this he's a millionaire if he'd only take it but he wont,
so you've come up here to try to talk joe into going back to the
ranch?, well not exactly, oh oh we're going to be honest remember?,
well i would kinda like him to come back, so would i, you think you
owe me that much, you would, i would, why donna, you've got a
head on your shoulders, well maybe i better stay at the hotel, oh
dont get nervous, we'll have this cleared up in no time, imagine a
fellow like joe bein a teacher, teaching's for women that cant find
husbands, now hold on partner teaching's a noble & important pro-
fession more noble & important than raising beef cattle for instance,
now you hold on partner feeding the american people aint such a
disgraceful occupation - I get an obscene phone call, a third steve,
said he was coming just as I hung up the phone, pretty lucky - & it
aint an easy one let me tell you, you let me tell you, we werent
going to argue remember, we're buddies, i'm sorry daughter, some-
times i fly off the handle, so i heard, joe's sore at me eh?, well you're
not exactly his favorite character, i couldnt let that boy grow up
soft, all that land all that cattle, i had to toughen him up for the job
ahead of him, & when you got too tough you tried to square things
with your money, well now i didnt go for to hurt him, oh if joe had
found understanding at home he would have had to try to find it
somewhere else, connie i want him back, what must i do, try a little
humility, try controlling that temper of yours & above all keep that
fucking bankroll in your pocket, connie there's joe remember, joe,
yeah, joe look who's here, mmm, shit, hello pa, hello boy, had some
business in the east yeah thought i'd drop by coming so close & all,
well i'm glad you did, been a long time & all that shit, sure has, i
know you two must have lots to talk about so why dont you go out
on the porch where it's cool & i'll finish getting dinner ready, yes,

come on pa, have a cigar boy, thanks pa i'll smoke it after dinner, still smokin those dollar cigars i see, why not son i can afford em, last year the best year we ever had down on the ranch, glad to hear it pa, oh yeah things are boomin down there, that's fine pa but how've you been, oh i've begun to creak a little bit at the joints i'm ready to step down & turn over the reigns, anybody in particular?, well a man like to think his son . . ., pa let me put this as kindly as possible, i'm not coming back, doggone it why not that dont make sense not any more, you run away from home cause you were sore at me, ok all right, you win your fight, here i am on my hands & knees beggin you to come back, what more you want, pa try to understand maybe i didn't take up teaching just to spite you, maybe that's how it was in the first place but since then i found out something, i love teaching, it's what i'm good at, you cant forgive me can you?, i have nothing against you pa, i'm tickled to death you're here honest i am, & as far as i'm concerned bygones are bygones, i'm a teacher & i'm gonna stay a teacher, oh hi joe, hi, joe simmons, archy, come on & meet my father, how do you do sir, howdy boys, glad to know you etc., pa came out from texas to pay us a visit, oh are you connected with the university down there sir, i am connected with 20,000 head of white face cattle, well you're alot better off you sure are, arent you gonna invite these fellas in to have a drink, oh sure, we'll have a . . ., thanks some other time we're late now, we'll take a raincheck on it, well so long joe etc., friends of yours?, teachers at the college, they seem like nice young fellas, well why're you so surprised, oh i dont know they just dont look like the teacher type that's all, well what is the teacher type pa, skinny sexless bald at 20, oh i didnt say that exactly, well you know the old saying joe them's can do & them's can teach, here's another one, feed a cold & starve a fever, well what's that got to do with it?, & here's another one, sing before breakfast & cry before supper . . .

July 4
twelve seventeen & ten seconds bright day warms up, I warm up, I have little mats stapled into my nails, owning elephants, this space for a field, remember? Ed wet went "to get some cars", cigarettes & money flew, HC-110 at 7:1 dilute B at 68° straight-hypo, into cans, stop bath in beaker, take temp. of HC-110, 68°, get time,

lights off, roll & cover on, shake 30 seconds, lights off, stop bath one minute, cover, do cold running water 2 minutes, permawash solution, 2 minutes, agitate, cold 2 minutes, or cold one hour, photo flo, 2 minutes, hang & squeegee (in photo flo), hang one hour, then contact: shiny faces paper, prints dull. *School:* I'm going to take a picture of it, the only thing I feel like doing is looking at it, is looking at it in a picture, it is ducks in glass cases in poor light, it's hard to take a picture of it, james noeth has no prick, takes his clothes off, revival, all in kerchiefs & a movie of me in the room across the way, a movie out of the window, a blond girl running with flowers, she drops the flowers, she drops her wig, she isnt blond, we sing a song: *Trip to the Moon:* rocket ships on ringed trucks & families going like trailers, & finally high school gets out, we're going to massachusetts, rows of girls in golden coats marching, I call to someone, I say "Hey that made me think of you!" & he gets angry & we live in big rooms in hotels are centers all is sex. & hotels are centers all is sex & ed swimming a fish a frog a girl in pedal-pushers a line the set, droplight, the stone couch the design. Dear Dash, it could be me or you, you are sinking in the pillows currents, more specifically, red frequency: dreams #3 asleep & where's the coffee, the sun is coming through the library window, yes that one, its against but cant come through the windows at my back, yours, at your back is a bed dont sneeze when you get up in the morning, white. Write: what where you get up it's afternoon Dash I took the camera with me Dash bye. Orzata hamburger chili sandals courvoisier scallops coffee cereal film tape piano pens candles matches mosquito netting gnocchi house in the country 8mm movie camera roller skates — the monster that was in here last night was the country, he was, still this is the sun still this is the city still the country was blue white & maroon with a long long tail, buzzing & making giant shadows by the light, feeding on the glue of a piece of tape on the ceiling, we put him in a box, country, slid a paper cover over it, threw the box out the window saving the picture we'd used as a cover, country, bye. One day I saw ed, eileen, barry, marinee, chaim, kay, denise, arnold, paul, susan, ed, hans, rufus, eileen, anne, harris, rosemary, harris, anne, larry, peter, dick, pat, wayne, paul m., gerard, steve, pablo, rufus, eric, frank, susan, rosemary c., ed, larry r., & david; we talked about bill, vito, kathy, moses, sticks, arlene, donna, randa, picasso, john, jack nicholson, ed, shelley, alice, rosemary c., michael, nick, jerry, tom c., donald sutherland, alexander berkman, henry frick, fred margulies, lui, jack, emma goldman, gerard, jacques, janice, hilly, directors, holly, hannah, denise, steve r., grace, neil, malevich, max ernst, duchamp, mrs. ernst, michael, gerard, noxon, nader, peter hamill, tricia noxon, ed cox, harvey, ron, barry, jasper johns, john p., frank stella & ted. I still see ed, barry, chaim, arnold, paul, rufus, eileen, anne, harris is away, i dont see rosemary, harris is away, anne, larry, peter occasionally, who's dick?, pat, gerard is away, pablo is away, I still see steve, who're eric & frank?, I still see rosemary c., ed, & david is a different one. It's impossible to put things exactly as they happened or in their real order one by one but something happened that day in the middle of seeing some people & talking about some, something happened that day (look it up in stories) & what happened was what began this: and this came later, the day after that: "one two three people I saw, money we spent, gave out, the energy it took to get to the country, drinking three cups of cof-fee to talk about anarchy, to write a letter to anne about an old worn out subject, the destruction of the tapes, feel the breeze the generation gap, think about watching another person, then creating one for people to watch, understanding the desire to watch other people to understand them or just to watch them, not finding any place to set things down then save this for later & wait. I saw I talked about. No decision. No direction. That's good. & No thought. Fans, the energy it takes to wave them. Flags. Get the pillow. The cake is in the oven. Get the beer. Why not talk about the energy of the weather in the city too, three describe it. Waiting toward something to come out of something. Placing something there. To think without thinking. Write without writing. xyz, thoughts with fine edges. So many noises people places things points of view. Put something out in that field. Didnt understand. Now do. The do-nothing school. Against technology. Energy comes from somewhere. Pay. Some way. I feel terrible. Why. Race against time. All the dreams all the notes all the directions nothing comes from it. Need drink. Empty slot. Cant sit up. Cake. The leisure to go beyond the tree. The time. Did ed take a taxi? No, but he did get a ride home in j&k's 1964 cadillac convertible." & then I have something similar, I dont know when it happened, but first there's some time spent in a luncheonette: the answer box, answers any question, any yes or no question????? & lucky nos. for today, we're in everybody's

luncheonette. I thought it was may 10, noon. It was june 5 noon.
Vito & the roosters, the day that Dash was sleeping, sinking into the
pillows currents dreaming, you remember? the day I took the camera
with me this was the same day: pick any rooster, my rooster's come a
capon, raphael's question: what artists do you know? Film, black &
white, slides, tv, movies, the american legion auxiliary box, what's
the matter with r. Sign: how to succeed in business (cheat), viva &
emma goldman. "Hi woody" & P lives near here. 10 am (sam) & I
am at 125THST, 74THST later nursing homes siring women scream-
ing I scream a woman with short hair sipping a diet cola, straw, a
kid says get outta here & gimme a glass of water what? water what?
water pure water & kathleen pierre clementi christophe whatever-his-
name-is & randa 302 elizabeth street. The kid runs out. A man makes
a phone call it gets crowded, everybody's cheeseburger rare & a vanilla
eggcream & a woman: "Mikey stop around the store, something to
show you, close for 2 minutes, minutes? that doesnt take care of
it." Lose my mind like eeeeiiieeeeh & I found out when that hap-
pened but this still escapes me. This is something, something like:
what's in quotes beginning with the people I saw, the money we
spent & on through the fans & the energy it takes up to the con-
vertible quotes. But now this interests me more: it is: it's Charlie
Chaplin brought up to make lists STRANGE IDEAS LIKE TO
STOP thinking about T. dream am shot by hilly or jacques & how s.
everyone is & what you already know & shouldnt concern you &
sudden mood & how h. everything is & all of a sudden cant move
feel stuck feel s. the clear co. makes two by fours. So, drama is real
is real in on a day & then some vision you are you are not so some-
one can know you are you are not the fleet the flight what kind of
information is that going forward tradition master you have the
time anarchy you are much busier to bring the tea out to the table
& do you want any coffee no thanks & I should go out to show
hate & fruit flies cant move bells stop in the middle of the most,
but, but knowing neil's energy who knows? But about that above
something must change most of it must change into something else,
the . . . at the door, the . . . in the door, the history of china the arts
of china the anarchist paper the year 1887 the year 1931, now we
buy: potatoes, etc. Looked wildly about me looked wildly about me
saw, three women at the door, a man in the door, the history . . .
a light in each eye, eye in each light, the woman who wrote the book

had two eyes, the book two volumes, it was written in 1931, she
said with the blue of the table cloth & an extra apron, she said in a
two room flat on houston street she said most had repeatedly given
her the same ultimatum, she said to go back with the detective to
new york, she said & locked up for the night men & women, the
meeting at union square, she said counting many thousands, said as a
result the air at union square, the state is the worst enemy you have
& it goes on, her name was not randa, the police burst in, the tele-
gram still in my head in my hand, said began to swim before her
eyes, said struck her full in the face she looked wildly about her &
then, who she wanted the money & the gun for, said never written
for publication before, the police got busy, said family need not
know about her plans, something unreadable my mind was made up,
the jury was picked for conviction, her entire possessions, besides
their common anarchist ideal & he had her released from the jacket
strait jacket, break the backbone of every economic struggle, steer
clear of politicians of politicians, had no idea who had notified the
press & the action of the police, protests by well-known men & wo-
men, her right to speak, that she should return later, the suppression
of the meetings in chicago, how could he have anything to do with
them, he might be a detective himself, hated to let them escape,
she said, returning to minneapolis, she again (something about
letters), in a number of cities in massachusetts & union square, the
laborlyceum in brooklyn, demonstrations of the unemployed, said
knew had come to stay, streets lined for blocks, that the owners
backed out, never invoked the law against anyone, five years on
alcatraz island, no redress or escape of the sources from which they
spring, because of a terrific rainstorm, her first meeting poorly at-
tended & the chance to send you this note: stay in mind something
new: like holidays in the city, we must've done some wash either
last night or this morning & hung it out on the fire escape to dry &
I remember being really tired the night before this. There wasnt
much recording to do this day though because everything was closed
or empty. Ed was still asleep when I got up. I washed at least 3
blue shirts to take to massachusetts & overexposed them on the
fire escape. Tom said the underexposed ones look like a casket.
Then I washed our blue hockey shirt, my 30's outfit, alot of t-shirts
including anne's tye-dyed one, two pairs of army green socks, ed's
pants & hannah's green & white shirt. Put them out to dry. It was

sunny. We went out. I had wanted to go down to the world trade center so we did. Couldnt get close enough to it so we drove down broadway to barclay street & when we left up deserted washington street, not exactly deserted but torn down, the whole north-south street of it, just lots & the most interesting thing about the WTC was the rust on all of the materials. We saw a pile of stones somebody had carefully cut out on washington street & one building was being moved. It was raised on a platform. Further up on a continuation of washington there were a few streets lined with trailers without cabs & they said dart sea & acl & it was late afternoon. We drove around & found a street lined with some kind of unusual tree, an uptown type street with two-story houses, gas lamps & iron, I think we were looking for a place to eat something & we had all our equipment with us just in case & I think we ate in the pink teacup, ham & greens, corn beef or something like that, then we went to a few bars on lower 6THAVE to check the sound. We walked into one place where we had met j&k once but the tv was on. We recorded alot in emilio's which is a really loud place & had a few beers & it sounded good even though two tv's were on because there were so many people in there. There was a whole scene with a few drunken middle-aged couples. We also went to tony's which was empty but we shot a game of pool two games. We heard some really spectacular firecrackers while we were driving around & we thought they might be good for the explosion. I cant remember if we went home in between or just on back to the west village listening for the loudest explosions & wound up at the morton street pier, where, walking out I met Lee Crabtree who I hadnt seen in a long time. The sun was setting & there we were with alot of people & firecrackers at the pier. We found some guys with a station wagon full of rockets & explosives & I saw a guy walking along the edge of the pier with some kind of walking stick & a pair of headphones on that must've had a radio in them & a couple of ships went by & flares continuously going off. Finally the guys with the station wagon agreed to set off some of the big stuff for us to record. They acted like lunatics. We got a few incredible explosions, watched some more flares & then they left so we did too. By this time the city looked some pretty strange colors. When we got home we listened to the explosions & they all sounded too far away. We had some cherry bombs of our own we had gotten in wisconsin somewhere a guy told us they used these to fish with just explode one in the water & all the dead fish come floating to the top & there's your dinner so we exploded a few in the parking lot across the street & recorded them. The echoes were incredible & some people in lofts down the street started applauding for each one. Alot of them fizzled after they were lit & we didnt have very many so we had to feel around in the dark for them, thinking they might explode anyway & relight them. We used up all our cherry bombs & the recordings sounded ok but later they couldnt be used at all. I guess we spent part of the night packing & I wrote to Dash, dear Dash, it's hot & i will sweat writing a letter. Vladimir nabokov's *Despair*, I can see the resemblance there. & a Joe Cocker record & I thought it would be easier to write a letter to no one, a letter to you in particular but, to wake up on a hot morning, have nothing really to do but everything & no money & no very little sleep & very scared in the morning & to start doing things, you better start doing things, like, the diary as a book - 'the lowest form'. Everything's high or low, Germans, everything's perfect, the stick, 'you got a friend' - grace & tom? Low German high German vladimir nabokov, it's you. 'With a little help from my friends' - make some sense out of this. I will. Who are you? The play's about to open, to 'brighten up the airwaves'. Once was too serious now not enough, Signed. & Tom said i'm really still very nervous about new york/what?/i'm really still nervous in new york/that's funny i didnt think i was nervous when we got back here & now i'm starting to lose my mind/i tell you i've got an ulcer/you?/i have an ulcer/no i have an ulcer/i do/i have an ulcer/ everytime i eat i, everytime i eat i start to fart it goes on for at least half an hour/i get such terrible stomach aches i have to put my legs up to my chest/is that right?/well we're both gonna have to go to the doctors/that's right/plus . . ./i know it's just nerves/i'm getting stooped shoulders/plus i'm getting, me too/i cant even drink a cup of coffee anymore/alright bernadette feel where my shoulders are no really just feel where my shoulders are in relation to my bones, are they up front like, like this, like come up close like this, arent they up front/yeah/shouldnt they be like this?/yeah well they should be like that it's true but not/my whole back my whole back, like i sit like this all the time/well you'll just have to start sitting up straighter/i do i'm gonna really start to sit up straight i'm gonna/ well you arent just . . . you have a . . . such a big chest it's really

funny/it's really funny huh i dont think it's so funny why is it
funny/it's definition, this is what i'm telling you it's definition/
yeah i know/i know/look pecks, these are the pecks/i know/go
ahead go ahead go ahead right like that, no up there/it's true that's
what i want that's why i'm gonna lift weights/& otherwise it can be
like this, now feel it when it's loose just push this but then when
you make the muscle - de fi ni tion/well feel this feel this there's a
muscle/that's not muscle that's just your bone that's cartilage/it's
just my tenseness . . . you're right i have no muscles there lets have
this . . . show/you want it bigger?/ ah, what do you think . . . but
then you have to move it around/well maybe i'll just put it on the
other side of me/if it'll go yeah/you know i've gotten my finger
caught/you've got your fingers what?/caught in the fan of the pro-
jector/really?/yup/what happened?/horrible bleeding/is that true?/
yeah if you put your fingers under here . . . /dont do that . . . drying
your wash/ok listen to this: he was in the clouds, with airplanes, he
with airplanes airplanes & him they fly higher than that, news, it's
you, all over all over each other rain all over the earth, tomorrow
rain tomorrow, the world what word rain earth, earth steeped &
staked through the coil it leads & you forget, you forget not for-
ward or backwards, in & out maybe, you think you forget, the
earth's core & pinned to it a sample of hunger eating the colors
of a line-up of words, excuse me now, the scent of the track. ok
this is the fourth remember that/ok/that's ed in bed/cant see him/
funny i could see him before maybe that's a different picture/great
blues/hmmm looks like a nice day doesnt it/really looks like a nice
day/the fourth was a nice day i was at a country fair july fourth/
really where?/sparta new jersey, not a fair, it's you know that
fourth of july parade/oh great, looks like some kind of strange
funeral/funeral?why?/ yeah doesnt that look like a casket to you/
she looks like barbra streisand doesnt she/yeah/oh that's great
looks like something/yeah this is the first time you've seen these/
yeah well i held them up to the light but i havent seen them/i dont
recognize that street do you/no but we can figure it out, b. i think
its broadway/broadway?/i think so because ah theres cobblestones
there/cobblestones right plus the lowness of the buildings, it means
it's very far downtown/yeah well its down here somewhere but
theres no cobblestones on broadway/oh great/da-dah/is that a dance?/
looks like a man on top doesnt it/yeah it does wonder if it is, no

it couldnt be could it/i think its the other crane/yeah its one of
those cranes/those buildings are gonna be so ugly when they're not
yellow anymore/i know/this is a whole series on them/see that
cross/its great blue sky/yeah/they dont look big do they/in relation
to what?/that cross, heh/it's true they dont/are those underground
caverns/yup only nobody can live there, i have a great one of a little
hole in a mound of sand, alot of little holes, where birds live/
whaddaya mean birds?/i went to this sand lot to get some sand to
make sandbags & there was a big mound of sand & the guy told me
that birds make these little holes in the mountain & live there, it
was just sand/under under/yeah under/that looks like the coliseum/
huh it really does/well i mean a little bit/oh you can see it well you
sort of can/what?/those, ah, see between the columns in the back-
ground those wires?/uh huh/they're all red yellow & blue/ is that
right?/yeah really weird/that's as close as i could get that last pic-
ture & i sneaked in there to take it/did anybody yell at you?/
yeah finally where i am for this one there's a guy just on the right
of me who, a really nice guy, who was like a guard foreign college
student type & he kept saying/did he say anything to you?/yeah he
kept saying you cant go in there you cant & he had told me that be-
fore but i ignored him i pretended i didnt see him/& did he yell at
you/no he didnt yell but he wouldnt let me go back in/this is
strange that's a whole sculpture that somebody made in an empty
lot/that looks like a nice street to live on/yeah except they've torn
it all down/there's apartments in the back/is that the, is that the,
quietest street in new york, remember that street/ that's the street,
that's it yeah/were you driving down?/washington st. yeah/what's
the name of that street/washington street/does that look like what
it is?/mud or water/no glass/that's glass on the pavement/yeah really
weird looking isnt it/the thing i cant believe about all this is that
nothing looks like what it looked like, you know, i mean no, it's
amazing/that's just because it's framed/it's the light/if you looked
at it, if you looked at it, but even if, even if you looked at it through,
if you could get the same filter exactly as the light that's there & if
you had it framed, you think it would look the same?/sure i dont
know/alot of wash/what?/alot of wash/did you know that the theater
was also moved/whaddayou mean moved/the whole building was
moved/about ten years ago or something from about ½ mile away/
was it really/this guy's playing . . . /huh/oh that's the place we were

gonna take the picture with the moon/uh hmmm/only the moon's
not there/that's nice really nice/oh great/that's great isnt it/great
dart sea that's great though/wow/you know what street that is?
you wont believe it/i'll figure it out. yes i do/what?/canal street/oh
shit/right?/yeah ahhah/doesnt look anything like it though, i know,
someplace outside nebraska or something, that's what it looks like/
that's a dream a dream i had/is it? you took a picture in it?/yeah/
i took a nap the afternoon of july 4th/that's great/oh this is a weird
street/oh jesus/this is the street that's like, its called saint something
street & it's, i had never seen it before, it's lined with trees/where?/
a kind of trees i had never seen in new york before/where . . . /st.
thomas or st. something . . . /where is it?/it's sort of near the lower
west village you know/great looking street/unbelieveable i couldnt
believe it/that looks like jesus it looks like charleston doesnt it or
something/tony's pool table/great mahogany/yeah/boy it's a good
thing i gave ed that shirt this year/sure is/christ/wouldnt it be great
if you could swim in it/hmmm/is that pier 17/umm it's the morton
st. morton st. pier/what is that stuff in the water?/i guess its just
lights/the next thing you see will prove to you that its . . . oh no . . .
oh that's great/whats that?/he's recording the sound of . . . /hah hah
which is it, is that a sparkler?/well its a rocket actually they set off
these great rockets for us/that was the 4th with the sparkers/yeah/
that was it yeah/you know how i ended up the 4th?/how?/with
gigantic firewords/really/i wont need, that wont need that/could
you put that light on/here's a rocket in the sky/oh great, i want to
see, that's what i wanted to see/where?/it's there/i just want to see
this/tastes good with that/ . . . you know who looks like him, the
photographer from, who was doing the pictures for, remember that
photographer/ oh yeah martin?/he looks like him/is there any hash-
ish left/yeah a little bit/just a little?/been smoking it every night to
beat the heat/but b. but b./ . . . & it lasts much longer than this . . .
he really takes you by surprise . . . ok you ready? . . . lights/lights/:
So, stay in mind something new & stay in mind something new age,
in red: it's still the fourth a sunday, we do the wash I was sitting
with it you could watch it on television, brown skin & oil. Sun why
bring that in: of wash on it: we hung it out to dry on the World
Trade Center we have done so much & we sat at it on it at sunset
waiting for it to dry, vito & kathy? R calls Leon mad phone caller
calls. 5 am & later today & while we are in the process of it & while

we are on it the tallest building in the world fallen into a diary of a
river in the book leads to this one, that one what is interesting & so
on, something about lines & bells, lines & bells, a fraction of a second,
ed lines the bed with no clothes on, ed's mother's glasses make good
bells we were looking for bells like the bell on a typewriter like the
bell to tell the time with must do this must do that: carry a book with
you to the top of . . . make a phone call from the highest point in
. . . take rubber cement to the high seams of . . . & the colossus of
new york & from the second tallest building its twin grace calls to
say that wash is done it's over you can watch it on television, ed
writes to say I write useful messages we order a pizza with sausage &
a pizza playing chess, what have you forgotten, it's a long way up,
let's pack & lets pack good. What's packed into that past you knew
who it was when they called before the thieves marched down the
buildings with your electric typewriter & its iron girders slide: you
say, ready to go

July 5
Chance it's morning you forget to see blue you leave it out I looked
at the windows do every morning, to see what the light is, how it is,
what the day is, what part. Yellow before, green after projected
large: the yellow before means too much light but what does green
after mean. White pants french tv-shirt is red & white & cant find the
sunshine going up & part of niagra's missing going down: I put the
film in the toycan a 2-lb coffee can for small toys, rain no rain
having coke sassafras cigarette so you forget to see blue was morning
was light on whatever was light was new but you return to 47THST,
47THST: new return nagra & stuff to arnold & fix the projector,
get t. into film course, 47THST waiting: I look up eagles soar at
signs cars sun on half of modern which half & I was & still am always
bored waiting parked no parking waiting on west 47THST, I've been
here before, on west 47THST between 5TH & 6TH aves empty
streets the street goes west it was sunday or monday it was monday
of the storm & revolution weekend, fire. You know this, that 47THST
was deserted the war's been over looking west through the wind-
shield, fire. Red car across the street parked in front of siegelson's &
someone's son & someone & stein's with a giant red car with black
top, you know this, that a man & a woman went by you forget to

see green you stare at green you wait to stare at green & in the country you see red. You know this that the sign of the diamond exchange looked better off better off for its shadows my shadows by afternoon . . . & waiting: a room with a family where are you where will you be let me know, R, V & K, T water the plants grace randa anne paul let me remind you: by afternoon we were up in riverdale parked the car packed with our stuff in view of the window so we could watch it, will paul get his door? No one was there but tom, did I expect someone whole family of blondes they exist now you cant watch them on television no one was there but tom. It was quiet. American flag hangs out some window heavy head near white & brick arch, the kings, & queens. We picked up a tape recorder a few things there left a few & ate a sandwich smoked hashish in a foil pipe took off very fast up the highway on our way to massachusetts, another highway on our way cia. Cigarette, get to see the trees moving like listening to them: what was that, I can hear it in my head as you begin to repeat . . . let's go back to that tree, that one, cross the divider, turn around, is that the one? is that the one that moved to listen? & what are you listening to is it the line of the highway rising you hear it mark X on the sun, say, ed & tom are brothers. Outside the city we stopped for gas, no money, turned around & went back. In detail you went back? What'd you do that for? Tommy? & this is where it all begins. Sings under that name, he was watching tv looked sleepy & stoned shirt off the sun was on the left side of the highway shirt off. Forget for hours smoke hashish when we left for the second time the flag had been wrapped around itself a few times by the wind I guess oblivion sleep day was the day you were tied up remember? the road was empty we were going against the traffic. Remember to look up ron the cab driver in astoria. Ed took a picture of himself in the car, we left the top down (except, for a month you keep your eyes open) had to tie our hair back & pleasantville hill pleasantville hill see swear a resemblance in going over it, free fly twice as free. We stopped at another gas station about halfway up for coffee, remember? Not abstract he said like the argentine pampas, we flew, I dictated a few things to ed on the way up & he wrote down in my book: expand: ed was wearing sense the blue hockey shirt with stripes who turned it down? what? the tv. I turned it down when the cable tv man called. You have to get the landlord's permission & the landlord said, they're turning

the electricity off so do what you want & they have to get the cable
down here by, on schedule. When you stop at a gas station on the
taconic parkway you can stand just a few feet from cars going by
60 mph drinking coffee, sweetheart cups. When you stop at a gas
station on the taconic fantasy parkway you stand & look. We had a
sandwich. A white car will pass by over your shadow if it's after-
noon. If you can control this the future will be easy easy to direct,
it will make sense, we had a sandwich. An old man in new dungarees
& a pale orange shirt goes by, 3 guys with cameras go by, a prosti-
tute with a camera too. Now I see - 47THST. Do you see the ar-
gentine pampas, where, here here a red car, black top goes by on
the parkway & the pampas the black-tops retrace your own steps,
they do the work for you, it'll go on like this. The bathroom looked
like a woman's prison & we took off again, top down stop still down
on stop down I took pictures leaning on the dashboard dashboard
of the car. The sun set. He flicked a pack of paper matches along
the dash to nick. This is the taconic fantasy parkway: you look down
a road to the left you look down a road to the right paradise: i was
on a bicycle, the bicycle was electric if you want, i was always wear-
ing clothes of yellow daisies green leaves, going down a road (a house
is a forest) the road's not dirt, a rocky road not pavement or asphalt,
a road through trees but trees dont block your sight, you can see for
miles, i had everything i needed with me. It wasnt anything. The
road through trees with colors, it could be fall or flowers made them,
or sun's prism, & things along the way, where would i sleep, in the
grass or in houses? whatever comes up, maybe a change in direction,
i enjoyed being watched sense the presence of other people, it was
not a road of one direction or a road getting somewhere, further on
it wasnt a road you kept to, later on i got more interested in flying.
On the road that would've come up anyway. With this road you
didnt need a house, everyone set the sun & sense the presence of
other people. This is about watching other people, then creating
one some for people to watch, understanding the desire to watch
other people to understand them or just to watch them, not finding
any place to set things down then save this for later & wait. I saw I
talked about. The sun set. We're at Near Road. The way smell detour
moon train & the golf course. We get to massachusetts in the dark
darkest to the theater to find out where jacques is living, would like
to live in a house that comes close to being a forest, & where we will

be living. They show us our room on main street we hate it and cause cause and miss malloy was in the other room, it was not a forest. & what about the seasons? Went to the stockbridge inn for a beer & ate a stewarts sandwich played songs A to Z & 1 to 8 chose nathan jones over a weak james taylor & what about the seasons in a house so, shot a game of pool & tried to find a house that we could live right in. Bought bourbon & went over to j&k's yellow or blue small house up a hill near glendale, k in j's green robe, we talk in the bathroom we like to sneak in the bathroom, there was to be a peter arrow concert in the hall so julia came by with some sheets, in the theater people move in a piece. Peter arrow was giving a concert in the theater where people move in a piece & they took us to a party for theater people. We drank the party but were bored, try to remember the downpour. A few people asked are you from syracuse are you from boston, what we were drinking was a strange old punch remember of champagne glasses, well where are you from? In destiny I owe you something if you ask that much, in the theater I do not. I am from the massacre & was the massacre night or day, we finished the bourbon under the table, in the movie will the massacre be night or day, the next day we drank with hitch-hikers, over, in a movie you replace a shadow with something real, you do this by turning around. Whatever that real thing is, it's framed in a mirror. We moved around a shadow yellow room & this is the hard part, exchanging identities, anne kathy & now kathleen, & now, turn around, there's a boy with blond hair, k called him over, replace him & his friends with musicians from woodstock born in texas & k is from texas they had dope but wouldnt smoke at a party so fine so we went outside & framed in an old car mirror we stood around passing joints packed as fat as cigarettes, they really were from texas, the police cruise by, turn around, there's a dog in the car, we went for a ride night. I took them to the bridge over the stream in the woods by the house I used to live in. Road was overgrown. We had never seen it that was in the spring or fall mirror. Stood on the bridge & talked about movies, turn around, k is in the car with the blond boy because of the mosquitoes and cause cause and of mosquitoes, she invites him to stay with us, musicians who have the word color or poet or earth in the title of their group & we stayed till we were bitten & then went back to get jacques. Shadow, there was no moon. We slept that night in our room with a family & how could a family come with a room? It usually does all right. I kept thinking someone was going to die in the house & then, turn around, you'd see them carried out. Now who is that? I think ed took a bath. There was an actress in the other room: in a movie theater the seats should face the back, turning around you see: you packed the car past hurry up beautiful bright sun in loft you leave nothing leaves, waiting: in a new state a schedule, on time: 10 am meet john in the paint shop which is the barn & 1 pm meet jacques to ride around for locations & 3 am experiment: Take as the stimulus a scrap of brightly colored paper about, say, the size of a penny & make a tiny pencil mark or pin-prick near its center. Lay this on a sheet of white paper & look fixedly at the mark in its center for perhaps twenty seconds. Remove the colored stimulus & fixate with the eyes some tiny mark on the large white sheet. After a few seconds during which nothing may happen, a patch of color will be seen. If we continue fixating, this patch will vanish, then return only to vanish once more; it may alternately appear & disappear as many as 20 or 40 times, growing fainter with each successive reappearance until a time is reached after a minute or so when it disappears altogether. Now, there are two surprising things about this image. The first is its color. If the stimulus is red the image is green; if the stimulus is blue the image is yellow-orange, if the stimulus is black, the image is white. These are the complementary colors. The second surprising thing about the negative after image is its size. If the stimulus is fixated one foot from the eye & the after image is obtained the same distance away, the image will be exactly the same size. But if the image is projected 2, 5, 10, or 15 feet away the size of the image will increase proportionately. It's intelligent. For beings. What would that contact be like? or simply, where are they? Anarchy 4 florence, exile 4 dante: you have a name, you explain; this image or effect is due to the adaptation, it is due to the 'fatigue' of the color- & light- sensitive tissue - the retina - which lies at the back of the eyeball, the eye, like windows, like cameras, like image in sound. Seeing the red patch, we continuously stimulate the same area of the retina until it becomes no longer sensitive to the red, can no longer feel or see the red of the patch (as we fixate the red patch, we may notice that it seems to lose its color except round the edges). Then when we see some other surface, look at it, this adapted retinal area is insensitive to whatever

red component the surface possesses & the negative after image re-
sults. The red is in the white. You leave it out you forget to see red.
As we continue to look to see, the retina adapts to the color of the
new surface, to all its color & the image an imagining wanes. The
important thing is that the image is the after-effect of continuously
stimulating you pay & so fatiguing you rest a specific area of the
retina you see

July 6

you see what did you have for breakfast? french toast & coffee &
today pears colors of the pears colors of the coffee, do you remem-
ber the day jacques & kathleen had maggots in their garbage can?
That's out our window, the room with a family, early morning sun
on screen & this was the day that everybody wore a blue shirt &
that's great isnt it & like a summer place at 4:30 monday so what'll
I do? you cut your prices in half until they'll . . . you see what did
you have for breakfast? different brilliant colors. It's one o'clock
& susan strassberg is walkin gaily down the street after a refreshing
cup of brilliant ochre coffee & a bun with rose madder jelly made
of fruit orange juice peach juice & a dim pear. French toast & coffee
yellow to brown with brown flowing maple syrup boiled down &
brown grass remember? Graham Brown sat with us he's black & sun
is yellow white light G is brown what light is ice & stockbridge is a
white town massachusetts a red brown & yellow state with shades
of tan & one green: we were up early: it's the oil added to lubricate
the tip of the pen that makes ball-point ink stains so hard to get out.
Can energy be stolen: I'll talk them out of it: the piano's there in
the morning with the score: 16 bars lit by candlelight in the morning
sun to get you high & screens make prisms of every color in a white
house gets you off & white garages fading into the reflection of the
sun on the screen a white fence connecting the two with a white
door into the yard I guess grey roof & black shutters. We cant live
here much longer. Clean windows. Remember, it's black: people
have different names, the movie: snooze alarm, chess & cool theater
of remote cocks behind? conceived of time & cool paint shop: we
see we talk to we cash Ed talks to Charles Projector on the phone
we go to e's rehearsal: an actor acts as though: you cant come in:
e talks about thirty thousand dollars from bristol myers sherry or

do I have it wrong & we meet M on Main st. & we talk about the
barn & we go to see it locked all around locked all around in a field
of dirt roads. Colors of the movie: raced to sleeping j&k's, they have
no phone yet, maroon cadillac blue sprite on a small mound of grass
in the suburb of yellow & blue houses house with a white chimney,
geraniums strawberry leaves old rhubarb is tough & a hex sign on
the stone step up to the back door the only one we use. Bob dylan
coming up the steps run hide the birds. **K** got up in j's green robe
coffee going up going down coffee to j still in bed in the early morning
rain of the blue room lesson just like a woman lesson filled the neigh-
bor's blue swimming pool, the neighbor saw a bear walking with his
dog one day. Ed wore k's blue ring, & all 3 of them 2 singing wore
blue blue shirts in the cadillac top down drove to town but we stop
off christ-like at the dump. Born in a small space edging to large
remember: I wont take them, not even for breakfast: french toast &
coffee containers, you should be a psychiatrist sociologist & anthro-
pologist. Applied logic is a sin: remember precepts? Bob dylan. We
left the dump & went to the theater to make calls, j calls about de-
signers k calls about her agent e calls charles projector & equipped.
the calls to calls outside I'm outside not calling taking pictures out-
side the 3 blue shirts in a way I forget myself, this is called profes-
sional the wandering Jew saw christ-like the figures at the dump all
connected 2 you to making movies acting in them smells a rush of
sensual a flood to flood over overflow its banks taking care of never
to be in charge. A policeman directs traffic. He arrests it when it
verges on the criminal: we want to go the other way! This is an
image a fantasy: I am outside in the cool office equipped with a
coffee machine. Take it it's yours it's for the actors rehearsing a
part of this a part of that & must it be as clear as this: you know
about your talent I hear a scout hunt in a conversation & think
about the bear, in a conversation over this part: I believe in this
play that's why I want you to do it & it suits you & it's what you
do best. We go to an antique store: k's ring was blue it was on ed's
hand and yellow wicker chair pose pose brown wooden one the
blue ring e's eyes are closed i'm sitting on the steps of the store. We
walked down elm street but the car was parked in front of the
lavender door red & blue make purple or red on a blue ground. We
3 waited 2 blue & one died. A car full of people waiting for someone
waiting 4 j with k: I spend half my life, the other half, the driver's

door is open & I am describing it. We look for Florida find it in 1957,
division street a brick house with roses in the desert low flags waving
over 2 people pretending to be children playing with a sailboat - son
in stream brother in river car floods mother before her house rain
when? I think it started to rain Housatonic paper factory mill turns
in the river too & jacques went to the bank of kathleen drove home
she slept. Down the road roses to the fork at the T, there's money
buried there to someone's red roses purple evergreen & spaces a
thin road with .no space for walking I saw the wild cat Ed fixes
dinner eat ham corn strawberries & cream strawberries' cream
whipped once to butter, cream & coffee & more b.dylan: focus
zoom telescope, there's a dollhouse in . . . Kathleen: My ring! A
telescope: we slept in our room maybe we looked in on promenade
all that night & on the way we fed some sour mash to hitchhikers
going to housatonic, how much can you stand later B & C? Vitamins
a foggy night the moon falls haze we take a wrong turn B & E lost.
Later the soap fell: to the theater to a bar to a garden of an inn, j,
e & x are cool the sailboats have changed hands, we check the last
house to live in before we move. K's gone to the city we take a bath
I wash my feet here's where the soap fell: parable of the lost piece
of money or is it the last, this is it: I am Dante Ed is Chopin I'm
reeling & falling over tripping over my feet. We go to the T in the
road. It's night cant see the light's in my eyes, E uncovers the cache:
it's a trophy engraved with the whole of the life & times of Dante
Chopin Peter the Great. Goya Beethoven Goethe Louis XIV. Colum-
bus Michaelangelo St. Francis Washington Jefferson Elizabeth I.
Napoleon Leonardo. We thought it was here. Note: Beverly 3674:
on Rte. 183 1.7 mi. from the Glendale post office going south you'll
see a green sign that reads tag sale. Now what is that got to do with
anything? I'm just giving you some old saying that makes about as
much sense as the one you just gave me, listen pa every thirty years
or so there's another generation of mericans a whole new nation,
160 million new people, we're in trouble, what's to guarantee they're
mericans, why dont they just turn into 160 million new people with
powerful airplanes & big bombs & an itch to rule the world, i'll tell
you why because they've got a heritage they've got a constitution &
a bill of rights & a declaration of independence & a declaration of
anarchy disorder confusion disarray, a declaration of jumble chaos &
clutter, litter complexity & knotted tangles & a tradition of fair play

& unlicensed nihilism & how do they know it, because the teachers
of america tell it to them not only tell it to them but sell it to them.
That's out our window, the room with the family, & do you always
get a family with the room, early morning sun on screen & this was
the day that everybody wore a blue shirt & that's great isnt it & like
a summer place at 4:30 monday so what'll I do? you cut your prices
in half until they'll . . . be moving on

July 7
Do you have access to a T? Do you have access to a xerox machine?
This is a major fate hate weigh your fat. So lost so you're lost how
lost can you be when everywhere you turn it's morning & a flag's
going up over a map: 2 bean sprouts resting on a snow pea pod &
then, it snows, it snows for the first time it snows buckets it snows
mainly. It snows rain snow gets rid of alot of germs, says X of the
piemonte ravioli co. we pack our pasta in boxes it's homemade &
speak about the weather: homemade stolen electric typewriters it
isnt one yet stolen cassette tape recorder he had schemes. Between
recorder & he is: the difference between me & the maharajah. We
dont we wont atone for that we leave it as it is so, lost you're lost
how lost can you be when everywhere you go it's morning & the
sun's coming up over a map: & the map a map to alford massachusetts
to a certain place in alford massachusetts within the town lines it
goes like this forward: start up the car past golf course along wind-
ing road across route 183 past j&k's house (blue & yellow) upto T
in road (chesterwood sign) follow the sign make left the road turns
to dirt follow the arrows who? till the road it's dirt veers off in two
directions always bear right on the dirt road. Veering right watch
for oncoming cars on this narrow dirt road you'll go by a white
fence just pass by it when you get to real road, asphalt, that's
route 41, take a left go over a small bridge quickly (it's green) you
go a tenth of a mile & make the first right up & around the black
surface of winding cobb hill road, if you're careful you see the
sign. winding & uphill until you read a complex of buildings that
looks like a textbook farm, if you make the right right in a second
you'll be passing a big red barn on the left, watch for the cows &
people on the road & incidentally here's where the road - if you walk
on it you'll see - looks like it was hit, the surface of the road, by a

44

series of small meteors burning holes making holes making burns in
the surface of the black hard asphalt brown burns. Go right on till
you see a small sign that's faded over it says alford five miles & some-
thing else, this is your first left on the road - if you're on a motor-
cycle at night you'll notice here that the temperature of the air is
considerably warmer than before, we are in some kind of valley air
pocket but after driving a few miles uphill it seems inexplicable
except to the people who live here, here we also pass a dreamlike
farm nestling in the valley's expensive soil, after making this left
the road suddenly turns to gravel - I think this was probably tem-
porary so dont count on it but the gravel begins as you cross the
west stockbridge - alford town line sign. Just after you've passed
the alford brook club or just before alford brook itself is almost
invisible like a light on the shore of the country we're making for,
we're almost there, go about 1.3 miles on this road & then stop at
the house. Before you make it you'll pass by blueberry hill & the
house of a certain dr. pepper a white house with a red car the doctor
has a beard, also some house with a title like swanns way or windy
haven, everyone here is dead serious dont go as far as the turn in
the road where you pass a white fence on the right & a winding
uphill road to a black & white house & dont go as far as the next
valley where the view is for miles & definitely dont go as far as
the strange house with a gazebo a wooden horse & carriage & an
empty reservoir on the left, two bachelors live in this house. If
you've made the right house it's the one right on the road on the
left opposite a yellow one & it's brown with blue doors with a
chimney of stone in the front, it's a funny looking house, stop
there, across the street is a russian prince who loves cats & a
princess who is vincent price's sister who curls her hair, stop across
from them, they have a station wagon & two 35mm movie cameras,
her name is cam so lost you're lost how lost can you be when every-
where you turn it's morning and a flag's going up over a map: pack
car get gas get j's car & tv equipment go to beverly's get key, she
had none we had to break a window to get in, buy an alarm clock
pick up the bed go to the barn see about electricity, go to j's re-
member eileen & call tom, we made a map which is sun which is
shade & how many are accidents we almost hit a car there one day.
And so, we pass jacques & kathleens house on our way home again -
3 white chairs in front reflect light & kathleen left for the city last

night dont forget to call the massachusetts electric company, we did. Splinter splinter of the headboard of the bed splinter of an unshaved dangerous support board for the body of the bed, the bed set up in the middle of the room, splinter's clear, we took the splinter out a foregone conclusion pasted it up with hydrogen peroxide bought bandaids & fell through, ed took a picture you are an actor but dont want to act so instead you talk about marriage by a sweet pond near a sound studio sound & sweet the whole story of the orange pen stolen from the basement. Someone smokes quotes if he someone's son were a few years older he could dip in the cool hollywood pool they provide at an inn, describe gold describe golf get married sink in the deep with no regrets no one looking after him just drown, he could get married he could think, no one would taunt him about it & if marriage had an open end he could think it could become misty in the light could drink light itself, add up the mileage conveniently open find out what's inside he could work live without light, he could candle & flashlight it, he could ride in a convertible without seeing he could create a shortcut write about prayer he could set up lights take them down take pictures he could photograph lights he could be forced to, he could let the light in he could begin a day without a proper bed he could freeze sentences in air, he could eat out, he could drift in & out of a blue room he never woke up in he could imagine a yellow one small, he could notice windows, how you see them, two eyes, ed read the new york times he will never eat a big mac again. It's as simple as that I am looking for 2 u-haul mirrors not fish. And again: legs crossed, who is hungry as I am who is sweet j laughs at cars point risk point. The cars last word, in them, who hears it fall direct a line to women fall by the side of the roadway, men? gouge out eyes? no, but fall by the side on one-way roadways of those not like to like. It's too loud a thud, swan swan silvertones comes down & down just a little bit a little bit too hard hard pat pat a person subtle system, laugh & swell life clear smooth & double perf of film, opaque a system system design your life not mine. It's clear: read genet to describe kathleen run hide give her something run away stay away hide you're in here i'm out again, hide resist fall get up run away ed smiled in the u-haul store we buy a flashlight. Ed the detective ed the cook & messy erasure, ed or mr. & mrs. ed & mr. & mrs. north, what of this take? 72 times in the year & still the same tone, never come true dreams that ring in your ear that way

all around the ear 360 degrees & elaine sets designs rejects set designs
one right after the other then, concentrate, set design, freedom a
moment a memory away, then one step more, get rid of a memory
& laughs 'come clean': "You're in the wrong doorway!" You're in
the wrong home you're sitting in the wrong sun writing in the wrong
car smelling the wrong burning hair all is wrong over is wrong some-
one said & someone said 'functional & ornamental' & the pictures
are like all pictures are lie like sleepers like a railroad crossing sign is
a skull & laughs comes clean at the edges & sign the sea is bluer
signed a book & sign in time, put dick paul in city hall, why two
men & are they both sitting down? Do you give up? The ghost as
well? Oceans right & left, since we're always aware of it, what
should we do a-men, men are able so just act sweet & go on: You
wake up you walk out a man is raising a flag merican flag in house
next door & nixon's the man do you like trees? is susan strassberg a
famous merican actress, woke up, walked out, owner waters the
lawn n' mows grey house of merican flag & mellow one with basket-
ball hoop, there's an merican mosquito under my shirt does it hurt?
no we moved. between the thumb & forefinger of my right hand, be-
tween those a splinter zooms in quick & the taste waste of a room -
i'm a schoolboy in watercolors, look around, its mountains in
merica zoom, what the fuck's the moon we're in an insulated room
we take our time runnin round we zoom no moon, we make, monster,
the greatest milk of all time, like this: one blue head with a black
wig on sitting in a window surrounded by skirts, & mercy like they
say another merican flag by god a whole display of em, pink, o mesh
& gauze cause you to faint for mercy wow up on a mt. top maybe
if you're lucky you prick think back: you saw flowers underneath
women's head eyes closed reflected in the window you saw flags in,
same one, shit man it was a beauty shop if i ever saw one, somebody
grabs a 7:30 flight to toronto man & S. is doing juliet on the Square,
what a gas explosion that was red engines galore & ten gallon hats to
boot the end. Not by a long shot. Cabs. It was the circle beauty
salon with a capital C. & wait till you personally see the Capitol's
mind's eye blower encased in space emergency glass - that's silver
& gold case you didnt know, you fucker. The mother's house was
bigger than the house of the fatter father. That's how it goes, both
mother & father resemble police cars & in the dark: a picture of a
stone a picture of a mother superimposed on a father, a picture, a

prize-winning picture, of bird on tree. We never saw that one, we
never looked at it, we didnt come from there, we grew up in the
city, we grew up in the shadow of the housatonic riverboat gambling
casino we grew up in a cadillac we saw a dog limping we saw a bear
in the woods in merrimac forest we saw a bear limping by the side
always by the side, they were constant companions, of a giant dog
a strange giant dog back behind the swimming pool we saw this
sight, it was glorious in the sense that it fit the exact size it fit
exactly it was just the right size to be framed by a single standard
size, the official size, basketball hoop of this century NBA regula-
tions. And so, we bought a berkshire eagle & a couple of side view
mirrors, there was nothing playing at the drive-ins, something black,
we got home after dark, no juice. No sparks. No gas. No flames.
No water at least we had ground. The moon was full the brightest
clouds you ever saw moved across in front of it the brightest night
clouds move fast, it's scenery. You think you plan you save this
up, your calm drink, black jack daniels sour mash whiskey from
tennessee where ground is green it's orange, no colors in the dark
fire flies we lit the house with candles on the stone slab center stone
is safe turn on the fire brigades, light up pricks & ready for the team,
we put out fires after they begin, they burn for a while you call
clouds passing all the while passing quickly in front of the moon,
when are they coming when will they be ready. Get dressed in the
middle of the night, on call, it's the volunteer fire dept. of new
york city we'd like to see you in action we'll call when we're
ready meanwhile we're watching these certain clouds go by by the
moon & I'll hold a candle to your face if you'll hold one to mine,
the fire flies in no mood exposure to the moon will . . . & ed with a
candle on ed face the moon behind we're ready for action, the mo-
tion's in the sky candle ed makes a path through the room dont
trip to the moon or i'll call in the brigade again & they'll sing
hearty songs drink all the whiskey we have in the house & sing no
juice how? in the sky ed walked through the room with a candle in
his hand how did the fire start sir, in the bed in the sink in the dead
of night, it must've been the bed in the middle of the room caught
fire in the, no, it was the matches left out in the moon. Light matches
& perhaps you can see fireflies ed with a candle on his face, the big
moon behind not long enough i'm lit candles in my hair my hair in
braids but not tied like randa wears it the braids coming loose at the

bottom so much action in the sky ed walked through the room with
a candle in his hand i watched through the big window he passed
behind the headboard of the bed, drank & smoked, left matches & a
candle outside, the candle got a feather stuck to it no mosquitoes we
bought sugar & evaporated milk, had coffee in real cups with water
from the pipes left there, boil it, new tv, notes candles nectarines &
many matches ed got a new kind of match today a permanent match
eternal one. Come out now men in your rubber suits for the permanent
match is a dangerous one dangerous to the touch & a flashlight at
the auto store, i demanded it, a clear light not from fire soon blow
up explode in a flash of . . . drink more, we make a match fire light
a cigarette & store or set fire to the end of one & draw in the smoke
into our hearts & lungs, the firemen are back to help put out a row
of candles sleeping, fifty or a hundred of them shaped like the body
of a man or a crown, we light them all drink a cup of hot coffee &
sleep in flames. Leaping around the notes we make about moon,
sleep, middle of room, wake up clear & alter. It's annabel lee or
something: sharp knives cut fingers & hands, splinters get in they
burn we swim at least we like to swim

July 8
Eight, right, & sink a foul shot, wait a minute wait a minute what
are you talking about, think back think straight, eight right, they're
just not gonna give you any electricity for free, well what's the dif-
ference I can see or I cant see: just glance at it, just James Dean.
And so, go ahead: red tide in florida: one carried gas the other oil,
they sank. Like a clamp like a mirror like a brace like a strut of some
kind like high school like college like beatniks like hitchhikers, I
dream of ed's parents like vitamins grandfather falls down like god
he goes to the hospital like in france, slide down the day you can
barely see, bernadette you can just about see, he gets x-rays like
film like cans of film like fine jewelry like silverware, glance at it
from the bed, from bed to bed bernadette, bath is trance, like clocks
like pewter like the everly brothers like bye bye love like watches
like photos, love, like radios love like phonographs or stereos like
television like appliances milk check milk see milk sleep milk,
ultramarine blue marie. You sleep marie: save them for me certain
moments I'm resting I'm restoring I'm gathering I'm hunting I'm

starving I'm you you say go on being peering owl on top of fortress
sounding out training sound to meet my ear drive & mark time I'm
a history her coil mark time, suffer a moment to let me be like her a
history, object she was determined defies all laws & rules is the lan-
guage I bought from passers by sea crate full of junk & language
twisting & twisting coil of all morning I met that guy the guide &
cast his bell aside I'd rather die in sync with just random tones, just
war can bury baby brick your foot's my foot core how late you
suffer core how late whispers suffer whispers into the tape a running
water sound at the bell rewinding a vision I got & mystery works at
the door if no one's there I'll stay right here adding a picket to this
to pierce you/me clear through I saw you remember we go through
the greatest horrors of the world at last together you turn over you
dont really wake up sink a shallows at the oceans deep deep malay-
sians sleep I'll know new dance the boxes taught today it's rare code
words can sink a ship in the shallows reform so dry a crease & saw
the same crack in the dream before sink down broad ship at dawn
home plate they hold it up to their ears to hear we years you go on.
I'm resting. I saw her once. Her pins prick my skin she makes me
dizzy she makes me well. You repeat: we were just in the process of
repainting the dining room, one wall yellow, one wall blue, two walls
greens & the window legends orange to look like the sun, like a
broken ankle in france like tom slipping on the west side highway
& falling into a hole, will a car come by & kill him, will a tour come
by & watch him, will an engine come by & raise him up, will the
police come with sideburns & arrest him: "I dont want to hear how
you got in this hole." I can hear tom's voice it isnt saying that. Orange
notes orange moon orange check for $10.25 orange reflection orange
log cabin orange food sing out loud orange car away moon no think-
ing moon orange map the same map as before. Sing this: W is a letter
I is a letter waiting for the phone co waiting singing I sing I ants I ants
& geranium geranium hum spell that: cicada, ambient & transient. It's
over before its begun that's a day & note, something's biting me, the
sun replaced the moon so we act like people we woke up feel good get
water from the pipes: the house through the window shaped like a
tree shaped like a house, luckily you work in time. Ten o'clock let
me take you higher the ants are going crazy it's hot in the sun it's
the sun I'm waiting for the telephone we drive breakneck: "I can't
act so let's just be friends as men," so, who'll play the brother?

once there was a man who wanted to leave things
where they were. but he covered them. a slow death
—the dope a fine powder under the cap covered with
stones. once was a man who worked at night his face
was close to the lamp, inches away. he added something
to the heat of the lamp. one man with no light in
his eye, 3 stones. he stayed, he talked about suicide.
once a man but the heat of the lamp was thousands
of watts & watts was riots. the man thought of
leisure built stick match bridges with a gap
between them. he began again: he woke up in
the morning. he remembers he's changed. he sinks
into the desert sun dizzy sick. the sun's dark &
he's in a corner he's treed. once man like a theater
there was a man like ugly dogs at the theater
was a man like yelping puppies, I was sitting
waiting. ed gets out of the car: once a man he
cut himself. he caught a girl in a faded net.
she was the shade of numbers on a phone. he
stopped himself, dried in the sun: you see it
I see it, shoes off, close to was where the paint
brush through the trees dots.

I thought that bursh was my memory closer from behind, in the
woods a gulf, a light crate for the phone, catch a car going by, wait-
ing for them, get lost, pink toad, the threads of the restaurant, we
eat. Blue. Blue in the eye, ultramarine on an imaginary line on the
road, on a line at the center the once was man parked his car, car
dashboard crashboard & all. He always parked at the capital with-
out hesitation. Pollynoses? come later. Blue sky strawberry plant
car pool. P.O.V. is straight but it's day lights are on, some kind of
curtain & some kind of curtain & some kind of bottle & a person
lying in the dark, the once was man. He looks like a bottle of red
wine vinegar he looks like a memory he looks like a visit in the
middle of the night while we are putting plugs in cases to protect
them from the water of the river he looks around like a clue: we
made maps he looks red, lion, log, cabin — all those places, a big
dinner was made we drew from it — scallops steak awful corn not
set by indians in the blue soil, drink water from a green glass glass
& once was drew out his credit card to pay to pay for two or three

once was's, we wrote a check for $10.25 good capital, start a plant in georgia employ blacks for once returned his steak it wasnt rare enough, a moments chance a womens club walks through sits down for heady cocktails in the autumn dawn & summer sunset which was which for once they all ate veal the same. Why consume cowboys rope steer they all eat veal, do you sew quilts for us in the dark dark nights in winter once lit a cabin with wagon wheels on the ceilings drop down from heights where rain & so on out the window darker & darker, little lights a green space on the plate a blue dot on the feel of the veal in veins in your mouth return it it's frozen that's what eskimos eat. Here, once in a crowd one bright one color & one costume. I'm from another planet I zoom in on a red car top translucent white appears from the head of a woman in turquoise with white trim a french twist, blue nose noses come out of a short-haired man in a suit he puts that in his pipe & smokes it down, he's through, a blonde in orange with a white bag is hanging on a cross, she sighs, a woman turns around, once was a man with his stick-arm leaning on the bannister, a man in a white suit what's the use of being a boy leaning against a white silver torch car a mixture that has to be stirred like a man he's bad extends his hand there's a coke in it for a quarter to a woman in white with a cool black sweater dragging in folds over an arm glisten in shoes high heel shoes she reaches for the coke, grabs it, once was holding a theater bill in hand hand behind him a man scratching his neck in white shoes the room waxes green of the exit door. For once in case the heart of once stopped like a light aimed at the floor & off to the side of the light in the light ed stands on legs. Power miscast his clothes left on the floor he took a bath & went to bed but not before we disappeared that day & were never heard from again: & once in the pacific we went back to our old habit of taking in information of all kinds & amounts, you know now or right away, you bend your left knee in the pacific of course you never come back, left knee like a stick match stick bridges in the sand you leave or will let limits defend themselves especially on the bridges bridges a fine line attracts friends from all over the world passing by once & once a name in print, you see it, one is done, celebrate the next, the people who have no interests are ahead & we go to bed but not before the race: detective, go to sleep, kathleen's braids are in a jar, shoot me shoot him shoot you center edges align a space together a

light repeating, detective go to sleep, but not before the race begins:
        once there is a man who sings as long as he can
        & he lives in a yellow house so, he sings as long as
        he can & he lives in a yellow & blue house thats the
        end, the storm was near, the fellows the guys the
        skies werent clear, they were clear & the storm the
        storm was dry, we felt it dry on us on our hands &
        ears & on the words coming up: let's just use the
        rain making something out of anything & the man who
        lives above the once is man was learning more & more
        about how to sing, he was green with envy for all the
        greatest singers of his time. I'm good at setting
        up a paradise he said, look at this one here. here
        is a paradise made in blue & red - all you need &
        you are not I repeat you are not riding a bicycle.
        The sense of it she began & she was not the girl
        who lived in the house, she's the girl we saw with
        that guy, the two of them just hanging around, you
        know the guy with the stringy blond hair, the tall
        guy who looks like anthony perkins in tall story,
        no, in psycho & the young basil rathbone.
They lead me around they lead me to the race. Sit up stretch what
comes first. Something come first comes ahead. You call something
something, it's in mind, it's at attention, if you do, if it is, then it
comes first, first page four then page one: if you call it something
if you do put it first then, you'll know later what you're doing, the
things that dont get called they come last if there's time if there's
time, you missed it you threw it that's an echo that comes last, unless
you play fill-in-the-blanks, you make a bet. Sit up stretch thin thing
red thing moving along the red dot on jacques watch is a person a
machine when he's in the movies? The light of the light I'm looking
at is the light that was shining on some small man a year before the
earth of something happened a quake make down come down some
hard hard things on the head of the man who did die he died shout-
ing reciting my name, it was in the theater but it's the same the same
thing as the thing in the theater now is the time for all & so on to
the end dash would anyone like to read this picture to the end: when
my parents used to bring their black friends over for a jam session
that was all I could remember when the police handcuffed me. Read

the picture, picture, now think harder, it races ahead of you into
some other time, it races you to the moon, now further away it
races with you you are neck in neck, you are making the fastest
moves, it's gaining on you, in close, it's coming in close, racing you
to the finish, finish not in sight, it races, you race no one's racing,
the finish you expand you expand your chest you are in some other
world you have been prepared for this you have waited the world
is wound around its other one, you think you shiver you are racing
still, it races ahead of you, you whisper, blast explosion a soft ticket
a boat a ground like fur, a bed of leaves, nothing new, nothing that
is really new, completely new you are in it, you are out, you have
felt the beginning of it before you have felt fear, races flash but
dont reappear, it's the end of something before, but nothing, no
song, sing wrack song & that plant that's the same plant as, that's
the plant you I am I & you know what red is . . . red of strawberry
is . . . that plant, the way it grew over, it is growing over now, what
sign what pebble & almost, some road some race you dont we can
talk like that we can talk like that it dont mean the same mean the
same thing at all that at all. When I recognize the strawberry leaves
down on the ground I'm back where I started from & to bear it up,
a strawberry , two dead ones, dead leaves, they're here in spring
past the bunk of summer, gets to sleep on top? Summer you never
saw, summer this summer you never saw it saw it before, I saw it I
couldnt see I slipped I skipped what was what it was, they were used
to it but I saw it I saw it I knew it would be right where it was, no
slip, fit that in: go for a fitting in every example every instance
every time like for instance there might be an actor moving in, there
might be him or her, there might be this or that, there might be
time for everything or we might be busy we might be strong we
might collapse, like some building blown up by the designer who
hated it, that's a thought: we're in here, tree, listen to this: I die
sigh resign I like you which of you is nearest, which is here, a bath,
a bath of trees a sea of trees, you think a fall of trees, that's there
when I'm there, to make a tree fall, why not, think tree does that
make sense? think tree does this ring true? think again tree can I
talk to you? & further tree which one are you? have I done have I
done it? tree do it over? tree think my thought? tree, tree? sit back,
a recipe, a ham, I cant go anywhere, I have to stay right here: veal:
in america veal is a misunderstood meat & the milkfed variety is

hard to come by. Veal should be tender succulent & white, if it is not there are 2 ways to improve it, one is to blanch briefly starting in cold water & the other is to soak refrigerated in milk overnight before cooking veal needs a careful cooking approach as it is lacking in fat & may toughen quickly although abroad certain dishes like veal a la meuniere or a la creme are severed both sorry & juicy veal here is generally served after reaching an internal temp. of 175° & it is roasted 25 to 30 minutes per lb. until weeks have gone by although a leg of veal may be roasted most out of its head large pieces of the things are pot roasted the long roadmuscle of the leg when cut across the grain produces scallops & then dial-a-steak dinner & he'll deliver it you soon, next time you hunger for a succulent steak day or night reach over & dial CH2-4100 & go right on doing whatever you were doing, at home or at somebody else's place or at your office, within 60 to 90 minutes, stop & start eating. A complete steak dinner broiling hot with all the trims. Serve on the sturdy service that arrives on request or use your own. Keep the handsome stainless still steak cutting knives with our compliments but be careful with them not to cut your own throat. Your steak & baked potato will arrive so hot it'll burn your tongue & you can keep this too. Packed separately is your crisp tossed green salad with insects with the steak joint's own seagull flavored dressing. Dinner rolls large chunks of creamery cow butter salt & pepper from the mines, napkins & utensils. Minimum service is for two: either or both of you may already own a fur. Add fifteen per cent for delivery & gratuities. Dial-a-steak service available noon to 11 pm seven days a week complimentary gift on request consists of a corkscrew. We honor all major credit cards.
Goodnight, meat

July 9
What's the difference who's in charge: when our experience is increased by the addition of observations which *were* future, down the road & relections to infinity, but are now past, we seek once more to order in the same manner our increased volume of experience: when it's this bright it's just as well to look at them small, how, can you see that? But in this increased volume all experience is of equal value, that which was future, reflections to infinity, is

in no way different from that which was past, for all is now past:
when it's this bright it's just as well to look at them small, now can
you see that? what are those are they trees or wild flowers? Down
the road & reflections to infinity in the bathroom mirror: in order
not to lose the light you do it with a mirror & the only way you
can get a mirror there is when the shutters close & nevermind &
when this light goes on: this is the first or last & those are the holes
where birds lived where they live, I said, what's the difference who's
in charge: the light says the money says the dawn says desert no
this is an incredible thing those are little holes that birds make to
live in a mound of sand it's in a gravel pit, I said, that's really strange
what kind of birds do that she said, I have no idea cause the sand is
completely dry & they must have to wet it some way the way ants
do when they build anthills I said, it's in a gravel pit it's not near
water anywhere is it she said, no it's a gravel pit in the middle of
the berkshires I went there to get sand I said I wander all night in
my vision someone said & I say lie down on the road in the dark,
say down on the road down the road & reflections to infinity in the
mirror framed in a color on the winedark road: it was green to my
house & I check first the holes in a mountain of sand where birds
nest, place: sand to make sandbags & what were they for, she said,
for we shot for we shot a film in the middle of the river & we put a
tripod down & we thought we might need sandbags cause the river
runs it's hard running water but the holes I couldnt believe it & I
took a picture of them & then the guy at the gravel pit explains it
what they are & you see the birds flying in & out huge birds &
they're big holes they dont look it you dont get any ideas of their
size I said, pterodactylls or something she said, yes birds with wings
of skin & long fingers I said & she said very prehistoric really in-
credible, she said. Place: 2 bean sprouts resting on a snow pea pod
& props: jacques I remember it perfectly, sandbags: he shoveled it
in, I held the bag 4 for $1.00 & something in great detail: that's the
rest of the gravel pit I said, I thought a gravel pit would be very
grey & look like the kind of gravel you see in driveways & I'm sur-
prised to see it's so tan she said, this is a mysterious place, it's right
around the corner from where I used to live & one of the reasons I
went there was that I know I needed to fill up bags with sand & I'd
tried to buy sandbags but nobody'd sell them they thought I was
crazy you know like a person from the city wants to buy something

that's right there in front of you so I bought burlap bags & some-
body charged me 25¢ each for them I mean for a burlap bag & I
went here because I was always curious what they did & they made
a loose mixture of pebbles & rock fragments coarser than sand &
sometimes mixed it with clay & they were very nice I said, is that
where you lived she said. I got a softball shirt at nejaimes free from
a man with no morals, he took it off & I dont have to go on with
this, what would you do? create laws? discuss the purpose of them?
disorder the order that has already been established? order the in-
creased volume of experience? or reject it altogether leaving nothing
to be ordered & everything lax in a mess in chaos in a muddle out
of place cluttered in a maze in a labyrinth in a wilderness in a jungle
in tangled skeins & loose fixes, a heroin addict wouldnt do it I must
have no respect for nothingness to photograph these scenes with
sand or snow off Monument Valley Road the road in the valley of
the same mountain monument mountain, a whole series of them a
whole series of photographs & one monument & I get a whole new
picture of myself, where is your driver's license he said, you are
drinking beer. It's loose there are no morals there's an absence of
authority in the subway: weigh your fate becomes weigh your fat
& what's new is crossed out in a convulsion of volition is intersocial
in this case the abstraction is order: kathleen calls & I've drunk five
glasses of wine in an unmethodical something or other before tom
called & a complex what was there a what, what is the music of the
moment, I'm here & someone said well there was a song & some
music in his ear most of the time he just went around with it and
to get off easy to get off loose or just to get off to desert to dethrone
to impeach to depose to abdicate to lose your drivers license on elm
street waiting for the fireman to come with his boots drinking beer,
where is you drivers license he said, you are drinking beer: no that's
just, no there are pictures later of the inside of the house, this is
just on the way to pittsfield because I didnt live on a street because
they put us in a house like that when we first got up there they put
us in a room with a family & I abdicated because we were making
films for a play because for jacques yeah & we immediately mobilized
our resources & went slack we tolerated we relaxed we misruled we
wanted to live in a forest & we got a house we couldnt afford except
that we shared it with an actor & they gave us each housing allowances
& we put them together & we got a house that was a forest but the

room with the family wasnt so cool because that's just another house or car actually & I think this is in white stockbridge & this is what I said & she said, they're really clear they're really bright it's pretty film & I said, kodachrome, that's the housatonic river at a calm part past where & that's a bridge I am looking out from a bridge I went over a hundred fifty times in a month & she said that's three times a day you must've stayed on the wrong side of it. John baker comes by one two three four lock the door where that blue car is parked the lock's broke or at least there aint no driver with the king's driver's license remember perrone's wife & is it hot enuf for ya because I went over the bridge over the housatonic expecting something & are you crazy you are a heroin addict & thank you very much it was a hot day on the same river we needed boots for river no. 183 near The Plains, Ticket, America I quit & switched to heroine Emily Dickinson signed her death warrant death contract here in Nathaniel Hawthorne's house, Lenox, in 1875 OK? That was in the river written, see it? no & that shore's for you to identify & estimate size estimate the size of there's a man on it small as a dot over hoover dam madam I'm adam spring water & close up the spaces of rivers for good. Bridge did you plan it that way: well stockbridge was on one side, j's house & our house were on the other side & was it a pedestrian bridge or a car bridge it was both & it has a something or other you can walk on it a passageway on the side like an old suspension bridge not a suspension bridge you know those girders those iron girders all clear cantilever I said, is that the same side or the other side she said, I think it's the same side so I say so & she agrees because of the trees & I agree yeah but she says I like that one better though for some reason it's clearer & closer it's different & I say it might be a different exposure but she says it's a question of height & mumbles it doesnt look like you are high does it. This was after I spent a morning getting props together & this was the day ed went to the city to get the equipment & I got props together too busy to take any pictures & now I'm on my way to j's house to wake him up so we can decide on a definite place in the river which we never did wasted the whole afternoon & that's the bridge it's a suspension bridge. Right she says I cant tell I dont know but I think if it has those wires I guess so but it's tiny though really tiny & I say pretty little stock bridge that's j's forest it's amazing that was the daytime forest so dark forests are very dark & she says that's a forest

I dont believe it it's too dark & this is a swimming pool: bridge did
you plan it that way it's all clear cantilever & why did I picture this
forest first? I remember he was sorry I came & wanted time to him-
self like blue comes up white comes down like branches hanging on
a vine, this will be a jungle i'm sure. No it's not for that a jungle & a
maze that dan called & someone from the nursing home called &
they're trying to get him to sign remember, what sign what sign
sign over bags of sand in the end in the end in the end no light just
2 cats & 4 pairs wading boots on monday night tuesday night wednes-
day night all: we're looking for a boat & ammunition of sand & blood
blood in a movie blood in the sand & a one-minute speech on mon-
day afternoon from the four-to-midnight cop you call him at his
home, mr. cop perrone, you meet 1:30 pm at the fire house & you
can have the boots till monday night when the volunteers drill & you
wait 1½-2 hours & it's 3pm now at 1957 division street, is that the
year from which we make our mark, yesterday & today eileen's
at home on monday between 12 noon and 3 with no lights 2 cars &
a minute to spare to make a speech on a page of scripts about sand-
bags, you call the cop at noon at home it cost you 70¢ a call he's
the deputy fire commissioner & a four-to-midnight cop, his num-
ber's 4706 & call him the fire chief if you know what's good for you
& you know what his wife's pregnant, I've invaded his privacy any-
way to pay me for that he gives me 4 pairs waders till monday night
when the volunteers assemble for a drill: who is the fire chief, where
are the softball shirts, how can I get a boat: jacques went in for a
swim & we spent a long time discussing the color of that reflection
& it didnt come out the color it was & the question is did you think
the reflection would have it's own color & the answer was it did &
the question was no but in the picture you thought it would it would
have it's own color & the answer was well it did & the question was
what & the answer was it should have come out in the picture as what
it was which was a sort of purple color you see the green trees in the
blue pool turned purple & made too much sense & the question was
well & it did & it well but the how did it but the white of the sun
must do it & the answer was it did because it was just very green
along with the light of the sun & the sun was very low in the after-
noon & it somehow made it & it forced itself to make it & it forced
out of itself this strange purple color which you will never see & she
said no & that's too bad & I said here's another one you can never

tell what this is & she said july was a very long time ago & I said july oh & she said it does to me it seems that was & I said I thought you meant this seemed that way & she said oh no & I said if july were a long time ago that would be nice & she said they do & I said you mean the pictures & she said no july no july always seems to be about two years ago almost as if you had been there & I said except that I have a thousand ways to track it down & she said how are you going to name the book july & I said maybe july & she said if the light looks the same to you then but it never does & I said no it doesnt i mean that's what's so funny about looking you've seen it & she said apocalyptic: there was a definite place in the river & a time to pick up the nephew & there was a drive on monday morning & there was a mother on monday afternoon & there was some off-white paper & there was something in great detail & it was friday there was hot hot hot sun & there was hot enough isnt it sitting in the sun & there was the firehouse & there was beer orange pen camera a hot camera & there was john baker coming by to talk to me & there was his camera & there he was wanting a range-finder instead of a nikormat & there was every car that pulls by & there were a look & looks & there was mr. perrone the fireman & four-to-midnight cop & there was sleeping j & there was the fireman's pregnant wife & somebody said he'll never know & a woman in the post office got a speeding ticket in elizaville she was going 78 mph & there she was going 78 mph & she was getting her third speeding ticket near hudson ancram & there was ropes canoes knives & towels & a way to dial a camp to get a boat so today's the day when all jokes jokes & gestures go out of joint: ed left for the city this morning to pick up the stuff as I might be able to recreate later recreate later from this & in my mind I would re-argue reascend reassemble & there was a reassembly & I would reassert & there was a reassertion & I would reassess reassign reassimilate & there was a reassimilation & I would reassume & there was a reassumption & I would reattach & there was a reattachment & I would reattack reattempt reawaken rebind rebloom & I would reblossom reboil rebuild & something was rebuilt & I would rebury. There's something I've been meaning to ask you about in moving you talk about reading dune did you really like it & I kept trying to persuade mary to read it & she wouldnt she said & I said yeah I really liked it & she said talk about making spices & I said yeah I could never read any of his other books

they're all shit & I read one after dune it was something called the
haven makers no it wasnt that it was called dune somebody & I
couldnt believe it was the same writer & she said no it was the same
& I said I have it here but I couldnt get through it & she said I read
that all his other stuff was bad & so I didnt & then I saw dune mes-
siah & I just looked at it & I saw that it was really terrible & I said
dune was great & she said yeah dune was fantastic & she said all
that stuff about the salt women & stuff about other kinds of women
& all that stuff about the usurpation of perception & I said & then
for that guy to come up to me & for me to know what he was gonna
look like beforehand that's just what & before I could finish she
said what was that like & I said I sort of described it I was outside
in the country & I fell asleep & I had I was sort of half waking & half
sleeping the way you are when you sleep in the sun & she nodded yes
to that & I said I knew the guy the guy in the house next door, it
was the beginning of the year & I had never met him I was there
only three or four days, & I knew he was gonna come up & intro-
duce himself at some point & his name was bob may & so I had this
sort of fantasy half awake fantasy vision of exactly what he would
look like & what he would say & then I woke up & I was just waking
up & the book was on my stomach & it all happened exactly & he
looked exactly, well he had a pipe exactly like in the dream & he
came up & he said hi I'm bob may which is exactly what he had said
to me in the dream, not such a strange thing to say really & she said
no it isnt & I said but on the other hand he couldnt have said some-
thing else & then I said I'm bernadette mayer with the accent on
the e, r, as if I were more may than he was & he was the son of rollo
may you know the philosopher psychiatrist whatever he is & she said
books yeah funny books very funny & I said I dont know what this
is it's a light it's one of those lights you know those candles they
have in restaurants but that doesnt look right at all & she said it's
some kind of shadow: well that must be the garden of the ed-red
leo-lion-jacques inn an in to the actors & actresses, it was hung with
a crooked fence & there was an addition to it an ad in the papers
for paperhangers, our nails were filed we were filed we filed in to a
neat white space with red candles, who's the fall guy: the boat
dealer, jokes the sandman, jokes the guy at agway, jokes jacques,
jokes come back later, hopes jokes dopes go look for a boat to swim
away in we are having a nice conversation in this garden with two

hitchhikers one is white one is black but neither of them talk, we
had a nice conversation it went on forever till the sun set no, i forget,
rise: there may be a glass there or something, yes, there's something
there look at it, it looks like the orange is distorted, the orange part
looks like a dressmaker's dummy, yes it does it does & there's more
of those coming, yes it is this is in the red lion inn where we were
having something to eat waiting for, no I dont think it is oh yes it
is oh yes it's really dark, yes it's an outdoor grave I mean garden or
something & there was no light there was no light & it was night
except, wait a minute, that's not outdoors you can see that that's a
window, yes curtains & blinds it must be, it looks like the house, yes
but it's the same candle or is it the same I dont know, it could be
yes it its, the color's the same but maybe it's not maybe it's not the
red lion, no I'm sure of it it was the red lion in, yes but what about
the glass, well I cant figure it out, it seems to come above the flame
here & in the other one the flame seems to come above the glass, yes
it's true, i give up I don't know where it is it could be anywhere, I
know I was in two restaurants that night, no three, but that doesnt
look like the other one because the other one was lit you know it
was inside & j told me the whole story of two books he never wrote
while we were waiting for ed & kathleen, yes she was in the city too,
we were waiting for them to come back, oh here's a clue, but what
is it, is it j's house, no it's a person sitting there, I think I know, shit
it cant be they have a garden, I know, everyone's arrived by this
time, ed & kathleen & tom showed up too & they were hungry so
we all went to the silver city bar, finally, which also has red candles
I was confused that was the confusion the muddle of red candles all
over, now this is the silver city bar where we had cheeseburgers &
there was live music playing & this is our house. Like I told you we
had a nice conversation it's easy I'll set the scene: a con man, spring,
you ignore alot, the sun sets, no I forget, rises: a man & a woman
have gotten up from their table in the garden of the typical summer
inn. They face each other standing across the table: her hands are on
her hips in an attitude of (there's money in it - the narrative cinema
& sin in a & sin M.A.) reprisal (I've got it - robbe-grillet). Shes in a
summer dress & he's in a suit they are standing still till we're back in
the U.S.S.R. Silver City Bar & the home coming has developed into
everything everybody turn the key in the lock, I dare you make it
work & sink ships the marauders bang they make their presence

known, carol faints, I the machine of the future of the future by
john mchale with live music, folk or rock, no identity, sorry lady,
slam the door, another beer & ten cheeseburgers with everything
on em I & you, but it looks empty, why? they've gone. Bob Dylan
comes in here: he places one blue book, one red white & blue
book, 2 books down on the red oilcloth table cover with an alligator
pattern, he talks to david silverstein at the bookstore but david wont
give him any of his poetry books, he holds back the poetry down then
further down he blames it on some black guy so he wont look bad,
he sees barbara roy, he makes notes, he goes past the left curve &
down the hill a hundred yards along a straightaway until he gets to
the part where there's grass growing in the river, steve told him this,
he gets to the part where grass is growing out into the river, he eats
clams, its the hottest day of the year, he gets the paper he gets rope
& special cigarettes & special off-white paper, he gets some sandbags
& he calls the gas rope. She said that's really nice & I said that's the
main part of the house but that thing on the side is like a loft & she
said is it really modern I thought it was an old house but that looks
new & I said it was an old barn but now it's full of glass & she said
now I can really see something at last & I said the light is really some-
thing & she said yes & I said yes & she asked who's that sitting on
the bed & I said that's tom & ed but they were moving & she said
the light's nice & I said yeah you see the recessed lights like that
one & those big spotlights on the top on the roof of the barn so
that you can point it to change the lighting you know what I mean
& she said well is there alot of natural light like alot of windows &
I said alot of glass you'll see do you see windows like that & she
said is that a window & I said yeah & she said that's a door & I said
no that's a window a window that's shaped like a door a really wide
one & she said but this is on the outside & I said no we're inside &
that's a reflection & she said oh & I said this is all at night & she
said it looked wonderful & I said yes a house where right out that
window in the daytime you can see a tree just the trunk of it shaped
like a house & that's another part of the house & she said everything
thinks it's the same but there are changes in the texture & the color
& I laughed & I said that was the only piece of furniture we had was
that bed & she said it looked familiar & I said see that's the big win-
dow in the background but it's jesus even a little bigger than that
when you look at it right on & it's just glass all over the house they

said two thousand dollars worth of glass the people who built it &
she said really & I said these are the boots we borrowed from the
fire department to go into the river which is very polluted but it
looks real nice & she said it looks wonderful & I said but we didnt
some of us didnt use our boots & got terrible insects in our feet &
she said there are chairs you cant sit in: there's a roof over a bat's
head a whole family of bats & E teaches T how to use to use the
camera but be me, the recessed light was on their backs during the
exposure the camera moves T is still I've got nothing at stake mis-
take I'll take as long as I will. There are 70 foot waves in the bay of
fundy delight dessert & all views of the same dot circle around dot
star tsar of the boots boom bogs stereo boot no. 22 S left that's the
size of it & erase a mental erase, sound, clear: dark blue, the lights
will, a black chair with a red velvet seat cover, I admit it. Move on
the bed you hear it hear this is the night K came in in the middle of
the night this night or the next one where boot no. 22 is blurred is
that OK? Reflections tell a story they are outside & not in & T the
head of is his is invisible will blur while they're still moving & I am
cut down paring the black off the camera with a chair, scared, stripes
hypes the water of the river out of chaos fear new shorts with stripes
might come, that fucking light it's the beam that was in focus & the
head headed with leader edit a magazine I'll tell show see it & say it,
Ed, how come nobody ever left new york city for new orleans for
california for somewhere for here, yes I've seen that before the roof
was pointed like a barn & the loft held hay or wanted to the windows
cut through, it was full of something & that tree the windows cut
through that tree down on them so I decided to move & you know
what & all this stillness is not an aim, then they seemed more in
focus & after that I forgot after that to infinity, cause why cause
there's some fires: I was glad that day was over I am glad that day
is over & this is a kiss, you laugh, a dent has been made in my
imagination: Big Allis & con ed & moon tom & the rest set along
a long bow & the archer flies: oh shit, dead? Jim morrison louis
armstrong & the end of the world the end of the something & all the
things come up do they come up do things come up & more record-
ing & more of it: lee frank julie & lynn living together in one large
room in the shaggy dog studio & one thing in great detail & some-
thing in great detail, one day, new black shirts softball shirts, nolan's
chargers: in order not to lose the light you do it with a mirror & the

only way you can get a mirror there is when the shutters are closed, where is it, something, never mind, when this light goes on you do something: those are the spotlights that you can move around. She said that's good yellow light, it's yellow it's not really red it just turns golden & i like it that way & at first I thought it was the reflection of the wood but it wasn't, well the light was very good but it didn't look that good I said it looked different somehow & it was really hard to take 36 pictures every day some days & she agreed it would be & she says what is that & I say that's aiming at different lights & moving all around & she says amazing & I say like cars going by, is it the same, yes it's the same you just keep going especially if cars are moving & I'm sure you've seen it before, yes you've seen it in the movies yes you've seen it everywhere, that might be a fire in the fireplace too or another red candle out of place, this is something i cant figure out, and this is another, this must be inside the house but i cant remember, this is like being a detective, there's one amazing thing & then some reaction, the reaction's diamond shaped, this is the light but it's done from the bottom, you see, here's the light here & it has brass or iron on it, yes I see how that's the same light & then the light's just moving out sort of out of the space it's in, it looks as though the light is moving right out of the canvass, what did you say, is that your hand right that something at the edge of the amazing light that looks like something but it may be just another reflection, no I think it was just more lights, the same lights, you see when we were still in the city there was a construction project on grand & broadway & now it's the same people & the same machines that work in front of our house, it's as if they ran it's as if they started all the way down grand street and reached our house just in time & they're going west & it took them as long as we were away & all that happened & now they're right out in front of the house, yes & I checked the numbers of the machines to see if they were the same, and were they, yes they were

July 10
As before well we'll find out we'll see. What's a break? slow pro gress lets get out of here and so, at least I see what I was thinking then, cut down & over: up in the morning & off to school green leaves &

a mess by the side of the house green leaves & no mess in back there are albany vines or are they lincoln ones, this was the dry runs for the films, ed in his patched jeans, the back pockets out for patching removed for patching & even yellow velour on the side where the jeans were burned in the oven, we were trying to dry em fast & that makes you giddy in the winter or summer will I ever have great grandchildren, he is standing leaning over over to focus the camera & jacques leaning his left arm on the cadillac door, watch on that arm, in the nolans chargers sweatshirt, pure soft ball, looking squinting through the famous eye piece of an mpcs arriflex which is mounted by a mount on the side of the car with tom in the drivers seat counting out the money right arm resting on the steering wheel left elbow down on the window ledge, hand on the top of the windshield of the car, top down, looking casual as ed leans further over truck & back of station wagon wagon carrying equipment & all the doors are open J frowns while ed adjusts the camera's position tom puts one hand on his head one arm leans on the top of the leather seat, you can see the yellow star on ed's pants as he leans, tom's arm in the rear view mirror, it's over, and done with a review: ed pulls his hair back squints at the sun or at me he is wearing t's black leather belt & t smiles at me back in his original position one hand on the wheel one on the top of the car, elbow resting on the side he is wearing the beaded bracelet I gave him anne gave me: ed his back to me still standing up in the car rests one hand on the top of the camera hair pulled back in a rubber band, license 838OYJ new york & ed sits down I see a tree in triangles J leans over, t's face is visible in the rear view mirror now J talks to t & e still touching the camera is thinking about something an orange car has pulled into the background there's a lawn mower still further back & J drives, top up, ed in the middle ponytail tom next to him, his bracelet arm hanging down behind the seat i'm in the back with equipment we're stopped we're eating cheeseburgers. And so, out the red curtains, a dead tree on 183: J talks & pets a dog who's come up devil to the table ed legs crossed rests his elbows on the table looks down eyes closed tom looks young he's in the dark & no its a cat a puma siamese cat jumping down out of j's grasp head first toward the floor ed hates cats & he's the devil in rare red light, housatonic riverboat gambling casino, nobody makes love much yet, cluttered weeds glisten in the mush, now: frances opts for suicide as a man's best work that a woman does

for him, rocks devils flow cant fall we rehearse all for the moment J
& E are in the river sun a dead tree the beautiful green river men-
tions something to me: psychology. It gurgles with T on the river-
side, he had a swollen wrapped-up ankle from falling in a hole on
the west side highway up in riverdale where he was running across
in his lacrosse shirt yellow flowers plastic pen a rock of water take
me home to the place I was born infection: will the police & so on,
those green hills are reeds in the current, down. The camera went with
it back of me & someone says back of me that's the extent of memory,
I caught it, I caught up with it: summer squash 19¢ a one-pound
green ripe tips no melons place red bats from texas in my mind,
red bags of onions from california E.M.Mallett Inc. you know the
guy? & sun in sky a truck load full main office stockton, california
not l.a. not a struggle to remember a struggle to include where was
I? at Taft farms, get out of me: cover, dont throw away & someone
says cover, dont throw away & what a thrashing machine, we talked,
the farmer & I & someone says you bend over the thrashing machine
& I'll fuck you up the ass, you see he wanted to get married & the
fields from the car glimpse a mirror there I recognize T in the middle
now. Mrs. Ebitz signed a release. The 7 arts gift shop: reclasping re-
classifying recleaning reclothing recolonizing recoloring recombining
remember to cover, dont throw away. Guys hanging out on the steps
I'm in the car. If the sound of the thing dont match with the image
recondition the machine: did ya ever try to live with lenin did ya
ever try to drive with lenin? There's two cockroaches on their backs
under the plunger & my time is race its full sense diminishes with
clothes new clothes & I'm suffocating them & we pick up K at the
theater home by sunset is the most unnatural way of putting it I
feel sick & am not interested I'm arrested, ed, we waterproofed till
dawn & K came bravely through the trail to see us doing it with
tom still with us with him with us what does that mean he loves us
too much love & that's a story that isnt here: was is this the tenth,
yes it is & what is this, it's the side of our house which had a stone
foundation & I've no idea what happened really happened this day
not yet, that's the outside of the house in the back with all the
doors blue & all the doors open just like that & now I know what
happened this day this day we went through all the films, a dry run
& what do you mean by that, I mean you know what I mean with-
out film & without actors because this shot was of someone driving

& that's tom in the car now but of someone driving the car & what
ed had to do was to stand pretty much in the position he's in now
except leaning over further almost in the fucking road where jacques
& that's him looking through the camera where jacques is & he had
to stand in the car & lean over & look through the eyepiece of the
camera & there was a move involved like a zoom in & a move of the
camera slightly over while the guy was driving the car down route 7
& talking, talking into the camera, so we were rehearsing this day &
that's the cadillac there & this is right around down the street from
where I spent the winter of 1969, this is the corner of the main road
that you turn off to get to the house where I was living & you say
there've never been any people in any of these pictures from the
country before & i just realized that there were people in the town
but you cant take a picture of just anybody stranger than the people
you are with I mean the ones you know well & in that whole park-
ing lot there were no other cars no others, well it was summer. & it
was summer & the real story's here: not one word for today until
quarter to two tomorrow but alot of open air. I took a nap at 6
o'clock I never take naps without sleeping through them. Waterproof
connections with waterplug from the basement & pain becoming a
monster through film & we're running some service organization, are
we safes? J all day horrible remarks about women down to a cute
little redhead she limps a little but in my grief do I know what I'm
doing: moon here & K visits for 3 seconds: tom has trouble with
kathleen still no dreams you sleep at sunset & get a can of paint
from the art union of lenox used to be the county seat where the
sedgwick's contributed to a fine library. Where are the boots? We
panhandle a florida license plate & I plan to braid my hair & eat
breakfast this morning I remember taking a deep breath once I
wish I could write backwards cause film doesnt seem worth the
trouble it would be better to improvise than to try to live with
lenin: if the sound dont match with the image then recondition the
machine & take it easy no struggle to get an effect locking k's pas-
sions in the bathroom to make up & I'm talking to the guy at taft
farms who wants to get married & even though i hate his advice I
seem to like to take it, it's just about ladybugs carrots & lush pale
vegetables the pale moon rising, it's hard to stop hurrying a pain
in my arm & ed falling asleep to the sound of the pen, felt tip, ed
the queen tom the prince a complete & udder distance: "the cows

are over there" between tom. I knew the boy at the farm would like
to get married & so would he & so would he & so will she even
though magic markers never expected a carrot to play & someone
says never expected a carrot, now whaddayou mean, this early too
soon or so small? Or this is serious business, tom's ankle astragal
on the night of the full moon now he is snoring & green all day &
every day more & more flowers ones that were there all along dis-
covered, snoring, moving, the water pump goes. Never discover
something new this way think of J's trip to new york the massage
parlor the gas station the fuck the mutilated blonde the sun rising
on the sink rising over the dishes the crazy room with broken glass
& black white red velvet chairs all over blue glass that's all in a pic-
ture, something new you give up, the sky, I think you'll bring the
magic markers I think you'll get it right, think hard. I cant wait till
I have my time & all our time a fine time: I felt a strong resentment
day for what was going on some stalinist decision-making lenin at
the helm of the cadillac ship so why not make it up as you go along
disorganized & unmethodical with tangled skeins of power leaking
in & out the plugs are waterproof, the nagra niagara couldnt destroy
unless I drop it in the river plunge with tom floating & I'm floating
& K looking like what vito is always accused of, assents to, dracula:
when she got into the car, when she got into the car, she is getting
into a car now & I am worried about her, she is getting off a plane
& into a car, we understand now like t's questions: why would the
prince ask so many questions? to keep the king at home? the
answer's in shakespeare & I'm the bear, my play's his play & the
queen stays home. The author of this play wishes her aunt was dead.
And so K walked across the gravel driveway the driveway was gravel
pavlov was the driveway gravel. In that picture & in that picture I
remember some energy gives me faith in what you're doing all you's
but movies & but movies I remember I have no sense of where I am
in this room & there are no crickets. No crickets? No wind no winter
too I guess. The people in our old house had to move away the win-
ter was too bad for them. Here we are on the road, looking at beams
all the time time every time I have to say what what I mean is to
have some idea where I am like a small bat on the window does &
at the bookstore someone says things were very different then &
that's where they were wrong when they were building this house,
the whole north-south group of them, this house an old barn loft it

looks like a movie theater & could be if you werent rich & how I do memory: I make a design writing this & later I make something this time out of remembering but later out of not remembering or doing it backwards including hallucinations & all liquid clear distillations of what is it? ice as if you try to remember by will & a choice is here the instant you do: I'll remember the instant, you dont have to you dont have to remember not memory but snap beyond the "past is so dead for me I have no way of checking on it": telling J about trips to new england to letchworth state park, you wanna find out about my life, the same as this no pictures no pictures please, what I couldnt photograph: bill macy & I'm trying to remember, dry, the bartender & strangers up close, two men fighting on 6THAVE&34 THST, policemen, construction & road workers. Note: the sheriff was here, someone says & he never comes up this way this far up into the country lands & it must be you or some longhairs, you stare at the old woman crossing the road at the farm complex, not a crow, a worm & magic, the wind blows assent, the mule on the road last night as animals are moving closer to us, many cats dogs the glendale bar cat & j's neighborhood cat, cat across the street & certain theater dogs, glendale bar dogs, we work like elves we are spackling plugging taping sweeping setting things straight, things nobody knows about just expect their toys to work, they dont even know they happen & then — a story an exposé a mystery a myth, where is the ocean? I'd like to see it cause there's too much green, too much green here like being in a box of feathers, bats wings of skin & where is everyone they cant speak & the wind blows assent is threatening me: people wandering around town I'm watching them they're watching I'd like to see the ocean sing a song the nolans chargers vs. the silver city heads & they are, closed for 15 days, it's easier. It's easier to write numbers than letters any day, letters to everyone even the aunt the author wishes was dead as ed's beautiful new belt, the belt appears. Learn to repeat like the indians, to have fewer words & the wind blows again, I wish, was that a well? & Over there where the head boards are? Ed's gone. Oh shit & drums through my chest & he's gone again. It's me. There's a creak put time put time aside put limes aside side of what you cant do - to remember is easier than to look in a dark house & when you think real slow: did lee jaffe steal the car, is he the one & cello the cello lessons a cello tape a cello between your legs a cello concerto a cello concerto for

70

cello and orchestra my cello's broke, I hope tomorrow will be a
better day quieter calmer for the prince & more exciting for the
author of this play & that the queen will glow & between the dif-
ferent gods kings queens princes saints rabbis actors & actresses I
have in my house I come up certainly, I can seem unsound & I'm
losing my mi my min my min n-n-d-d on tape & on direct & two
butterflies with two dragonflies blue are fucking so let's fuck the
new gravel road or is it gravel or is it asphalt, vitamin o cello: the
bar in the pit in the drift is the drift of things, e's & a's, john's book
a-z corso's book no name picture my book memory the tripod with
the fluid head, did you ever tripod why no not yet, meets the dead
at dead center flush with the earth's dead center of gravity at thirsty
elmhurst yes this vehicle is wired negative earth yes this vehicle is
wired negative earth yes this vehicle is moving yes I'm going down-
hill in it yes brakes yes the drum, his chest his swell high pitch voice
of the trees voice of nowhere voice of somewhere voice I cant still
go on come on see swell & sea alone decide for me I'm high on sea
I'm on it I'm with it I turn the page slowly I sink in the stream who
are you, I breathe do you, did he, byron yeats & hawthorne a wo-
man & down above what I said what I did before, I mean it I made
it there's no one no one there's someone it's over what will it feel
like to do this again. Repeat it. A question & sink into the stone &
sink into the stone big bed design right screen america flush dont
move, a moth, dont move north move outlet & every time you right
an M are there three three screens three rights & a bear a wood: I
net a picture draw it make it stone make it some relentless weaving,
dead? repeat it: storm drum mill: put it out on the stone, it's out,
it's completely out good night I burned my finger

July 11
You can see that the question I started out from has been almost
completely left out by now: I go to a place where you cannot reach
me or you go to a place where I cannot reach you, no one can reach
you I am alone & you are examining, I can finally tell you that you
are examining the reenactment of the crime the reenactment of the
crime, to see what it suggests for the future, for future experience.
I can tell you this much - there are places, different spots, to move
between. The crime's already done so you can fool around. The

photographer comes with us to the scene, with us what does that
mean? etc. This is Kathleen this is kathleen here is kathleen here is
kathleen kathleen is here she's doing the dishes why is kathleen
doing the dishes why is she doing the dishes why the dishes why not
the dishes Kathleen doing the dishes she does them she did them last
week she did them again she didnt do them right the first time why
does she have to do them again do them again, she said. I'll do them
again there she is doing the dishes again look at her doing them she
does them typewriter teletape tickertape typewriter tickertape tele-
tape kathleen is doing the dishes she's doing them again when will
she finish when will she finish. Blessed Virgin Mary. We stand in the
water of the river there is no time. E & I dont wear our fire depart-
ment boots, the fucking kid & T on the banks again: anything that
happens befalls us & someone says anything that happens is just we
fall. Cues queue up & J in a red mared shirt me on sounding nobody
fell. I fell this: my life doesnt work the tripod spread wide & rivers
no flow river flow no glint glistens back & black turns to green, the
plastic over the camera over christ in boots like J with the garbage
at the dump & its shoulders make st. christopher amen, this was a
very religious day as murders are. Someone reaches the shore & we
shot: "If I took something . . . attention." A show now here in the
morning everyday get high hair small from the boy in the smile-
shirt with flag-patched pants & indian-fringe boots, a look looking:
two eyes saying I know you & I know he didnt know & tom puts
"bored" in his hand & in his mouth. He's wearing our dungaree
jacket & an F-shirt that says something backwards he's wearing it
inside out & cars lined up for the kill, kill the pavement while two
hitchhikers by a volvo station wagon backpack it on the yellow line,
two sleeping bags, neat prepared, a car whizzes by a neat white house
& I am walking their thumbs toward the centers of their bodies, E
& T walk toward me on gravel while E's head is tilted, a part of
crime's return to grace. Back in the USSR there's a motorcycle
gang they pass the bank & then . . . we were up all night, the tele-
phone pole & you, mist, on the fucking golf course you come & go
but here we are, we played a joke within & you look at us like us
like solid frozen summer greens packed as they unfreeze packed as
they can be, we eat there's nothing there. Ed in the dungaree jacket
eats all the eggs with orange juice & drinks the juice with cream &
the cream with coffee & white balls of pastry on the curtains we had

ordered by the window & further away where does the light come
from it's ok but no wind to assent to it. We exit by the door & crash
whim a square table reflected in a window becomes round old ladies
chewing slow & I hope the table's set as Ed covers his mouth from
the sun that's up like they made us write too much in grammar school
& now it hurts especially if you play the end. No, the butter knife,
we used it. I was looking out from a car I saw 3 VW's & a country
squire parked in front of the bank & somehow J K & I walk in the
woods in darkness, we see white people's house through the trees
with swimming pool & a strange mound & leavings we leave the
doings we leave the bear, there is too much light there is too little
light, we shoot the typewriter we take two fires black ceilings make
two fires a fire on the ceiling like a crotch emblazons something
there: never forget, as poe comes in the door here now. & E hangs
another gauze scrim skim scan or something & it will blaze it will
blaze again with beautiful J's red shirt as the lion in the fire. I stamp
it out the bull & K the spider is asleep: we all do our part for hours,
click viewfinder P.O.V. well find 'er p.o.v. We figure it's a hoax & at
dawn we took a bath together with a stained glass bird bath yellow
red blue it's you the dawn I love so few I love now lock the doors &
wait for breakfast on the river of the li.e. of the li.e. of the l.i.e. Both
sides of the river gentle velvet wet better than people someone says
& who? the car smokes at dawn it's cold I wear K's fringed jacket &
we run into monday through moon & clouds all over & clouds all
night we shoot the typewriter with jokes crazy moths right & left &
the one with glowing orange eyes orange water gun, I sleep & dream
of k's father burying food all over texas so he could vacation wherever
he wanted & dig it up dig it down, there'd be food for him wherever
he roamed & he says who's crazy you or me & who is it & which one
is crazy which one which one, we were in the woods we were in them
we werent crazy which one is crazy which one we were in the woods
we werent there we were we were there we bernadette mayer quotes
ed bowes unquotes how do you do & how are you today & fine &
fine & fine fine & where were you yesterday, there's water, water,
everywhere, but, not, a, drop, to drink, to drink, drink to your
health, there's water water everywhere but not a drop to drink to
your health. It's calm smoke rises vertically. Tom hitchhikes home
nose peeling he's the holy ghost after all & steve's a snotty kid. Ed &
I come on stronger amazing grace & want to cry cry without stopping

sever all tones all relations see all things glistening those reflecting
stare at carpet crouch like an indian calm. There are feats, the feats:
walking in the stream like astronauts then seven hours of work at
the typewriter & we wind up faking it & we've been here a week &
it seems like a week & there'd be food for him wherever he happened
to go, house down low some farm form of alliance I see between you
& me do you understand everything & how so what comes later but
come on stronger, camouflage? laziness, ridiculous, wrong words but
many of them traveling traveling on a train you take your time, in-
fected foot your foot could write a boot about you, why not, get
it? We were in the forest mounds we were in the forest rounds but
never deep deep deep breathes & more than fashions leave, how
many days will it take to tell the time, get back maybe to somewhere
I was before, back to where we both began, these dragged out days,
& is the thinking better & if you dont sleep is it more, with the
same two people & with tom & tom with the same parochial school
& have you gone to the public school & what did they think there
of the blessed virgin mary & of bernadette frances catherine mayer
& of frances st. bernadette st. frances st. catherine & mr. mayer &
little bear who lives by the bridge & mr. bernadette mayer & mr.
mayer the kamikazi pilot & little wonder woman little wonder wo-
man & little wonder man the man & woman are wonders little
wonders they are real wonders & where do they come from where
do they come with starry starry eyes starry legs starry feet & starry
images & st. starry & starry rolling stones & janis joplin & anything
anything anything just anything anything just anything anything
& fire fire fire anything just fire & just fire just anything fire just
just where just fire anything & somehow at some point you get rid
of everything, there are so many things you never think to do there
are so many ways of predicting the time there are ways of remember-
ing it are there more ways of remembering it: yellow cover, red
cigarette pack, white ashtray, grey green film, silver cans, yellow
bag, blue chairs, golden reels, black bag, blue shirt, blue pants &
black belt yellow & white striped curtains stained glass bird red blue
green & yellow bird black & silver camera blue & silver ring black
shirt red pants brown moccasins white door green book black pen
grey tape black box brown table & yellow floor blue cups yellow
pitcher glass pitcher white window grey grate white & gold chan-
delier tan & white butts grey & white ashes persian mat & red blue

white & grey-green plant blue glasses & inlaid salt & pepper shakers,
turquoise green pink & white, orange coil, orange light, white light
green plant, red & white milk: some of these things are worn or faded

July 12
The fats in the fire from noon & the fire inspector's here he thinks
there's a problem, last night ed set off 3 cheesecloth fires cheese-
cloth or scrim floor fires & ceiling fires it takes a long time to
notice a fire flash fire when you're throwing joints around the stage
& chris cuts into 600 volts, he does it by ear & a girl appears naked
holding an airplane mechanics we had slept off the mechanics of
that we hadnt slept at all, she's a cartoon she's a groupie she is cut
off just below the navel where a record appears: ed had had his
silver breakfast & OK I had breakfast too liverwurst & swiss cheese
on oatmeal with cold cafe au lait, cf. liver cow oat bake bean cow
hops & leonard in the a.m. harriet in the p., we did leonard in the
early morning sun on route 7 & there's no recognize of that but I
recognize the same tree in the front yard of 1957, division street
was near the barrington town time line & it's one hour earlier than
you think so the day goes slow as you sleep slow over the day as
the parking lot, no, as the front yard blends into a parking lot & she
cant learn her lines, no way, lions over blurred grass & chiggers, & S
jumps over the sun for me ed bends over s looks on h scratches her
neck & is the sun set already it's been hours so I should've bought
cake but not any further than 1 am: tree wrack tree wrack yoga liver
blood we went to the restaurant speeding, alice & famous photos
of the hills people speeding we agree: k in shades a bottle of wine
from next door the food is shit, it's st. emilion saves the day, crepes
for dessert like tonight with h & f downstairs who say this building
is beginning to take on character, so they move out what is that
sociology? K in shades drinks elbows up j & I on an uncomfortable
bench e leans his head on one elbow other arm rests on the criminal
table wood table & they go on outside of us with country road take
me home summer fall etc. red green & orange light makes magic but
not magic enough: I light & we're on the road American Sun. night
to Mon. morn. regular or lead - free K drives all nerves no style in
the cadillac & we go the thru way I look to the right ahead to the
right again there's a truck being fixed five trucks beings fixed snack

arrow cafeteria boom sleep moon? orange plastic flowers & a mesca-
line coffee pot: ham salad plate 1.75 fresh fruit salad 45 cott. cheese
35 tossed green salad 40 fruit 40 cole slaw 30 & in the middle dr.
pepper & jello 25 pie & cheese 50 pudding 30 & in the middle
prunes 25 & pastry 35 & a picture of some fruit & ½ grapefruit 45
pies 35 juices 25 catalope 35 cant elope the great outdoors on ice
induced a sneeze the place was air-conditioned but a woman is not
a seal or even a walrus: & more American in the distance now as we
pass the Pennyam express Express red lights all around doze I'm not
right there with the lemon pies holder for coffee on the seat a bridge
thuck orange & no green-blue from 2 a.m. WRPI orange lighter orange
light on songs in the restaurant the berkshire hot shoppes, this 1964
is like an airplane mechanics we hadnt slept at all we're in the doors
on WRPI & all trucks buses & cars with trailers on them cars with
traitors in them, construction 1 mile, con ed's gone to sleep with
jacques big allis, riders on the storm & waves in texas 70 foot waves
in texas you wave a red mark on your car at 60 mph. See alice in
the restaurant & 3 days melded into one july 11 12 13 sun mon tues
hard to remember sleep how do your eyes look sleep your face is tan
it has some color in it some mother someone says from the catskill
region in the catskill region at the catskill game farm skill game skill
farm still game still farm: b. 1945, the tools are under the coffee tray.
It's cardboard twinkies & pies one blueberry two lemon 25c, for
dinner we had a knotted tangle of indiscriminate scallops au gratin
from a garage with vermicelli in a health food place crepes blue-
berry custard jacques & arthur penn: K says he's a jew & A says he
could never be a jew. When we were in renssalear, green, i'm not
driving, after a long winter counter of hibernating we are in a house
a barn all over on our way to new york kathleen is driving she had
beaux by the bridge these bridges & a whole network of bridges a
whole new mythology an imbroglio a jumble a litter of the four of
us but not close enough or dose enough, now kennedy's on the radio
where am I: get me water, water! the tall more toll more sneeze it's
morning is it, we change lanes neatly there's a 10c toll more orange
than suffocating light is that light but this is clear, we got off at
18THST. The garbage truck on bleecker street glares see the garbage:
one, the number one, lights glare on horizontal glare tilting up to
the left or down to the right, this is a test, there are no red lights
at dawn: legislation, underline. Clear more down than it was or

dawn, as I learned I learn ed up sixth, carnival, down la guardia, wtc
& now is there less dawn than it was or a bottom a bottom-top to
the dawn dark windows are upside down & someone says I lived in
my somewhere a bomb shelter my house was & you have to look
around that sentence: look around speed no speed makes clear better
a mess a little a better mess than green, a red electric electric guitar
& rugs I sway three in a bed they say, ice beer the jersey something
& law west of the pecos you know if you dont know somebody
know the justice of the peace & pearl the famous roy be, sticktuitive-
ness, do not send cash to the judge he will not reward it & who are
you thinking of? an invitation & a light who said the famous judge
wore headphones a number & dials it all in above a girl naked hold-
ing an airplane merican airplane silver & gold the mechanics of it
we had slept off the mechanics of that we hadnt slept at all scared
that K would crash in on us in one more show with mirrors like
this one here, just me & her looking out of joint & tangled turbulent
& labyrinth, two rumpled women looking at themselves: that day
the next day a million hours clocked up on my face K makes up a
century in bed already streaming dirty the red towel I look like that
now kill yourself you've won, kathleen pushes her nose to the left
right I look dont know it's in the mirror yet a purple streak some-
one else was there my face is crooked dented riotous my hair a hair
caught in the fan like being afraid to go out afraid of voices moving
voices in through the window that's dark of voices moving inspired
me who are you to do a thousand things necessary measure smoke
& sit on dimes a thousand times I have a hundred dollars stuffed in a
book somewhere, for postage to a foreign country one I came from
I found ten in pope this is a diary bang you say for the say for you,
the spent, bang again there's someone at the door, the twelfth, it's
open: 10 to 5 am of the continuing days all the highway clear as a
picture & me looking for dreams, searching out certain people in
half-sleep, they wont move their voices move: rag doll still in cleve-
land & just passed the george washington bridge, sides of meat lamb
legs? sun rising emergency parking black streaks in the sky over
jeremy's apartment sun rising emergency sun rising emergency park-
ing bme bme bme bme bme bme bme bme bme bme bme be me be
me be me be me be me be me be me bemebemebemebemebemebe
mebemebemebeme rememrememrememrememrememrememremrem
emrememrememmembermember bememberrememberbemember

rememberbememberrememberbemember

July 13
The royal sky's way before autumn it's a phony drop. Woke up won-
dered where ed was found a better pen & it's a new day wake up late
3pm a phony drop behind the view: dreamed michael died, grace
was there, we were going to a store a department store to prove
something, the lights & the cushion between the two front seats in
the cadillac that's all I can remember cant remember more, called
the church twice & they thought I was bernadette devlin cause I
said bernadette again. If I'm bernadette devlin if i'm b. devlin I must
b. pregnant, called julia she has something 'important' for ed at home,
where hannah is, voices on the phone & laughing house of mirrors,
nick says anne is at the laundromat, jacques roast beef is in the oven
in stockbridge, kathleen is at the bank & I dial o for operator, define
it, stockridge eggs rockridge is burning there are no fires yet today,
I dial 413 plus 123 plus operator's reading for stockbridge I am try-
ing to call the the ate r & I call deluxe at 850 10TH AVE 2473220
& speak to I try to speak to the expediter for 16 mm color film, I
speak to otto pellone & he's the wrong one, it's high speed ekta-
chrome for a print delivered to you brought in at 9:30 am this
morning & when will film for the theater be ready, so finally I get
him mr. meany or minny, I ask frank to fill them papers out & he
says will you hold, I'll hold you right out the window I say & out it
I see the nyu flying another merican flag the washington square
apartments, you will hold will you hold & how did I get here? Irving
kay at deluxe says 2pm & I believe, dial 201-9483519 to talk to nick
talk to michael they're pissed off I have coffee & last night's lemon
pie the thru way pie. Ed's gone to return equipment drop off film &
outside it's bright at the loft but the light just wont come in it's not
coming in nature food centers at the coliseum: I'm in the back of the
cadillac down the road I'm in the backseat, we pick up film, pass no.
7 broadway we're on the avenue of the americas what americas, a
school a color yellow, a scoop yellow schools yellow cabs again block
before radio city music hall, get into the sky before autumn royal: let
me see them fast says ed kathleen i have to hurry talked to tom &
what'd he have to say I say & he says nothing, well did he want
those tickets or anything & he says didnt say anything about it, no

so ed went over to k's to pick up dope: yellow cabs yellow saab yellow
car in two lane black top & red yellow & blue filters over the camera
lens aimed at a light: royal a taxi's for door to door, the terminal clean-
ing contractors fill my house with what they've cleaned or at least
they try to, I wont let them him & they're the ones always pounding
at the door, middle of the night, trying to get in & banging: one
yellow cab three yellow cabs blue sky over manhattan slide fade a
new bike cycling central park & the next one's that guy you wanted
me to take a picture of remember & another yellow cab & yellow
light a guy standing on the corner in a pink & blue tie, blue shirt,
suit jacket no. 62 over one shoulder, hand in his pocket, a black
suit, a black dude walks by coat over his hand, hand rests on his hip,
three men walking all walking forward left legs bent to advance, cor-
ner 72NDST&5THAVE no commercial traffic, the black tire of a
white white car: ed feels a little bit crazy his hair blows all around
with it, we were on our way to eat at the pavillon the little one a
french luncheonette across the street from where were used to live,
york AVE&75THST: the sky looks one way it looks another, high
rise apt. bldgs & a whole different story up here sun sun sun sun
sun sun window in the suburb now, Maxwell's plum, yellow cab
we're going up york now across 72NDST about to turn left uptown
on york I can see the 72NDST bridge the green one at the end of
the street over east river in the distance not so far hazed out, we
pull up behind a car stopped for a light next to the car another yellow
cab crossing york with the green light there's a yellow cab on york,
a newly renovated bldg sun on it low window reflections sun on the
other side, I guess the bldg is a freak: orange fire escapes a man in
black suit a man in white shirt sleeves two women together in
sleeveless dresses the branch of a tree with leaves on it, that's on
our side centered I centered it: the side of that new bldg or maybe
another one more orange fire escapes unless it's rust proof lead a
metal under coat: we had just bought an orange water pistol the day
I went to lenox to the new art store to try to get some cheap white
acrylics & had to go to the hardware store instead to spend 39c for
white paint but the art store gave me a few things away, some
brushes & a phony license plate & I think we were together the day
we shot & shadows haze out the bathroom windows we went to-
gether we eat our old window late afternoon shadows on the old
window on york but not the ones above it, there another high rise

tree beautiful skinny tree not like the one in the parking lot & two
more yellow cabs pass as one steel bldg top reflects the light: across
the street from it, something white, site of a new 40 story residential
tower the last of the red hot lov no more. We looked at a handmade
shiney new yellow saab sports car in the window of the saab place
we went to the beekman i think, ed wanted it I wasnt sure, curtain
up front row balcony half moon sunrises on the stage & there was
james taylor sitting on a fence & another yellow car a mercury a
dodge & another women's head of a color with a long black wig
was she yellow or blue, just a head dizzy light, the light in the
kitchen was on with the electrically taped wires hanging down &
the shadow of the ladder fell cast in front of it: three filters in a
case on floor: red, yellow, blue & a candle raised to baton rouge I
guess we were waiting for the film that night: red with a yellow ball
in the middle it looks just like the sun & next, pretty accurate color
with a tint of green to it like a fluorescent, that's blue & Yellow (end):
orangy yellow at that but the sun is pure white, a little lemon in it,
I was holding them on, by hand, like this: yellow gleams yellow
tawny, the color of gold butter or ripe lemons, changed to a yellow-
ish color as by age or illness like old paper like jaundiced skin &
have a yellowlike pigmentation of the skin like mongolians like
mongolian people like the yellow people of asia like yellow eskimos
like yellow north american indians like their straight black hair like
their eyes & yellow jealous or melancholy & yellow a coward he
cant be trusted & yellow a cheap sensational story appears in a news-
paper & yellow a color that lies between red & green in the spectrum
& yolk of an egg & any or several fungi or virus diseases of plants
causing yellowing of the leaves & stunting the growth & yellow a
jaundice in farm animals & yellow, jealousy: how can I explain it:
le petit pavillon, two lane black top, cheese omelette boiled po-
tatoes meatloaf string beans no potato pancakes ice tea & mary's
on her honeymoon: how can I explain it? there's one in the trunk,
this is the music & there's the lens, what else? it may happen that
the order set up for the original experience works for the new ex-
perience that we have that we now have & the parts that are added
can again be seen as just instances of the order we set up as a result
or something of the original experience & if that happens we have
no reason to change our order our design. But if that does not hap-
pen, if the order if the design that's set up for the original experience

doesnt prove workable when the volume of it is increased, it's the
thirteenth, then we have two alternatives: we can reject the new
stuff, orange pen, or we can change the order the design, orange
pen: washed hair here, rampage, heavy heavy air here, talked to anne
& M is still pissed offf about videotapes & now peter too as well &
larry & gertrude & harris her going to the coast & grandfathers state
terrible nothing right nothing wrong, a kidney infection jaundice
dehydration oxygen intravenous feeding hardening of the arteries,
can you break this seal break this seal his first movie in the english
language, grace is in the country with the magicians children: the
arsonist a hit & run, I saw it all at once tonight that words are lead-
ing me on, the ones in imagination, saw, in leaks in indian leaks
somehow, I can erase I can modify I pick up, least it's not a nautical
sleep affinity for words like genet some flow to stretch, stretch out
& pull in, to masturbate: & it is in honor of these crimes that I am
writing this book & so on, not a use or function like V., perform a
service, work words into a system, words put in a system, its some
play, some death, nautical, at sea with them & I started to write
that, what's put in, watts, what's put in creating problems, everyone
expects a rearrangement to suit not to suit, expect spectrum: yellow
but the sun is pure white, a little lemon in it, I was holding them on,
those games, jokes all the time, nothing to do with time, what can a
diary be not a reconstruction, something put in, use the time, pass
it, stain it, pass it, it's stained, it's magnified, it sticks, it sticks in my
mind & my hand always hurts always hurts still does when I write
in this book: book, took three rolls to be developed into seen. Some
place, something to drink to change my whole way of feeling &
something to read, transform, transform translate transmute trans-
cribe transfer transfuse, transform, camomile does it make a dif-
ference? Everyday, I'm saying there are no days, of, we've made
too much of days and, thinking & write another way, it's changed,
special, special social tea, special milk, special tea, open the teas &
make too much of them, grass, what is that leaves of grass growing?
Open old things, remember, grandfather, notebooks those poems
about organs, body, fuck, monkey & when you came in, & when
you came in, & new things on the desk a pipe a seashell a tv guide
things I've never seen before but can recognize, not in my own house
& two books one about tea: teas: camomile, anthemis nobilis,
manzanilla, maythen: a low creeper or trailer plant with large

feathery flowers from the greek, groundapple, from the egyptians
it prevented aging can be used as a poultice & it's a triangle star
triangle; sassafras, officinale, a tall tree in mexico & eastern u.s. for
syphilis for rheumatism for the blood, circle line circle line circle;
mate, ilex paraguayensis, jesuit's tea, large white-flowered shrub in
a mate tea cup, come, sustains the body without food mystery this
is a mystery, contains caffeine & tannin, circle star circle; herba
santa, for hayfever; hibiscus, star star living in a tent summer; violet
leaf, tom likes peppermint; orange blossom, try cornsilk, made from
the threadlike filaments of the husk of corn; golden rod heals would
heal wounds, pleurice root angelica & sassafras breathing hops tea,
I drink some tea I go to bed it's been with me, summer spring winter
fall a home here, one there, monte hellman, kathy was going to move
in here but H. has been living here alone. Three pictures, the light in
the loft with yellow red blue filters on, I was holding them

July 14
On Wednesday, I am saved from hanging by running away: I work
at the museum, later I'm saved by a petty bureaucrat who takes a
liking to me but also needs my services, dream, do you want to
turn me into antonin artaud, dream: on the afternoon of october,
four days after my marriage, my wife surprised me by attempting
automatic writing. What came in disjointed sentences, in almost
illegible writing, was so exciting, sometimes so profound, that I
persuaded her to give an hour or two day after day to the unknown
writer, and after some half-dozen such hours offered to spend what
remained of life explaining & piecing together those scattered sen-
tences. "No," was the answer, "we have come to give you metaphors
for poetry," & this was in 1962 & now I light up a beautiful blue
cloudy sky over grand street, probably it's not. Do you want to turn
me into dream, yeats, dream? & do you & I walked up mott or mul-
berry or drove or red green & white flags flap rain in a green car in
the too dark shade of the park flagged off mott street & prince I
think & when anne & jonathan were visiting we walked around with
justine who ran out of shoes & later I ran out of shoes & we found
the same solution, shoes for 29¢, you can find them on the street,
mott or prince or houston, anywhere & down from R's house through
the fire escape, I have a better one, through the fire escape black &

appropriately there a bright red car, I had the cadillac, a purple one
with a white top & one maroon & one blue & one olive, well that's
just how I felt too looking out of R's dark windows with the pale &
dark plants, you keep them here to remember you by? are you you
cause your little dog knows you & so on & I remember R complain-
ing about the view out her window & the people looking in on her:
one old man who makes obscene gestures, why she doesnt even know
the meaning of the word obscene, lovely obscene puerto rican wo-
men working in the factory waiting for ed's erections, you see he
gets up during their lunch hour & it's wonderful & gina says, well
they've seen erections before cause neil is always walking around
naked & david says I never knew he & he meant ed was an exhibition-
ist, is that a bigamist? & R must come out of some novel written in
new york about the slums of milan, written fast, an emergence at
the bank: something was accepted there & now I cant remember if
I had the car with me at all, K must have had the cadillac & they
say no pictures here, I might have been planning to rob that bank
that beautiful old bank at bowery & grand street I'll tell you one
thing I photographed the windows with just a little thought to the
built-in alarm system, like the antennas built in to the window of
your car, if you happen to own a buick electra, mourns: death, for
which reason I deny autobiography, or that the life of a man matters
more or less & someone said we are all one man & someone said I
count the failure of these men, whether they are jews or chinese or
whether they are me or my sister, R., I count the failure of these
people as proof of their election, they are all divine because they
die, screaming, like the first universal jew the gentiles will tell you
had some special deal: the end, not by a long shot: one chinese boy
holds out his hand to one chinese girl about seven or eight years
old in a short dress in the bank, sun streaming in long wide windows
encased in marble, curtains up sun rise: the sky is colorless where
pictures make double exposures, city gin, I wish I had some city
gin while R. is at the grand street subway station, R. & the subway
maps in dark glasses a dark scene subway exposures or R. exposures
suffused with green, tile, she is my sister, scene, as I hate the man
who saves me the petty bureaucrat who takes a liking to me but
also needs my services, dream: this is duress this is coercion com-
pulsion this is the german last of her race: down lies the posture of
my fathers all stricken deeply down & I fall down & echo what they

cry, all silent to the last when sudden starts the moan, one moan
ending last all which might have been or been bemoaned & I'm power-
less I cry silently through the echoes, dying last & in repentance,
half-man & screams out the window of the elmhurst general hospital
screams it was still a beautiful clear day & was this the day I took R
to lunch, no that was the day I had the cadillac & we picked up a
hitchhiker who said he knew ridgewood well, hangs out there, you
would hang out in ridgewood to scream that's all & that day too we
stopped at a first nation city skunk bank but this day we saw GP in
the hospital, alot of shit alot of west indian doctors with no informa-
tion alot of charm & how much money do you have & phone calls
to lawyers in ridgewood he wouldnt talk to me, his secretary reveals
all & it's a fraud & I say let's just forget & if they want the money
that bad & I was right: richard screams, he's ruining our lives, with
money I say & he just screams & it's still a beautiful day out the
window of the hospital with phony tudor apartment houses & still
one crossing the l.i.e. with a view of n.y.c. from the bus from elm-
hurst to ridgewood just one arid patch to another: the towers of
manhattan are towers of manhattan green shrubbery & l.i. or queens
lace yellow parched out ground & cars going one way all one way,
no cars the other, but we're on the bus on the other side of the
world traveling with strength within that other side from one place
to another, what further way to be lost could there be? I'm lost so
lost how lost can you be when everywhere you go it's morning &
the sun's coming up over a map: hashish the ghost is rumored dead
the slow boor had the rheum, worm & bug gagging him higher than
a gourd shouting whoosh, a shower & the rum you piggish shrew to
oust your mother from the same shroud as you: owl bitch hog &
whore met at the bog's mouth to bludgeon the womb & it was only
a gag, at least the author's brought his luger, he's ogling that myth,
a gob of rum for the wretch with the hookah & the oil-rout grew
bulging the gulch with rush & shout there there boils the ocean: you
are my chattel this is a shuttle from the other side of the world to
another part of the other side of the world, I will never go there
again, metropolitan avenue not the most cosmopolitan street in the
world & the next view is a piece of my mind, three-story buildings
as far as the eye can see, a sky like wisconsin, we're on madison street
near the apartment house where the only black man in ridgewood lived,
he was a super, they're sloppy & dirty, looking back towards fresh

pond road where the oasis was, never heard of them ones did ya? I
had a jewish friend there & no one said a word I think cause I
didnt tell: where the german people are it's more angles there's more
angles involved, shiny storm windows on every opening & crack,
some of the tiniest storms in the world blow here & they dont get
in the house not one inch, stone & brick stairways & stoops up to
the house: at one point everybody got a new door, GP had to get
one too even though we had one of the most beautiful doors in the
world, but marauders marauders might break through the fine
heavy glass, part of the front door was glass & so it had to go & tin
awnings in green & white stripes & cornices reaching over to keep
out as much sky as you can get away with without joining the bund,
I didnt know anyone on this block, except I think the somebodys
who once cooked lobsters live in front of me in a pail turning red &
green, the Steffens rosemary steffens & I think she had a brother, on
the next corner we met k.maher a high school person & she makes
conversation: she has a little boy she had a little girl she has a little
boy & a little girl I am visiting my grandmother I am a nurse & I
answer how right & she tells me just by accident about the nurses
registry who we eventually called & she acts like life if shit is at
least cute & this is what I saw while I talked to her later, met her
again getting on the myrtle avenue el: a clear blue sky towards eve-
ning puffy white clouds thick in the middle with streamers, the day
doesnt always deserve its sky & from here every day I saw for four
years & now you can see the wtc twin towers from here: I remember
getting on the el at night to go to events. A relief I guess I got home,
we shoot pool at tony's, finally the safe streets & interiors of man-
hattan manhattan pool halls: one yellow ball on green table, red
corners a game two yellow one red in the foreground ed sets up a
shot, with one of the yellow balls his forefinger over the cue join-
ing his thumb, three fingers resting on the green cloth, arm extended
as far as it will go hair falling down but caught on one side behind
his ear, a break, the white balls left & the light's in on it, someone
comes in to watch & on our way home I waited till the light was red
& green at the same time, at that point it was red on the other side
too & a clear outline of continuous bright red with anger, one color,
a reflection of green & the regular green of the light whited out, ed
sat down, next to him still from yesterday the candle not lit now
that lit baton rouge & it was & still is mounted on a ricotta can from

alleva which is mounted on the phone book so's to reach baton rouge
by fire when it's lit & it must've been still higher for the shot, what's
in the hand? ed in the gulf of mexico close to baja california, a fire in
the ashtray started on purpose & the ones that I deal with asserting
themselves & ed lights a gratuitous fire the veins of my hands are
bulging, there's a brown paper bag on the table & a potato a tomato
an apple coffee cup rope two candles mounted on jars, one an old
blue brioschi jar hannibal with the label taken off & a pack of
cigarettes closest a jar of sugar the fire's higher ed likes to light
fires & on the table as well rope ed ed i'm further away glass ashtray
& I've figured out what that is first what it was I see I saw: a hazy
yellow scene with some orange & splotches of purple, electric blue
electric electric purple into the ashtray on the theory of close out
of focus while the fire's still going I wanted to get this close to it so
I did, like moving around the lights, no limits but light or darkness
is all myself under the blue lamp it's more I mean less than an ellipse
a gibbous moon above my head making light, my face old my hair
orange my arms tan in an army green shirt, I hadnt seen myself that
day mouth like a clown eyes ears shadows dent too white not far
enough away the white sink with hannah's bottle of moldy spring
water on it more like sea water & not a drop to drink, a clean glass
wine bottle, reflections in the back of the stove & after that I
thought I'd gone to bed, no, three brown paper bags in different
stages & the rest of the house in the window more windows, a safe
glare from manhattan from the light above the sink & a green plastic
bag in the garbage & the top of the orange coffee pot above the top
of the black silk stove in the inside stripes of my blue coat those
stripes what I liked about it in the first place even when it had pleats
on the bottom in the eighth grade & I wore that one on the myrtle
avenue el alot, ed was still up & I made his pose for him: in the
light of the fluorescent light shooting out between his legs from in
front legs white out a background glow hair whites out hands like
fibers a back straight & cool as a girl's the coat the peacock ed's
wings the light goes on up the sun tree sky centaur & giraffe, cur-
tain shower ropes & phony ceiling, tops of the valves of the hot
water heater bows & arrows and stained mirror top of my head in
it close to the ceiling ropes of the shower reflections above it birds
fly across start & the rest to write it down is to repeat myself I al-
ways do I'll cut it all out later & go on, I went on out to the bed

striped wall pin striped picture of the indian god woman who stood
on a cracked off piece of ice in the river woman, pillows gone we
rest on yellow velour pillow & the one with the english garden scene
on the cover & green fringe comes from somewhere, the god is next
to the extension cord, narrative before, I cant keep up with the sense
the sense runs away with itself dashiell hammett hash simple sen-
tences: I went out on the fire escape. I rested the camera on one of
the ledges so I could make a long exposure, facing the windows op-
posite me. One floor is always lit, this night two floors were brightly
lit. The Baker Brush Co. I made them brighter. I waited for Baggies
elevator to be at the top floor. It was red bright red, it had been
other colors before including white. Red exists lights showed in the
place next door to it. In the background blurred are the lights of the
telephone company building, radar on the top not visible, guarding
manahattan from the south or from attack, which is it? Down grand
street before the pipes came making piles. Fluorescent light can move
of its own accord, ed can moving into these fibers leave after them-
selves the lines of the light: if the light has lines then that is what
those images are & up top a brighter more concentrated light & a
thin one like a match struck. Ed smiles in the yellow pose, one of
him there & now he's above himself, the sleeping prin/cut off by
sleep: you do as you always do go over this again: the brooklyn
laborlyceum is the kind of building that grows small & you grow up
you go away, emma goldman spoke there my parents had their
wedding reception there, now it's abandoned & in between those
events it was a knitting mill with a full front yard all around sur-
rounded by an iron fence, authority doctors & nurses in front of
me: dr. attoh dr. podell mrs. leo mrs. sampson: miss boowegbir
what about your parents? do you live together? & how could we &
do you live in the city? & are you married, no, so, I guess it's up to
you you two & I say he needs a mind of his own, I defend GP's
states of consciousness & no one can see them & I see two eyes &
a narrative: see kathy maher, still dry stiff sarcastic eats flesh I
guess & empty in vacuous vacuums white as though nobody had any
feelings at all, you say solutions to problems a speck of dirt,
whisked away, I say I see a peck of dirt & leave it there, grandfather
isnt dying a woman eats potato chips & someone says I'll have to
speak to my husband, I'm not saying anything, my husband will be
home at 5 o'clock, we are trying to find out how much money GP

has in the bank, it's simple but she wont talk it's the water gates
for her & they like anyone would did a fraud as fast as they could
& they think nothing is happening nothing is being done when there
are only women around, where are your husbands & I sit & we sit
lined up on opposite sides of the room D with her mother with their
interests to protect, lined up, I sit next to my sister: I am the imp
of the perverse I have nothing to lose, this is addressed to you rose
of the sea, marie & rose-marie our secrets yellow on a black field
on a field, sable, the letter whose imprint is red is black: Theodore-
Nathaniel & Bernadette: you've got her name & I've got his eyes:
Bernadette sinks ships: Marie, I want sex, I have Leonard in mind
now. Theodore looks in. I change the channel right in front of you,
no, I write in front of you now, addressing R: secrets are ours I'm
talking to you, rosemarie, keep the order keep the peace — the gun
I kill you with & the reverse: you're all there: listen to me, it's
blue. Watch my black eyes: the large skies of queens with the large
clouds of wyoming neat vistas, rows, fields no life anywhere, do I
want to be cut off from all people or from all of my family, when I
saw GP I thought of my mother mouth open gaping into the atmos-
phere of a room hospital room no power neither protesting I dont
want to die in a hospital: hear the thrusts deaths & sighs or was each
a soul scream head-rending at its heart & horrible, is the sigh the
soul or does it drink only lightly at the top like bees from water do
the words come through piercing, who did it & are he & the things
of him one or do they start stop fast now one now him & is he dead
thinking sweet is the joy I long for or forced stopped thinking in
the cool green-yellow of his body, does he faint can he hear his own
sigh & is it shorter than it sounds, ring or rattle, clear through down
the bones & at the moment then the things pure death comes has he
gone did it touch & is it clear then or will all pass by without sense
& what's above yes or no & why ask how is it thinking that we die
with nothing or with all & why isnt much to say, say power, say
money: graham avenue on the canarsie line: what would emma gold-
man do & what would kathleen do & the catholic priest, father o'fry
em from ridgewood, he couldnt commit himself, commit communion
commit an omission, commit a forgetting where you are & what you
are doing: his haze not his halo, smile & freckles, G's been in the
hospital a week could someone work the magic on him, catnip leaves
& the rest. H has to study so desperately to work such daily anxious

magic, the secret to good health is contained within this book, within this razor blade life over death in the hospital corridors I'm still myself no matter who dies: 1STAVE,3RDAVE union square wyoming clouds till the end of the day & saturday nights in ridgewood, there's $13,000 in a joint account with D, eat creamed corn mixed with potatoes tomatoes great bread wine coffee summer meal summer spring & so on ed sank the eight ball yerba santa tea & janis joplin yoga & the rubber man at the circus/cut my cut: I fooled the ape virgin foraging for a grape from his purple groin I gave him pale apples his uvula ingraining with my leer's earful: lion pears gore the reigning angels to avenge the pope who has pale nirvana in his green vagina, meanwhile the papal pig is ripe feverish & angular, my lover veered to a prig like purrs from a nigger his legs liver & unpurged loins ravaged to a flowery orange by the profane green plunger, rape purple, the sexual etiology of the child: she wants heroin. The I-character is usually the she. Let me just go quickly through pin-pointing the fantasies, touch on each one, sherlock holmes. There was the blowjob, the heroin, touch tongues, the list of men, the dance-model scene, the violent scene in the doctor's office & the one in the country. The first three are real & were the touchstones of the others. More came later. I came home: quick blowjob, want heroin, think of touch tongues: the list of men. I was trying to think of a man who would grab me. No, first I'm tough I think of L & wonder what grabs me to him suddenly, it's the way he grabs you, pins you down, at least he pinned me down without even knowing me, just right, not for them & not for then but for now why? I go through the list of men & try to think who could do it, it's nothing that I could do at all nothing for me to do, it has to be done, I think maybe T could do it but no he couldnt do it, I imagine presenting myself as the vulnerable object at L's new loft. When is he moving in? saturday. I'll go up there I'll just arrive, but he always has so many girls around no he doesnt it's just an illusion he makes there wont be anyone there I'll go up there & wait for him to do it, in fact I'll explain to him what I want. This is why he is perfect, he wouldnt care I'll explain to him exactly what I want & he'll do it, no it'd be better if T could do it, no it'd be better if i just waited for L to grab me & start to fuck, the whole thing, no I dont want to fuck I just want him to grab me, that'd be enough, just the grabbing by the arm & maybe the pinning down, I'd escape.

& M couldnt do it, he'd laugh & P would be too serious, I couldnt
be serious with E & E would just freak out, more trouble, too much
to bear for him & another she's crazy I thought so & just like all
the other ones I've known & so on so I'll go to the poetry reading
& see who's there, there'll be somebody there who'll be perfect, not
L, he's too nice & doped & I know the perfect one, a stranger, it's
C but I dont like him. L. or the poetry reading, just cruising as usual
& this is where she sort of branches off for good in the bed. Hours
must've been going by. She's modelling a new sort of dress in a new
kind of sex-show-modelling-show, it's the dress you center your at-
tention on, watch: she comes out onto the stage in the dress. Do
you want to know what the dress is like? I'll describe it later. There's
a man, close on her heels, she's got no shoes on, no I put that in
later. She walks to center-stage, the man behind her. He twists her
arm & pushes her out onto the runway: it's a thrust stage: this is
where you get to see the front of the dress: she acts in pain. The
man, keeping hold of the twisted arm behind her back, grabs her
breast with his other hand, it's a low-cut dress, maybe he even lets
one side of the dress drop down, he keeps his hand on her breast,
her act of pain changes a little towards pleasure, an ache, but the
moment this happens, this change in her attitude, this lessening of
the pain you can see in her face, he turns her around: this is where
you get to see the back of the dress. It's black, low-cut like I said
& full-length, maybe her leg can be seen through a slit up the side of
the dress, maybe he caresses her thigh during the act, but the black
of the dress as it falls turns to violent red & then purple, the bright-
est deepest shades & the back, in shades of the same quality, the
back is deep blue & green, the dress is like a tree, it must be painted,
she is very credible because she is so beautiful, will people laugh at
her, they dont. He turns her around & takes her hair which falls
down her back & pulls it forward so you can see the cut of the dress,
she does nothing but act, her movements are directed. The man &
woman speak but cant be heard, you have seen the back of the
dress, then the walk back down the runway to center-stage & here,
if I forget exactly how I staged it, it doesnt matter, here I think he
hits her & here is where I put in she is barefoot, cause she runs
away, she runs to stage left & here you see the beautiful dress moving
& when she reaches a certain point she stops, gives a look of total
desperation to the man across the stage & just as this look is passing

90

across her face, she begins to extend her arms outward to take a
slight bow — her head bends down after a brief look at the audience,
a look without pain. & just as she has begun this bow, the man, reach-
ing across the stage, extends his arm in her direction indicating that
she take her bow: this is done so that there is no doubt that the per-
formance is over & that the dress is for sale. Now that is all there is
of that. & the consequences of this scene bring us back to something
real, like the list of men, combined with something less real & this
is what it is. but first I have to introduce a new character, el al aaraaf
israfel ishmael helen thy beauty is, but I am like a stone & the new
character begins to be the he-character even though some of the
feminine engenders a kind of relief from that being true directly
true, you see, he must be a sister-love to do this. She will use an
office to set the scene: it's raining out & she becomes hysterical she
is out of control. & he hits her there's less embellishment, there's
none, he simply hits her you dont have to know why it's the only
thing he can do, he hits her, I put in a reason why, it comes later.
He hits her & she hits him back. These are just theatrical hits across
the face. He hits her & she hits him back & this infuriates him & this
is where I put in the reason why, it's cause he wants her so badly
that he is out of control, he loses control even more than she does,
out of frustration, this is the reason I put in here & I put it in be-
cause he gets so infuriated that he punches her, his fist is big enough
to hit her mouth cheek & the lower part of her eye all at once, he
hits her really hard & she falls down. He moves across the room
not looking, she starts to bleed, maybe she loses a tooth, she's
dazed, falls down, starts to get up, spits out a tooth. She wipes her
face with her shirt & remembers there's a door to a kind of garden
behind the chair, she makes for it, he tries to stop her, the table gets
knocked over, the lamp, he grabs her, she puts her head down. There
are all kinds of things that could happen next, what I'm saying is
there were many variations, like, the noise brings somebody down
from upstairs, there's a scene like talking between doors or he goes
out to take care of it but cant because she'll run out into the yard
or there's someone waiting & he says there's an emergency, you see,
he cant let her get away. It's obvious he cant cause there's this in-
credible bruise beginning to show on her face & blood & a black eye,
she's very happy about it, what can he do with it? maybe he even
takes her upstairs, maybe no one's home, maybe no one's waiting &

it goes on forever, go over it again, maybe he even has to call up someone on the phone, bring in a new character, there is another character involved with this, no, it's just between these two, what can they do next? nothing, there's nothing to follow it, el, al aaraaf, israfel, ishmael, the only one left, wants to suffer

July 15
In the country in a room. Do you assume in your creation that humans have an understood love to begin with & when I get that from you, I can make you any one, then, I can make you another, even the persecutor? Brights lights big city baby you knock me out, yeah have a life, nurses, it's twelve o'clock & fifty seconds bright day: bright & gifted children top soil red wood tubs & boxes hot lunches & terrace design maintenance care of aged & sick this is the book telephone book & mr. h-o-h-l the lawyer wouldnt talk to me write him a letter in anger, A, write to show, specializing in psychiatry gradual planes garden design, the nurses registry 5 N.Main St. Spring Valley, nyc#5626255: 150 a week to nurse, 15 a week to registry, 30 a day for replacement, 1 day off, 6 days a week live-in, pay carfare, mrs. wulfurt, $195 times 4 = $780 a month plus carfare, you set up the bed. This morning pictures the dark windows of the loft in morning, afternoon, the blue windows of the bathroom window & more of the extra now, the dark handling of the morning windows & last night end myself in the mirror & ed in bed, he's asleep, he laughs the shutter button gets stuck the camera shakes lines & jimmy reed gets stuck for the seventh time got me runnin got me hidin baby what you want me to do & that's pretty nice too & I feel heavy with three meals today because of bacon & eggs & veal & greens & home fries & peaches & beef & greens & wine & someone says it's all shellfish all right & someone says yeah we were in boston that day, you remember, & braids tickle my ankle & I am uptight distant & far away because I got up & went to canal street, ed, & I passed the public scales on 6THAVE, that's commercial weighing by water ron said & it's a trial: you get on the subway a black man in a straw hat is motionless & a black man in glasses, their heads go down are cut off & a sun-tanned black woman, you see ads for cheeseburgers you see ads for radio station WXYZ, you get off at 47THST&6THAVE & what does it say sale what, I cant read it from here something for

49¢ & someone says I can read that & I can also read 1st quality
stockings & I guess you can read 49¢, no you cant read that, it's
light bulbs in a glass case & I met ed at arnolds saw the films we
try to synchronize sound: nightmare alley with tyrone power,
dante's inferno on 47THST: it's red white & blue & you eat dried
cheeseburgers dipped in sauce, cell sauce, you've been in the city
two days & that guy in the picture was sitting right across from you
& he didnt even know it & he doesnt know it now, no how cause
you took his picture in the mirror with ed & ed's arm's black &
the waiter's black in white waiter's hat & you see a jewish man
eating food in a big brown hat with striped brim band, bands of
deli deli deli & franks franks franks lines lines lines fluorescents
fluorescents fluorescents fluorescents lights have changed my life
& it was brighter in there than it was outside & that was very
bright & bright green to make you sick, construction green dark
on a bus on a bus, grass: a place to relax excitement confusion I
guess we separated & I went to the hospital again you see a patient
looking out a window dark & read time magazine & R's not there
we're back at arnolds, ed talked on the phone & the floods are too
high, high orange doors to the construction palace & someone says
that's the reddest thing I've ever seen & that's three sets of teeth
& you look down like girls on toys through a hole a hole so deep
it makes ed black & ed in his black-green shirt t-shirt looks dean
james green & you must be in the subway against bright green
bricks & R-green he makes a face & you mug they say, one hand
on his other hand's elbow & what's that: you see the bank in the
park, that's right, lights on & wait till you see what's next it's so
dark in here & it's nice, yeah it's lions in buildings, right,
gradually coming down in a fabric of glass, no mistake: we took
the subway home. Later we stopped at smilers 6THAVE & fruits
prices quality reflect on the car, as before: bright lights field big
city field baby you knock me out & fuck GP he doesnt trust wo-
men or just women with children & he wants to live in his past so
he leaves us out in the process that's his states of consciousness &
you cant accept us just floating around with no identities except
we're teachers I think I think we say we're teachers & I guess we
memory young to him to seem: can he see us you stop time & I'll
stop time too with you & could he see us & his sister-aunt bob gone
to the coast for her 50th wedding anniversary fuck her & fuck here

now's the time to fuck, aunt bob's the one who wouldnt admit me
to the hospital when i was almost eighteen cause she didnt want the
responsibility in case I died, who moves: the moon & jimmy reed.
You listen & you become strong in your resolve & you move never
to give anyone a way to identify you, a sense of your ease maybe but
no word & what's the word it's poet, son. It's lamppost fence: you're
a fence & you're perverse, thief, I hope & a woman was an outcast,
E & a woman was ugly & her tongue was tied & a woman was blonde,
what century & in what city do you see & do you see a faster way,
find a faster way to get to the line that goes in all directions flame
no continuing space a space to live in flame you can see it right·
away no figuring & most of all sleep no questions that's the end:
there was a guy who tried to pick me up on the subway & he said
why dont you trust me & he said well if you're in a hurry then why
do you walk then why dont you run & you take pictures I see pic-
tures for me & another like me & so on. Notes: previn glenn miller
columbia decca prestige audio fidelity is a command enoch light &
numbers at sam goodys & someone says we should have a small pro-
fessional specialty store for what you want & he's queer & all I want
is old black magic & he talks an english accent, says this stores too
big & he comes up with enoch light & up with friendly hippie con-
struction workers smile like neil & dope seems to reign supremes
in the store for a while with nathan jones & chaim arnold & mrs.
kerlew legister calls & signs her name in her own black hand written
by the other black nurses out of the black house in black jeans with
black coffee besides the black mrs. sampson & lilah's black & she
says what records do you have & i have that old black magic & janis
joplin real as life & she says as soon as I start singing one of those
songs I have to go out & buy it & I'm much more at home here black
with blue notebook, store it up, than in the country passive in the
city sit back & be in pain queens plaza. I pass an indian spice store
on broadway of elmhurst & I buy spice tea cause the store is there &
I'm black & dr. attoh the west indian is my friend today & G says
get that thing off me & demands a glass of water & the F train goes
to kew gardens & I buy cashew nuts & the tea we couldnt drink it &
the indian man stands up straight to tell me that assafoetida a bad-
smelling gum resin obtained from various asiatic plants of the carrot
family is a natural laxative & he says or he adds to keep your emotions
pure or was it emulsions or motions movements bowel movements fine

powders real time: ellsberg, victimology & I remember that assafoetida
is the substance they use to see if babies think the things adults hate
the smell of smell bad & the answer is they dont especially shit & a
woman in the hospital elevator says to me because of your braids
they might need you in that play & I say what play & she laughs
as if I know & if they all knew how old I was they'd ½-shit jesus
christ the spartan restaurant & where was that asshole priest today
we go black to massachusetts G burps & I know what P means about
seeing all these people before but now I dont & will it make me put
everything into words & who is P always formulating for me he never
leaves my thoughts alone, it's fifteen to four & the 5THAVE crowds
are waiting for the RR train & I'm all alone in the hotshit crowd,
they get off early, just waiting for some room: nurses internal what
balls not all to have a family. Power money room. Gentle witch the
orange pen & change of $20 in my pocket overwhelms me, how to
run the splicers & the rewinds & who has films that want editing we
all do & can I have the mylar splicer & take away that spool we want
this over here, a loud buzzing, you want that? background talking &
walking & A sitting at the editing table says can I have a reel, emul-
sion side down it sticks that's gelatin & the raw part of the film is an
original the viewer left right, emulsion side down print up base side
straight up & down correctly wound it must be rewound, any ques-
tions? emulsion side upside down. Flip it for the image, this is a
viewer: a hippie runs off the train at 42NDST he almost missed his
stop, pinkerton gent agent getting on the train whizzes around, the
kid must be a criminal he thinks pink, punk, sits down & looks silly,
holds his hose his hat & his brief case he has a good tan not time,
that's G.Gordon Liddy says: if you've got the time we've got the
beer milky beer looking up, this is a detailed diary of my rapes:
now the pinkerton is taking notes, he couldnt stand it but I have an
orange pen & he's not looking up at me, his legs crossed mine apart
the two of us writing furiously on the train at prince street he crosses
the other leg, he's writing about tom, a traitor like jean genet he can
only write in the dark, notes: 522-2222-030A just charge it & say
you're mrs. roy pierce personal loan department chase manhattan
bank & how do you cross a palm with a negative sitting in the regular
studio there's a chair there where two birds artificial birds fly by &
you may not be interested in artificial birds in the sky but Paul is &
he makes a fish come in right over the sun as if the fish were flying

& I turn the volume up & we're sitting in the regular studio in the
fucking chair & we make a memorial or stars to the sun sinks down
toward the fjord where Paul came from far away from twolaneblack-
top art & but there's still a tree & this is drawing drawing's cheap an
optical printing'll cost you two bills you draw the bills out of a num-
ber of them 354 356 357 & it runs to nine bills on the A-wind under-
lined & in other altered states on the opposite side of the space there
is tom please per-mix me to tower a bone & knot over hills where
your ground makes sparks in the air no ground blue once easy yawn
rolls through the box car with a simple engine on it rolls through
the mountains on tracks: there's something to that story & I say
wow I know what that is you know those apartment buildings on
the west side highway & he says yeah & I say that's what that is &
he says do you have any memory this time at all & I say not so far
& he says you will I think & I say that's pretty nice too & he says
mm & I say lights & he says butterfly & I say that's nice you know
that sign & he says yup & I say teneco I waited long & he says auto-
matic exchange lanes keep right & I say we were as far as riverdale
ten cents & he says i dont remember this day very much & I say
we're going back now & he say I think we had K with us too didnt
we & I say yellow pail & a blue jar at the gas station & he says was
K driving & I say this might've been the hitchhiker night & he says
it was & I say how do you know & he says I can just figure it out &
he says what's that & I say not me & he says lights on & I say I dont
know & he says J's friend from topeka was there was that it & I
say a mystery & he says I dont know either & I say next morning
& he says we & I say I slept on the side by the window & he says
I slept by the door & I say who's that I dont know who I was who
I was sleeping with then & he says obviously & I say obviously so a
moth flies in & we're sitting in the back seat of the 1964 cadillac
convertible K & E in the front up the west side highway the miller
parkway listening to pres. nix. announce he'll visit china but the
date is secret so is beethoven's motive for 1st symphony & so is
brahms' motives same screech cars pile up not on top I'm with the
machines on this one & jim the drummer called & E gets stoned then
the h-hiker who got part of the next page turns out to be a preacher
for the jesus revolution of teen challenge an ex drug addict he says
& he says when I saw a pair of white hands on my back I never took
drugs again & yes he says I saw white hands on heroin no I wasnt

96

on heroin when I saw them yes I was & I never was again & I spoke
in tongues he says a tongue freak revolution from the top & so he
says regina coeli brother he says blessed mother mary magdalen &
christ you know the preacher got into the car with them but he
didnt notice he preached & as he left he cautioned them I got a con-
tact high amen & sends us high literature later & when we get to
massachusetts it's topeka but first we leave off jesus in poughkeepsie
he belongs & when I see the woman from topeka my first thought
is well could she be his very own ex-wife & we come in laughing &
we file in laughing & we seem much younger than psychology & I
write the end of a note to michael says I cant believe that anything
in the outside world is that important I surely didnt do anything
vicious love & I'm still awake at dawn for the fields to watch me &
the field watches me, ed's back the field

July 16
I just received your letter
Dear B. it's over
So you're downtown to stay
So I just thought I'd tell you
To turn back the other way
Same thing I been telling you
Day after day: it's over & all is now past & it may happen that the
order set up for the original experience works for the new & if it
does the new part can just be seen as a sign of that order & if that
happens we have no reason to change but if not & if the order wont
work when the volume is increased when we see more then we have
two alternatives & they are we can either reject it altogether, what
is new, or we can change the order radically: the first alternative
is never taken if the second is available & the concept of prediction
does not enter in unless you can hold your love in disorder the whole
night long, hold your love in disorder & the whole night long it's
sunrise-sunset when you get up & when you get down: tom is still
limping we help him limp & I have a job in madrid helping a sea's
captain we are at the ocean shore in madrid it's sunrise-sunset waves
waves waves and so on altered waves absence of authority altered
authority I am on the ground dull & I'm afraid this day may bore
you but again this red day bred you feudal, planetary whip of the

sun: ed in t's soccer shirt biting the top of one hand the other resting
on the table & J cut off the blues vs. the tans on a white wicker chair,
someone threw in a yellow towel & we made calls that cello day to
find a moviola first we talked to jonathan & ann: ed figured out
why the sheriff was here cause he was involved in the eviction & to
see if the same people had moved back in & that's not us: tungsten
ASA 80 & a thousand dollars worth of rocks in the back of the car
rothstein silverstein & epstein & sunday 6-7 for the cello be back
tonight or tomorrow & can we use the heat here & can we work it
out & can we use the theater, calls, & should we take the tape re-
corder & noises of barking & intermission music & call ballou &
call R & get brakes & K gets a postcard from L through B with no
message on it it's a connection like having a baby, be me, & a pic-
ture of us in the stream appears in the public papers & there's a
telephone strike 411 411 411 the end & ed & J play feudal warfare
all day one forfeits his life for the car for the bear for the alimony
for the laundromat, the cello's bow is soaped so it wont play & e's
play is a jewish play the end of the play is not the end of the day
this play is open today so someone says in it take a few steps into
the middle of the beach & maybe perhaps i'll meet you there & J
reads to us from sleep & jon's blood runs hot when he hears the
word moviola the cummington school of the arts has one, hillary
harris amy greenfiled & davids (3) steins & g.stein says roommates
must always do laundry & with this forget it rains stops brakes
girls who look like bernadette devlin stop brakes: K reading philip
roth all over lying on the couch feet up near the game with the ball
& the numbers on the ball-bearing wood frame: I moved to the left
further & further away from K to the window & lamp sea water
color on the wall & I went out: J&K's yellow shed: the back door
of the shed is a false front from a to z & old rhubarb plants old
green everything green in these pictures old looks & they'd caught
some curled up dead leaves & apple trees among them & did we go
home then no, a house made of grass again does that deceive you
yes it does some very very ordinary weeds I'm down the hill red
berries & who cares they got a laugh I was roaming around from
just inside the forest wall towards out of it, that's beaut. yeah that
is nice tall stick tree in a hole, see, plants get no response are shots
in dark & I got fire far away from house a weird shaken shot in
patch of light on ground wet leaves on blackened trees & light comes

through & ed gets into bed & turns around all the time: two black
trunks one curling & yellow-green behind & what you do now &
what you did then you smell a fire burning then a library of photos
a million slides of everything that is, look them up many of those
tall thin trees are there some fallen wound around some fallen down
with side slide branches up on the roof & you pick two trunks to
choose from a yellow chair me on the ground & ed plays the cello
I put blue notebook down on a big white car at the theater next to
someone's shadow & a red bag floating, the windshield wipers were
stopped up we had no brakes we went home late the lights the house
spots across the road across the house still on still house in mist &
ed's legs in front of the tv a war movie for hours & hours: tom ball
mountain is on the map el. 1993: I wanna take you higher

July 17
Had I quit yet? Ed at work with his earphones on. Julia came & made
up M's bed like a hospital. Ed took his shirt off & pulled his hair
back. We went out. We left the screen door open. Ed went back in.
He didnt close the door. I went across the street. E turned around
& stood in the doorway. The roof of the house sags. Peggy drinks
courvoisier, the pen got caught in my hair. Posted no trespassing,
C.A.Price. I turned around. I went down the road. I stopped in front
of a row of trees. I really have nothing to do & no sense of it. I
havent been able to sleep nights at all. I crossed the road & crouched
down behind some tiger lilies. I crouched lower down & opened up
more. I didnt know where I was. I bent over some yellow flowers. I
went further down the road. I sat down in a field & faced the road.
I looked across. I tried to make everything look yellow & still catch
purple. I tried to make yellow keep its yellow against the sky. Things
were blowing. I watched out for bees. I found a bunch of things half
dead half alive. I went further down the road. I went right up to a
sign & looked behind it. It was pointing at light a curve. I trespassed.
The shutters of the house were closed. I went back. I bent over a
mud puddle. I walked around it till the sun was in it. I went behind
the house to the field. I went right up to two leaves on the same
plant one was green & one was turning colors & a hole in it. I went
over to the gas meter on the telephone pole. I tried to read it. I
found a heap of garbage in tan plastic bags. The garbage was hidden

in a grove of low trees. The trees seemed to be bending over it. There were flies all around. I found the pond in back of the field. We went to zayre's for tape & a record. We bought wild horses & someone says does ed know it was sagittarius keith richard who wrote wild horses which is probably why jagger sings it so bad. I looked up at the sky above the building. I looked again, We stopped at a dairy queen for ice cream. I looked out the window at a family of cars. We went past the farm. We went past the golf course. The sun set. I put something on the stove. I scrambled eggs. I looked at the tape deck. I put something more on the stove: this is what really happened reading backwards. Dinners I'm supposed to go to dinner I already went I go again & again in long addresses in long dresses, tom, we take acid before a dinner & then lose track, or, take acid before a dinner then lose track, somebody's father, strait-laced I'm strait & laced in long dresses my camera with me, the gas man comes he says this is a conceptual piece lacking conceptual data & he says I got no expectations: the gas man comes today & last night mist fell through the spotlight of the spotlit house our house is unspotlit like dreams & last night tv bats flew around this room on the outside whirring, little crashes & a twisting buzzing sound, little patters creaks bangs sneaking around sounds to which you listen with both ears, listen, they're nesting under the roof out front we saw their ears & ed's doing the dishes listen it's orange water gun in alford close to the state line, I get the blue toothbrush ed gets the elegant tan colorless one & ugly pictures are fathers trying to ask a question about women & the answer is me in spite of myself: women reading backwards. Where the fuck are the men when you need them? I hate x here & I'm glad I dont take very good care of a good notebook put to good use these days & I'd hate alot of other men too if I knew them knew them men in a room womb tomb alone with me like a young man from Japan I am highly dissatisfied with life as it is or let me reform that for you wanna go higher you want an unsystematic slovenly mess that is chaos for all, then come along with me & you'll have a journal & no survey: ed & tom are soft on women but hard on lines & edges remember to be reading this backwards & why bother a yellow bird a yellow bird & why bother a beautiful day I'm A. The mailman's here. Sun out in a white pickup truck & still old coffee stain on the white pants alot of car doors slam & it's hard to strike a match anywhere, the gas man's on the cellar floor & maybe it's saturday maybe

it's saturday what was yesterday the cellar floor's a good place to
strike em, men. Julia no first ed at work with his earphones on, then
julia & tim-ted-tom from the homestead house come a big bee chases
them a big bee chases me a walk through the orange green screen
through paradise & I think about e's play, FM should be here today,
I wanted a picture of the spider web on the downstairs bathroom
window july 17 & havent paid the rent yet well have you ever &
keeping track of the moons wounds helps remind you to pay the
rent soon helps a wasp a big bee a wasp in a hole I take colorless
pictures cause green is not a color & lose more style in my right
arm than in left, what little style are left right: something about a
sock hop & julia tells the wasp to fly up the sun comes out edison
the earphones with his work in an old pollynose on the porch pond.
The gas man fat mustache sideburns the sun gave a heavy breeze
here a door slams no it doesnt a black & white bug now I chase him
away sun again & put an ash in his path, you are a star. Yoga today
sun gone & green is silver to touch some days green is gold rustling
today & blowing the weather is changeable lemonade to drink. Musak
candle melting into the porch wood the dream sun comes again sky
too bright & gone again brighter a flag at the end of the field the
buzzing bats asleep a day a buzzing thing dips through the sky &
the yellow bird dragon flies top of many white flowers & buzzing
will I be stung by a bee, clean up this wiring robbe-grillet is a fried
bear in his fathbone in his bathrobe fatherbone he is father in his
bathrobe & jacques, marcel apple? Trees went to sleep this morning
no pictures they were gone a furious short duration phrases words a
sentence is over it runs not a period not a pause for breath from one
memory to another is it faster does it move still question marks & a
picture of lee I hope identities change again exchange again change
again home & you move & you need another bed is my right as a
writer to smoke all I want but a bug on the cigarette we need a bed
you need a bed & so much smoke from the match into & out of &
turned off it to it into it not into wishing well was that a well talking
muffled talking beyond the field the porch the deck all around the
house is weeping willow tree so please come in through the window
you see the minds that changed places were well on their way already
they were very much into that change & well jealousy is all you own
jealousy & some jalousie windows & I've brought in the dictionary as
I'm into it & is it easy how easy questions run into each other into

how questions run each other into great walls so a man in a yellow
shirt looks at me he bends down he's on my private property I didnt
think I had one & I think we cannot swim are not allowed to swim
in his stream I think we cannot own each others rights at all at least
not me & him so what does he have to say I say these questions of
private property always end in periods. They do. Trees went to sleep
this morning they had every right and zoom to write smaller sun out
in a very much into the sky where are the purples i love ya kind of
way type of way a whistle rustles through big clouds but grey blue
sky very pale very bright a truck goes by tomorrow i'll look out
front, this is out back. See, the property, the periods, me. The
flowers are ok the man stood next the flag next to the flag which
boundaries the markers of our property what time is it july 17.
Ed is on the earphones ed at work with his earphones on we have no
phone here a car stops is it for us & still muffled a door slams ours?
there's no mystery about it an actor is moving in but that knock
was mr. flaky foont aka mr. burnt u. thru the telephone man to
remove a white princess belonging to mr. dennis jensen formerly of
this address of this address, orange tiger lilies mr. thru you came on
like a nice guy long hair old jeans not just a public servant a tele-
phone remover summer style & you waved as you drove off towards
alford, a church, bear left on this road away from stockbridge &
you'll come to it especially flaky or hokey, the wooden horse the
carriage the gazebo & the empty reservoir, those people across the
road are nuts. 2. This fly on my page like orange & this orange comes
off on your fingers mine a mine of information like: the fly's back
flying over a sedentary fly prince princess & queen mother I guess
in bobby socks beautiful flood lights on the yellow house, mr.
prince waves but dont look too happy as he drives off he's a prince
to his wife's price, miss price, sinking feeling as the price of the
prince's yellow car goes by: I'm out front by now on top of blue
car. Red waving truck passes by box 108A flying eating orange but
not the pen point more ornament for the white pants ann & tina
talking about us at cape cod everybody talks about us with the
brandsteins this time on the beach at chappaquiddick & a whirr
it's a gold car old gold people burnt you thru my golden foot is bit
ouch: pink garage the fly's on me now i'm on the fly 2 flies love me
I'd be quitting puddle pine needles rut I guess ditch ditch it crack a
twig to show you're there cracks & muffled buzzing I'm flying or the

queen at the garbage can behold the lid on tight no fights on this
road & now & beetle he flies the fly on my leg beetle bent ruffles
& flourishes nourishes food nourishes lettuce & tomato sandwiches
with 1,000 islands sauce & coffee lemon lemonade whirrs, tree noise
tree tone gimme a little orange posted it's halloween at the queen's
house tiger lily radio stir up noise an experiment pure sure one
plant blows this way another the other & four or five more a million
anarchists came we had logs for dinner & the n with a cedillla. Sun
on pine needle tray shade on tom ball mt. el 1993 aunt el's was
high & the stones are free if you buy the whole piece only eli wallach
bought it & all the squirrels too double exposure I cant afford it
broke the train broke the beak of the bird eating seed broke his
carburetor, pump, motorcycle goes by sings broke the icy revolu-
tion in two instinct parts by pending in suspense with one and so
the end & the two teeth biting one a woman the other a man & all
trees still hanging down down around 10 feet clearly marked &
clearly marked the right record for this kind of moon, thank you,
through august 6 so read a book. Tell you: own a dot on lily a huge
expanse & keep it keep it well, red flag up mr. dash man fly foot
white the car with pants sitting in the shade of the learning apple
tree with harriet sweet williams: i imagine myself caked in cement
they have to chip through holes to my nostrils so I can breathe,
poison something on my ankle, first I imagine myself covered with
something sticky, I say cut off the hair on my legs & first before
that, shave it off, but the razor gets stuck, leaves my leg a bloody
sore, a rectangle, poison something on my ankle, her privacy, the
man fishing alford brook like muddy brook her granddaughter
visiting do you need anybody I need some body to love do you
want balloons yes ballou I walked up the road town road toward
alford quiet in her ear ed is on the ear phones making speaking
noises with a magic marker cant hear a thing, I'm in the hammock
with the flies in it but I walked up it to fields flowers smell burning
cigarette against a wooden match up a narrow road on a small
weekend I came to a closed-up house maybe a weekend house
another house behind it also closed black shutters green ones
white hydrangeas thin a curve sign fields posted at the peak of the
curve a rolling uphill driveway to another white house white fence
along the road this house a larger one a flower garden occupied pur-
ple across the road tennis courts & a view of the top of a mountain

tom ball the first on this road & from there the mountain's leg of lamb was white from too much light I couldnt take a picture of it so I think instead about being in the bathtub with ed after shooting movies I've turned around so I can see it rain & the wind is heavy turned dark by 4:15 at 4:15: let's go into stockbridge so we can buy some batteries for the tape recorder foot stopped itching soon thunder & lightning like hunger the bathtub when we were waiting for breakfast in the bathtub & so depressed about being here that there were pictures I couldnt take & that was the night we stayed up all night willow trees waving doors slamming them some days are longer than others & someone says it might take a while it might have some value we have to have everything together or half each including a tree a chance to do some thing an involving yourself in something, lets go. Out: backwards manny kershenheimer in the dining room of the cummington school of the arts or agawam near holyoke the bay state film corp near springfield & at 3:30 pm sunday sun at the school you will hear south indian music in the office: watching out for the thorn bushes allergic it'll go away it does, agawam, leaves foot with used look, like it, jack blue eyes pushes his hair back with one hand running his fingers through it anxiety & magic thinking there's more to it, vistas you've got a friend james taylor a mercedes benz in there & what'd I say alice cooper caught in a dream touch me in the morning we're in the silver city bar again & k&j fought & fuck you they go to claire's knee does k have to do the dishes & j reminds me of T, meet terence & f. murray the arab from pittsburgh, texas, & friends they all went six miles instead of point six & wound up at the state line all the way to the state line amen, noise shouldnt go too high the speaker rumbles the noise interiors out fast it's too fast lower the volume of the noise before the crash & add the add the explosion lower the applause does the noise of a small crowd milling seem too small have any appeal the noise of the newsroom is not clear & the noise needs bells turn up the treble lower the bass, a door opening slow, that noise speeds & that noise needs selection lower the base keep the treble normal then lower it for a while but not all the way to silence then up again & try the noise of the silver city bar & get closer to the cash registers when you listen they ring up & maybe the noise of dishes would work & the noise of musak & the noise of the street's no good & maybe the noise of just cars mixed with street noise & the noise of the bar needs no base at all: I put something more in. I put something more on the stove. I looked at the tape deck. I scrambled eggs. I put something on the stove. The sun set. We went past the golf course. We went past the farm. I looked out the window at a family of cars. We stopped at a dairy queen for ice cream. I looked again. I looked up at the sky above the building. We bought wild horses & someone says does ed know it was sagittarius keith richard who wrote wild horses which is probably why jagger sings it so bad. We went to zayre's for tape & a record. I found the pond in back of the field. There were flies all around. The trees seemed to be bending over it. The garbage was hidden in a grove of low trees. I found a heap of garbage in tan plastic bags. I tried to read it. I went over to the gas meter on the telephone pole. I went right up to two leaves on the same plant one was green & one was turning colors & a hole in it. I walked around it till the sun was in it. I bent over a mud puddle. I went back. The shutters of the house were closed. I trespassed. It was pointing at light a curve. I went right up to a sign & looked behind it. I went further down the road. I found a bunch of things half dead half alive. I watched out for bees. Things were blowing. I tried to make yellow keep its yellow against the sky. I tried to make everything look yellow & still catch purple. I looked across. I sat down in a field & faced the road. I went further down the road. I bent over some yellow flowers. I didnt know where I was. I crouched lower down & opened up more. I crossed the road & crouched down behind some tiger lilies. I havent been able to sleep nights at all. I really have nothing to do & no sense of it. I stopped in front of a row of trees. I went down the road. I turned around. Posted no trespassing C.A.Price. Peggy drinks courvoisier, the pen got caught in my hair. The roof of the house sags. E turned around & stood in the doorway. I went across the street. He didnt close the door. Ed went back in. We left the screen door open. We went out. Ed took his shirt off & pulled his hair back. Julia came & made up M's bed like a hospital. Had I quit yet?

July 18
There's a wreck in the sea I recreate wreck member be me remember this see & while she was pushing her way through someone asked her now I ask you can I say that & I'm gonna shut myself up in a

room honey & someone asked her medicine would do no good
there's a wreck in the sea: we sailed. It's cool today finally at last
it's too cool kathleen & I set sail together & while she was pushing
her way through someone asked her, we woke up well into the day,
i looked out the window to puffy luminous white clouds dark in
the middle & of all sizes but there were all sizes some just wisps
in the air close to us, some full of dresses some clouds of boxes some
of dishes some of churches some full of women some children some
teeth some had mice some had wives some full of knives some with
leaves some with theives in them some ladies some babies some
cities whole cities no countries & blue sky thru the diamond window
is green blue & white like a flag or an army armies are made to look
like the sky, it brings light to the ceiling pointed & you make sam
cooke a little louder, he was shot in a motel room with a woman in
it & someone says he would've been as popular as frank sinatra &
gwen gives me her record & the window brings light to the ceiling
pointed to bring out the inside to white out the outside, pastel it,
black tv on black chair with antennae up ed's feet up & a pillow on
top of him, clouds that are losing their substance at the edges as
though the sky water melts them down clouds that fly inside is out-
side ed in tom's soccer shirt. The tungsten wreck yesterday just
trials off into three hours in the theater listening to sound & san
francisco for clouds ed singing that old black magic & f warming
up in the basement enunciating gesticulating orating articulating
ejaculating epistolating theater personnel & star divine movie
technical & mouth open tv distant divine repeat writing letters
is a thirst rehearse repeat george eliot & f. motorcycle bailey with
cardboard plates he's rehearsing a good place to sit a good place to
be this morning, some dreams I forget more two's more towers &
bells or these wooden struts trees & all the rest shade a good shampoo
he's yelling both decks in the shade are in the shade. The ride through
the glade my shadow on the ground, receipts, i want some mail
ballou ballou cut come custard mustard away a way think sense
cant today a way cant get comfortable cant concede darker darker
darker deed I rhyme I got a pillow & pictures: I woke up & out the
upstairs window out the other one the tv then big fat white clouds
light from behind them out the windows dawn an amazing day
delicate ektachrome sky & keep yourself out of this delicate sky or
eye, less light bluer sky & later the blue in the blue in the blue in

the clouds full of airships rivers clouds of engines clouds of inches
clouds of pain of lamps of ovens clouds of rugs clouds of uncles all
over the place & clouds of noises clouds of addresses strait & laced
clouds of oceans right & left clouds of gloves of hills some of ice-
bergs some of election clouds of cars of the car clouds of undertaking,
fast slow hard old clouds that fly inside is outside ed in tom's soccer
shirt squints at the sky the tie is tied up to the top & ed's large hands
were clasped around his knees his hair loose & then he looked down
to the right yawning the sun was past the house moving quickly across
the road my foot was red from the rain on my moccasins the top of
it hairy love & fascination is her middle name to my heart to my
heart a sick sweet young rich cheap late sensation of thrills she brings,
the hell with the heels of his shoes, we went through receipts ed's
feet on the floor of the deck, our notebook crumpled red paper pack
of smokes an empty pad the pad i'm using now a wax pad I bought
for paper that wouldnt reflect the light we needed paper that wouldnt
reflect the light just as the curtains, freeze they close over the late
bright short clear friezes hanging up in the movies the old candle is
there with a feather stuck to it about the bottoms of ed's pants are
frayed from stepping on them with his heels the heels of his shoes,
the hell with the heels of his thick strong clean deep cold shoes, John
is small. There's a wreck in the sea the sidewalk & ground in the
kitchen & the waterplug opened upside down la rosa rigatoni empty
coffee cans jack frost sugar an orange & grey towel a screw driver, I
couldnt find one today only phillips heads, the water pistol orange
& 8 eggs in a yellow carton with the sun on them they pose feet on
the floor & wood counter they come clean we go out down the dirt
road & chris called the s.s. & someone says he's so wonderful & down
the dirt road at the treacherous part once we met a car there's a
fence to keep you from falling over the cliff the sun's always right
around the corner & now kathleen's putting up the sails. E & j went
somewhere but first j brought us over to the mahkeenac boating
club a kind of club no jews aloud there are those kinds of clubs a
lot of wasps & blots on their record & lots of boats & most of the
boats are private property instead of where they went a pair of us
went sailing in front of the boating club into the big lake in one of
the boats, it was easy: mr. stokes seems to be in charge of lenox &
he hates jews so we went down through the pine forest to the boats
& house & K put up the sails, two canoes float on upside down

aluminum & I took the camera anyway K smoked as she raised the
sails & someone says her energy & later I smoke it's getting dark I'm
freezing K wore her maroon corduroys a pink tight shirt & short
sleeves blue slightly tie-dyed shirt-jacket a red canoe dips slightly
into the water & things look bigger, it's wood inside, take off a
piece of your finger & I forgot the most important detail of all her
green shoes with long ties on them & ties are sleepers together K
bends over under the erected sail the main sail visible were her
arm hair one hip & legs & feet feet standing in a maze of cords ropes
ties our boat no.962 & backwards that sails in any picture a white
sail becomes the sky the land was all water the land like a river a
thin cord rope around the lake ties the lake in tight K in charge looks
around posing the sun on one side of her face in the middle of a
lake it's easy to determine the light the boat's tipped there was
little wind all those clouds of before had blown away k's green
shoes in the alabaster boat, it was poured plastic a lucite boat a foam
boat no ties at all of a piece, the sun on it to our right to lee her hand
on the rudder sail too white for the sky measures of water water the
surface of a piece the shore with the sun on it, this was a lake on
top of a mountain we were in the middle of it trees shine docks &
3 layers: water land sky or ground mt. sky shift we shift in the boat
weight on the water weight of the sun on water yes he will soul
stirrers the clean cut of evening light two other sails they went in
earlier than we did we had trouble getting to shore no wind up now
towards the rim of the boat water mt. cut by sails & sky with hori-
zon: sun: I closed down we fronted waves a sky writer in the sky
one boat in sight topped perfectly by the top of the rim of long
mt. sun set more sky more golden pink light on k's face was seeing
lines that arent there & I was freezing chattering in a boat: eyes,
we went back sat by a fire that gave out no warmth drank coffee,
ed & Jacques had come out in a canoe to pick us up we declined
assistance, ed in his black leather jacket jacket I took it I wore it &
back to the house to get stoned & eat we went out for dessert ed in
his shades so stoned we couldnt see I sat with KE with J we ate 7
cheesecakes I had two sherrys Jacques drinking brandy & coffee K
& I went to the ladies room I think I looked at myself in the full
length mirror white pants & this shirt or the tie-dyed one tied up in
the middle ed stands up in our room & has m moved in I lie down
ed is invisible I picture the picture of lovers in bermuda over the bed

it's too white in the light of the tensor lamp all electric electric
light we have many pillows we arent actors: meat & sherry sherry &
meat hashish to beat the heat there's something to this there's
something to being lost in the middle of something it makes you
wanna shut yourself up in a room & pour honey on the thick strong
clean deep cold blue sky with its clouds of dresses & closets & so on
& see black black dog comes by looks like plato approaching me
plato from before, this is a life, this is a whole new life: what have
I forgotten should it have been: every night what I remember mem-
ber every day remember later the hall of fantasy exclude f. eyes
red e. eyes ed b. eyes bread & light on my head on stone bull whips
whale & that the headline buzzing in head under the tensor bulbous
light like christ like light on the cross of window cross hanging down
ed is on the window cross T is like a bunny snoot once was once
there was a last record, song on tv it goes: when with me, once was
once there was, when you're with me, once I see, sitting there, once
I was, everywhere, this song, end there, how many feet foot to foot?
Do you know F & xyz you come in here you you & you & there I
cheat I cheat I put you in I throw you in you dont know it I feed
it I burn it nothing happens burnt u thru nothing leaves then you
come in you you & you another & you you turn yourself in you
are sitting down cross-legged on the sand what sand? do you remem-
ber the sand? you are free to move move around it comes in nothing
happens happens indians birds sing they come in how? they? are
sure. In a way helicopters are. Sure of flies you bring a certain num-
ber of them in you have to, sure of one or two others, you bring
them in you dont even have to think about it cutting it cleaner what
was it, to save some purpose some porpoise in the sea was it? to
something to ing to she he & in it later will nothing will it happen,
they come. They are out automatically in the room stays back
throw it in, use it used it's used throw it & now a bee comes in I
wish he'd go away a bee walking that's weird he's looking for some-
thing, nose to the ground, see red: on the deck he walks over to my
book climbs on it looks around plays with a piece of tobacco he lies
motionless on the blue paint of the cover the back of the bee vibrates
back & forth I drop an ash near him, I go to get a pad, I can no
longer write in the book, the vibrations disturb him he is still again
now he climbs on the spiral binding,yellow legs wrapped around it
he's out on deck again a grounded bee, can he see, he's still on one

leg & one antenna on a spiral vibrates again I could write in the
book but it might get stung still still fly, an electric typewriter
could never a comodate a bee, bee still out there climbing on the
pillow i'll shake him off: coffee rice pepper carbon paper a map
to the cummington school, 8:45 at the dining room, still the bee's
gone he was on the pillows currents I dont know if I mentioned
that & then gone ed hadnt seen him on the pillow & I find myself
imitating K we ate coddled eggs, left for j&k's talked to manny
kershenheimer went sailing instead of sounding, studio, celia the
cellist & thought of seeing clark & susan too celia the cellist went
off suddenly back to her husband & child, sailing the telltale ariel,
connor & nancy from charleston south carolina are freshmen at
williams & anxious to please to prove his something or other but
then j's the director of a play & k an actress in it I keep forgetting
why they're nice to us my poison something left scars & where am
I, sailing preparing to come about tacking K fucked just before she
left for college heave to trim in the gradual sunset on stockbridge
bowl streaks of dirt the air plane the cold air plane, cold warm
water white boat K is the captain of the ship the man fishing the
end of the world the lake on top of the mountain, a bowl we also
live in a bowl, alford bowl of elephants, & the brook club is here of
giraffes, j & ed ja nd ed row out to us ed looks like he's wearing
corduroy until we get closer they're paddling a canoe it's black
suede I look close cause I'm cold as the wind dies down lake placid
trouble getting in & colder wait for fire coffee j's feet & pants wet:
mr. stokes blah blah poor nancy comes on very strong she's no
racist pig herself & they're married or something. Dinner. Corn peas
pork chops wine talk to R she fades in & out sailing, oh, my father
& the corn. & someone says did you have any idea what death was
then, yes my father cut the corn off the cob & later I think of
answers to that like you get a good idea pretty fast & you get a
thick strong clean deep cold blue cheap ideas come cheap real fast
& j's questions of life & death: the burnt egg the sprig of parsley for
good breath apples & nuts vampires garlic the stars the bats stones
fred lord's house for rehearsal the sock hop over sit down at a table
in the lions den for cheesecake golden strawberry almost sherry
coffee sherbert a chocolate sundae everybody's so stoned tea brandy
k very stoned gets into j & women a white soul is invisible & j asks
us our ideas of heaven clouds & flowers reincarnate no & K is in

france now with castles & townhouses in paris, elizabeth marie
antoinette & then she begins, a night club singer she was a night
club singer & something theater begins as we sit in heaven cut the
actor tony franciosa or sergio somebody or other in white rough
linen suit cut in straight from a thousand dollar ante poker game
cut in tan from easthampton something easy some love easy life
something else going on: 12 ears of corn cut down cut off ear
cornsilk & my father cut the corn: elvis presley robbstown, an af-
fair with elvis, 1958 music k & b jazz sarah vaugh billy ekstein why
doesnt some body do this well why not, leave, outside vw bus with
people milling call us night pope people, cop car by riggs flashlight
flashing red & blue lights for sportscar to j&k stars the milky way
dipper there & home here cold f.murray in bed ed in shades all the
way down the night honesty rollo may dehumanizing come in lights
clock & so on, except for the beautiful young brown & orange deer
who came running across west road I stopped he ran across the road
as if it was a suburb filled with houses & then he runs back & down
the road in front of the car bounding & off down a road to the right
spots of his filled me with relief again I am there I love the deer we
dont hear messages from you anymore the bidet's very hot the bed
very cold tv very light & golden everywhere this light from this
house making sparks through trees that deer jump through, that
deer in my place, come over, the deer my father & the corn

July 19
You get into bed at night you whisper, you whisper into the tape
another person is there he whispers he speaks he could be awake he
could wake up, he could wake up out of a dream & call you by the
name of his sister & you answer, he asks you what you are doing,
you answer, he doesnt wake up you whisper into the tape dear
mother dear mother the church is cold & sleep you whisper death
father, this is the way things happen could happen this is the way
things fall they turn out there is no design this is a risk there is a
chance that he will waken there is a chance that he will live there is
a chance that he is lost & this is what makes such a wildness of going
to bed after your lover is asleep, you whisper: dear father how did
you first start to drink coffee, do you believe in magic, corrosive
remember we wrote a book in bed, where did the car go sometimes

111

learned where did the car go finely polished lines, our act was no
good for the campuses this is the day the night was lost but the
night's not lost, it follows these thoughts word drives down an
avenue & memory laughs: what'd I say baby what'd I see & when
you see that will you laugh at me I filled your baskets with bread
& tea & the games up for you you're not tough enough for me &
baby that aint me. I just had a cheeseburger we went to rehearsal
for the first time, our car parked next to a red car with black top
next to j's cadillac & beaut. green fred lords barn mowed lawns, I
thought he was a lawyer a basketball court, ed in his jacket & all it
was cool gets coffee: nick kate dick jacques barara murray marilyn
& probably bob & kathleen filling out forms it was their first day,
nick in sneakers & tom gorman a bracket of folding chairs over in
the corner a bracket of folding chairs metal rain again & the two
little girls one red umbrella one blue I dont get the red umbrella in
time they're running it's closed their storybook exists on a farm &
dick or somebody questions me, high speed film, black & white & I
say no i'm just shooting the light behind that green stuff not inside
not inside the barn & that was a lie: 2 doors open to vines you cant
get out you could through vines it pours look out the doors & dick
says something about the feeling of rain in a barn & two little girls
real floods down the road I guess it's something you have to go
across: little girls can play with umbrellas & under them & I say
something about that feeling you have under an embrella & one is
dark: we're on our way to north adams we stop at the new friendly's
on south street a girl eating a large yellow ice cream aluminum cone
it's grey & suburban & crowded my notebook's out & the envelope
of proofs on the counter of god we vow never to eat at friendly's
again, we never got to go to the top of the hilton: ketchup in plastic
bottles & on one of the turns we turn to follow rte. 7 it's tyler street,
it's still raining E is driving & it poured more the printer's fluorescent
lights this is mr. ballou, thank you, plays golf on wednesdays we went
over the proofs of moving saw the cover got a copy of the proof of
it saw negatives of the drawings & mr. ballou says I would do any-
thing to avoid working on that book he says that in his neat shop,
we pick out stars & I ask ed to pull up but too far behind what looks
like a salt factory in north adams it's raining so hard the lights are
on it's letting up it's under construction: wet cut unpainted boards
in wide wide windows men working a man in one of them & it looks

like townhouse apartments giant puddles in the streets & a wet black
generator or concrete mixer windows are holes the corner in adams:
tearing things down: I look crane piles & massive theatrical factory
sky adams blooms in heavy thunders it always rains in north adams
the sun never shines: that kind of day: they work in the day-dark
go home to rows of small windows since 1880 something & long
before a mill on the river for paper tearinghousedown but they keep
off the street one church bell tower still stands red bricks make
adobe puddles the light behind the crane clouds by themselves force
a horizon the death is missing I walked out of the car & down the
street for what I knew about adams: bricks at the bottom of a pile
flowing away melt like clouds like: who lives on the lives of the
who works on this block: passive: windows are holes all the way
through that light & clutter: pepsi that the the co. with ice on it:
who needs it today & sweats we went on we stopped in cummington
to visit but even before that after we sailed high speed ektachrome
ASA 160 that's the American Standard Association that makes pic-
tures in the rehearsal barn out of rain & 2 girls with umbrellas one
in blue with a red umbrella one that I missed & one blue, very
green, dick was brought up on a dairy farm & remembers how secure
he felt in a barn on a rainy day & b & t in easthampton clothes
amagansett agawam sweatshirt & f. murray in ed's purple jacket we
eat friendly big beef cheeseburg specials & peter's right in the berk-
shires they leave the er off of cheeseburger & I think about K saying
last night liquids maybe that's why I'm so pure while I eat clam
chowder & not before the rain & not before we pass dolphs inferno,
dox drug, colonial pizza, & williamstown to north adams to adams
to savoy to windsor to cummington mr. ballou's voice says he will
find any excuse not to do it & it takes a week for kodachrome a
week for proofs another week for books & mts. in cloud under rail-
road bridge following silver blue truck this color color of the ink
puddles flooding rains the something hunting machine co. pass cen-
tury & children in a diamond sign & southview south on rte. 8 the
alternate way the north adams vietnam veterans memorial skating
rink flat as a church can veterans skate bear right onto church street
past general cable there's a T in the road stop ahead this is route 8,
railroad railroad XX left at the T twolane road for the veterans past
chute arco atlantic richfield paper co. entering adams a gunfight
midway restaurant gene parr used cars rochester paper co. bertoli

oil co. road under repair flat tires flat long houses surface on the
road a front hoosac valley oil & grain national pride car wash
angelinas sub shop & I say the night's lost & I say the night's not
lost but death is missing, we visit cummington justine has no sense
of time makes a face at us she's shampooing her doll whose face is
painted like an indians the doll has holes for every kind of intake &
elimination but one, red roses climb up the house the old stove is
on the porch justine is wearing one of her outfits she's wet the
whole place is wet & every time the door opens it rains & everytime
the door opens it rains & do you want to know more, we pulled in
the driveway justine was standing there a tan ragamuffin there arent
many she had just washed the doll's hair but the doll had no hair
left, in a rainbarrel justine was in a rainbarrel & A & J welcome us
they just ordered the death of a cat so the death isnt missing I dream
about adams & do you want to find out more about my life well
check out the garden it's overgrown but things are growing there
it doesnt matter: giant zucchinis in pictures of the garden of jona-
than's stages he doesnt have them he has a row of cabbages the bees
are dead there are 3 distinct places or 4 dollar signs, what'd I say,
alot of shit around in piles shit of the horse boards to walk on over
it & the snow peas we took some the ice & snow & what are those
white things they're blooms the remains of the volkswagon with a
blanket over it rusting & wet tires all around like an old open car
no motor though & work in the barn the cat & her kittens she keeps
them across under the bridge over the stream all but one she tried
to get that one to come with her for a visit I tried to help her but
the kitten wouldnt get wet at all that's over where the grass grows
into the stream & later still garden green raining & every time the
door opens it rains & ann in a long dress swatting flies we eat
brownies she tells stories about beverly the pabst blue ribbon beer
heir ess & our house here used to be hers was built for her but she
couldnt live in it cause igor the prince across the street tries to kill
her dog because her dog threatens his cats & I know he poisons wood-
chucks to keep them out of his garden so he poisons her dog & igor
who's a sculptor lives in the house & he paints his windows white
her windows white so he cant see out cause it distracts him & then
rick & erika live there & they get evicted by mary who rented cots
to tanglewood people for ten bucks a night she put up curtains in
between & served coffee in the morning & mary helps evict rick &

erika & at some point in the history of this house igor cuts the gas
lines & he's totally nuts & this is the house we are living in & it's
for sale for $75,000 cause alford is expensive there are black cadil-
lacs going down the road all day sunday & ann tells us more: about
brownies & venable & beverly & mary & alice & there's the scene of
the cats under the bridge the kittens wont come one gets left on the
other side of the stream & the kitten wont come & she keep three
more on the other side of the stream & one under the boards by
the side of the house & ann tells us more: they're selling the horse
that wont foal selling it by the boards to kim to kim & her father
joe, we meet them, & her mother's an alcoholic she broke her wrist
& had a cast for eight weeks & joe commutes to work in westbury
or new jersey he's a printer & there's a town meeting about zoning
& kim babysits for justine & justine should babysit for all of us we
have coffee ed takes a nap he feels aches there's no snow in cum-
mington at last & the barns arranged: jonathan got us a moviola
at the cummington school & he tells us to come to a concert on sun-
day south indian music the cat feeds her kitten on a log it's
threatening we pick at the garden green beets we get beets jon plays
the violin to the plants it's somebody's birthday pete joanna & joey
come by, we play more instruments recorders ann plays ed on drums
& we should leave we talk about exchanges exchanging places we
pick vegetables snow peas beets spinach greens radishes & jon plays
the violin in the garden we plan a poetry reading with music a list
of all the things in the house I'll read the list with music right out
back with no clothes on no body, jon's got baggy clothes we show
them the cover of the book they had been to cape cod he plays in
the rain i should write to them, jon in baggy light blue pants a yellow
shirt torn over them & a tan one over it & the mare that never foaled
behind her electric electric fence drinking water, the goats are inside
the plastic barn some casual construction going on we didnt stay
past dark promised to come by when we used the moviola for lunch,
we didnt, we went back & I feel better & memory gets improved in
fact it's exactly doubled by the recognition of other people & I sure
explained the whole thing to ann if not jon except we couldnt figure
out why we were friends it's a stranger connection including ed as
much as me & that's why jon & I talked about a poetry reading with
music & I said I'd list all of his possessions he wasnt much interested
in that: we stop in pittsfield for cigarettes & paper no paper & A&J

seem happy & justine says to me we're in school & you're my
mother in her silver vest with her doll's scale the doll gains weight
weigh everything in town we look for jacques the theater has budget
problems no jacques he's probably out to dinner, we leave notes at
his house & a new map, he never came, eat a piece of white bread
with jelly & friendly's before drive though mist again home bath cat
movie on tv with michael sarrazin & bad women actors eat snow
peas fix indian tea, it's undrinkable but could be used as incest in-
citement to incest it's incense it's essence of pepper it's emulsion
it's out of hand it's $1.20, f. murray comes back the actors are being
invaded with machines surrounded with machines in the play I
never thought of it before they dont like it it fucks up their cues:
the night was lost and the word vixeninny in magnet plastic letters
on jonathan's refrigerator & I found the night F brings ribs of beef
from the red lion inn & part of a potato I peel the beets lose my
appetite & take a nap cant fall asleep but ed does again & still is &
F reads a separate reality & tom has & I havent: we had already
built a fire which we sit in front of & F strong presence in the house
& B a little bit uncomfortable actually she's in jail again but fighting
& E i dont know tired, wrote to anne felt distant & wrote about
writing, trouble with words, longhand, we could write good plays &
she writes back she says you sound serious like a serious artist writer
& she says my eyes are still spinning the kodak float had rippling
moving flowers turning into a panorama of the moon landing made
of flowers if you can imagine that & you're right about the dumb
playwright scene there's too much suffering psychodrama in it all
we should really take over soon & I'll write again from the lowlands
& that was float after float of amazing girls each one presenting a
meaningful theme made totally of flowers, they do this, talked to R
twice & GP is coming out maybe thursday have to set up room, may-
be take books away & arrange for coming home & the people down-
stairs will be pissed off & I say what'll happen & ed says GP will die
soon & J says did you have any idea of what death was then when I
was 13 & I say weird far out blew its mind & of course, quickly,
the nothing at all: numb? no, something, me: dear anne: what's
going to happen the green rain's good for me & animals good &
words mixed up come out funny so I think about vito & kathy but
not too much & not too much about tom: something else, do & is
this revealing enough, jackson - you see I try to make everybody

happy no the night's not lost it was there & it followed these thoughts
these words driven down an avenue a false front a false perspective like
memory laughs at the intuition of time: beyond its borders extends
the immense region of conceived time, past & future, into one direc-
tion or another of which which we mentally project all the events
which we think of as real & form a systematic order of them by
giving to each a date & the relation of conceived to intuited time is
just like that of the fictitious space pictured on the flat back-scene
of a theater to the actual space of the stage & the objects painted
on the backdrop, trees columns house in a receding street & so on,
carry back the series of similar objects solidly placed upon the stage
& we think we see things in a continuous perspective, when we
really see this way only a few of them & imagine that we see the
rest: what'd I say baby what'd I see? & when you see that will you
laugh at me I filled your baskets with bread & tea & the games up
for you, you're not tough enough for me & baby that aint me &
lights out, patti, here's something about rivers & something about
time it's the number of times in the tunnel & drifts, bill: one bell
in a tower, the best bell: tough & tired she bends to train rain drain
crane & all these words mean the same thing: vixeninny

July 20
Double exposures, live memory. Do I need music? Well then touch
me in the morning then just go away it's shorter than life, I bought
a ½ gallon of wine to finish the second diary it's bigger than life:
james mason & marta toren in: he's a doctor who's stolen alot of
money they fall in love but he's loved before & been broken they
wind up in the lazy town in mexico she convinces him to stay but
finally they have to go back to settle with the mob they do & plan
to return to mexico for real life so it's all set he crosses the street
to phone the airport & gets killed by a car someone says, it was no
one's fault: double exposure: the house is a tree, do I still figure in
your life, the windows come together but brighter & the rush of
light is for the giant plant before the blue bottles & inside is out-
side would a house made of sod for the eskimos in spring look like
this like some kind of green thing in the grass that I used to make
the house winds up in the middle of the window like a giant manu-
factured grasshopper, a drink maybe, in the window & the window

still has panes but the curtains fade into the ground I mean blend &
snap something new could happen: some body's pouring blood on
his face: orange crates & I kept that feeling about orange but this
time I put them through a transparent blue awning & the awning
only gives them more light night delivery grocery delivery bakery
delivery deliver me everything from & joe cocker could cover this if
only & only in the supermarket, frances just called, the plums: I
forgot to cover them many plums ed wont eat plums I eat german
plum cake many plums glistening in their plastic already covers a
tree & sky against a building or over it with a white mercedes benz
parked in front is without pretty consequence I never thought of
this day in terms of what I did I only saw, joe cocker & not the
beatles, we went to j&k's to the supermarket for food the only food
we could get, plums, to the theater & back home to work out what
we had left to do: the trees gave us enough light but no trees just
papers our script cigarettes coffee mattress to sit on sky over land
clouds close to grass clouds in the house the house in a cloud ed
reads he is smaller on one side than in the middle he sees himself
from the back for once & from the front at once looking down in
my softball shirt his ass coming out of his falling down dungarees
& fire gets out of control there's a door in the sky a half cloud is
strange to begin with the house is half window so what was in the
middle it was the same, repeat it: where the fuck is tom, i shall be
released, ed in the clouds & in the clouds too much he's a woman
it could happen to anyone he looks, his hair is wild in my small
shirt, ed from the side has made the grass his hair by sitting on the
edge of the deck & making me look past him to see him over his
own shoulder the deck stops to let the grass be hair & stripes on his
shoulders fuck the record I'm through with love I'll never fall again
I'm walking in the sky I've washed out the trees my notebook's up
there with me, ed the biological element: he has a hat on his head:
it's a plate of beans rice & snow peas delicately boiled & to top it
off above his hat is another hat a similar plate of a different color
the salt's in his eyes & for a lung a plate of salad & cheese & bread &
for a heart beets in a yellow plate, there's a fork in it & he holds the
fork of his heart to his tongue: a carbon copy reaches for his ear:
all this in front of the trees: he's taken his shirt off to show these
organs of memory: his mouth is open to receive what's on the fork
he looks down unaware of what he's revealed, a simple one a field

I would gladly give the earth to you & the, ed takes a nap in the sky
his arms up hands clasped behind his neck the stripes of the mattress
he's on encounter the trees & one of the trees has made it on the door
& one of the trees has made it in the door, finally. Everything I
have is yours no but ed & I are one except one of us is a little off
center my body takes over our necks seem the same we are a woman
with breasts: the shingles show how off we are, two identical pieces
of sky, we compare feet 3 of ed's 1 of mine, just picture a penthouse
way up in the sky: ed's hair is the trees & he's put up a strange sort
of blackboard in the forest, well, there's a door in the mountain
now but it's too dark to see, I had planned white flower on white
flower but forgot to stay to leave it alone as they say, they're play-
ing the piano about it again on the roof, I wonder what it would've
been like, she's going to start again: it's: dont worry about me I'll
get along I had written I'll get by on myself: go out again see four
giant daisies worshipping two setting suns in some kind of reflection
or ceremony by the farm over the head of the farm, an exact dupli-
cate of the farm below, the one we know, it gives us a light feeling
& with a prism of the sun to boot, sky of morning at night through
a hole through the trees pink & blue you might know I want on
without remembering we stopped at the store standing by your
window in pain I looked back in our car at ed, blue & yellow lights
in my eyes what was over me: home we expel them for social, forget
it: we built a fire & cooked on the stove, I burned an egg carton but
triply I liked the red wall near the stove & lit the stove too & made
the sink white & counter glow copper with pots on it cooking our
dinner flames all over the place all lit nothing on them & lights all
over the place interrupted windows blurred lights beginnings of
diamonds & in the bathtub some light shining down on the tub that
wasnt there: I should've stayed with people I guess to avoid all over
the place, straight & laced. This is the second part, you lay it over
the first like a correction: double exposures tea men to connoisseurs
for over 250 years, lift here for the sound for the image: I dream my
sandals fall completely apart & lie there, K dreams she's trying to
get uptown with men raping you you go up a stairs men put their
hands between your legs e & j are in the bedroom talking e & j em-
brace fm's an arab I make notes: supermarket old black magic toilet
flushing bells dog barking car pulling away car passing interior taxi
silver city bar dishes call mr. charles get the bus schedule, who?

119

deposit check who? last night i went downtown who? paul delany
WQRB will try to locate old black magic & ed's wandering around
at the red lion inn we've been to the supermarket & had lunch
there to the radio station with bells & a defective scotch cassette,
they light candles in the thrift shop I feel awful & someone says I'm
quite concerned & someone says the play might not be to everyone's
taste & berkshire broadcasting is worried & porter is worried due to
nudity & vile language I wonder what indians' feet look like, red
stains on my fingers from beets & green vegetables taking over the
refrigerator, red stains on inked moccasins & snakes no snakes we
see porter doing exercises here & birds, ed in softball shirts & jacques
in same today little bug on toughened red foot red from rain in
moccasins not into a different gear different way to write & it's an
old way anyhow after all & we talked to the grandson of famous
mr. charles the projector man & ed is cynical about clear eyes, toe-
nails red what do I have to do, what is being clear here birds & wil-
low trees many bugs, storms, should I shoot should I shoot at all?
one roll out of focus? supermarket: un-toothbrush 4 j&k, ok harris,
mature measuring spoons copper-colored measuring spoons coffee
choc full o nuts special blend instant stolen, bought white river rice
saff-o-life salad oil regina red wine vinegar planters p-nut butter
frenchs people crackers 4 dogs bananas eggs for muscles cole poultry
farm freihofers canadian oat bread 2 packs pall malls sweet life
cream style golden sweet corn grandma browns home baked beans
friends brown bread with raisins big johns beans n fixins stella doro
almond toasts durkees black pepper polaver pure blenheim apricot
preserves wisconsin longhorn cheddar cheese, six dollars fifty three
cents I hate door that you cant push open with your feet. One day
I hate myself in a row feel crumbly lost ridiculous worried about ed
& his turn in our get rid of his her mood with a bad one of your own
our work in a morass what to do next it's pilgrims progress time
hurry it up will grace come was she at the meeting last night when I
called adrian to talk to R & I never thought of it where's the other
A, Anais? Ed & I working together the old american flag filing of
separate duties makes some kind of excitment that they've trained
us for we're used to it & I dont have to tell myself anything cause I
start to write even a letter & it comes up I know it all already WBRK
A-OK MAORI Indians & how does you mind work? Sun out in
cloudy bright double exposure GP I hate the people downstairs &

everybody who reluctantly cuts themself off from you & everybody
who reluctantly anything some obsession with the truth they just
never come out with it just ok's & groans & some words they've
said a thousand times before I hate the thought of spending time
with them & then with R who can get imposed on she can get per-
formed on so easy by me & by them & lose identities in all in the
morass of school teachers unmarried & not married & answer my
questions I make the demand I demand it suck my cock, if any but
most of all volunteer information: ten years ago I wrote this poem
to the nirrengartens, the people downstairs, I said St. Anthony is
in his hole but will your green suck-off thumb yield it's sun suffered
unripe ovaries up on hokus pokus day or has your symphony gotten
still further out of hand with a still note an unspoken note without
no asshole, well my stone is hard & white & half transparent it's a
mountain & you can sometimes go without pajamas & grandfather
farts all night so when you let him play with your kid do you think
those heavy leftovers are lost on him & do you think he turns yellow
from just fear is what I said & I say volunteer information, their
possessive compulsive guilt about GP & his money & J says get what
belongs to you & their total helplessness when it comes to seeing
he's a person & GP sees us as half-people women without men &
families at best he's amused he must be confused about our ages &
the whole world we live in doesnt exist for him he's a monster
without tails & we're little toads I hate him but defend his only
states of consciousness which are few & the people downstairs see a
good deal for them & the helplessness so I ask you how do you show
faith in a good deal? that he will survive & recover that it's worth
it & it's a better deal for them they think if he dies & it is & they
have all these religious principles they're full of them & golf. & the
next time it rains up here I'm putting all our clothes out to dry & I
put my shoes out on the road 2 B run over indian shoes & a white
car passes by I'm sitting underneath the tree at the entrance to the
berkshire theater bob makes me sick I think I'll buy a bottle of brick
amontillado & two running girls scotch pass by we are drinking
scotch I am drinking scotch & what must j be thinking now & some
remnant of high school in the word creativity I heard its sound,
someone says creativity & someone says how do you see this &
today's a bad day for anything that will last in the notebook I feel
cut off need to see no one being a woman you can make a campaign

of it I dont wanna be forced or forced to be only with other women
for a while this is a junk image so volunteer information for the
splayed, you look for the self that isnt full of shit & quiet other
things bring out & how do they bring out bring out spring cold
harbor & then a full out spread eagle metaphor a junk image a new
wind rewinds it will it hit? under the tree did? metaphor meteor
where? porter a porter a good beer where were the men when we
needed them, were we brought up without them, you set up your
life so you can run it I cant get the money but sometimes do so why
the rest of the shit & will this ending change it & there must be a
way & someone comes along & says this is eddie's car but this is my
car so you now have a place: when you need me, call me & when I
get back I think I'll take a few days off & drink, hope nobody comes
up: my eyes, fire, the room doubles: god, I found Tom. He says
what'd you say that was & this is the third part, you lay it over the
first & second parts, it's extra & I say god that's a wrathful angry
god & that's j&k's window & their tree & he says that's great you
do that on purpose & I say these are all double exposures & it goes
on: on purpose?/a whole roll/really?/yeah/& he says that's quite a
day you had & I say quite a day/is that a double exposure/some
of them are triple I think & that's my idea of a house/of a what?/
of a house/jesus & I say beautiful what? & he says something very
clean looking about all the/yeah they really/what's that is that a
grocery store?/yeah it's really strange isnt it?/is that the day that
ah what's his name was up?/bill no somebody else had that same car
who worked at the theater a guy from west virginia/& a house in the
sky/mmm/that's great/camera bernadette?/no . . ./that's great . . ./
you were walking upside down? is that you in the sky? & I say
that's my notebook in the sky & he says ok & I say that's great &
he says hey you look so sad & I laugh & he laughs & I say my body
has taken over though & he says I know & I laugh & I say who do
you see first? Ed. Ed's head & your body just because ed, ed's
exposure is a little bit higher, well the first thing that catches your
eye sort of is that very light area on the left hand side of ed's eye/
that's two different areas of sky & I laugh, god/what's that?/god a
wrathful angry god & he says he doesnt look so wrathful he looks
like ed looks really strange & I say great hair though imagine if you
had hair like that/who god?/anybody & I say I dont remember this
day at all or these pictures I cant remember & it's fire the fire

crossing the stove & look at this & inside the prison grounds, convicts
& that there will be no administrative reprisals for the riot & took
command of four of the five cell blocks of the prison & wow, where?
& was a model of security, attica, new york & saws, drills, WNBC-TV

July 21
South to argentina from massachusetts down to ny to downtown to
uptown to back down to ridgewood to elmhurst back to E uptown &
north to massachusetts one day: this is too hard: I think I feel bad
but I never felt better like the day we drove from mass to new york
& back the same day how did we do it: we thought we felt, the night
they drove old dixie down & on, the house is dark it's strangely
quiet maybe I dont know how to work anymore: when you awake
you will remember everything: tyrone power in an instance of total
recall, nightmare alley, he gets screwed but goes back with the carnival
& finds his wife who'll take care of him the great stan had become a
wino, when you awake, she bet on one horse to win I bet on another
to show, ans: maybe that's how I survive? on hash? cigarettes should
be better than dawn mist on the meadow: it was a golf course the
best meadow in the world we picked up kathleen early & took her
car, left j ours she wanted to leave at night but we picked morning
about 7 o'clock & this was the day this was not the day ed got the
ticket for making a wrong turn in nyc they look away they took
away his license since for not coming to court & anyway the meadow
mist is frozen at first & then rises but this first meadow is the meadow
of the four thousand dollar an acre farm before we met k we stopped
many times for the mist different mists: eyes, two trees & at the
corner where we make the turn onto cobb rd. the cows were acting
like suns two of them were acting like suns the others looked right
but with the cows like suns we didnt miss the sun to our left it was
in a tree: maybe the reason for the cows was this, reasons: it must've
been about time & something about success & just after dawn k says
to me you couldnt get that one you couldnt take a picture of it &
i got it but better I made a tree longer & rested my thoughts heavily
on a light morning mist to make it clear but not before I could push
it: it's pleasure sun still in a tree: we're not bored mist is always in
the distance but mirages behind trees are tales blacken out outline
& makes less real within the music stopped I quit little thin branches

are clearer than the air tail light in red brake I looked at the tree with
the sun in it I looked across the road into the meadow gold course
then further away from that tree but still facing it I turned around
a different shadow lengthened out I made a different tree longer
almost like two twins I was close to the car it was too cold to leave
the door open this spot: should I have stayed there all day or was
this moment the only one when rays direct at everything but me &
so me, rays like stick marches but something must rest on them for
it all to appear & we did, you depend on things above the ground
your pleasure puts a pressure on them, you dont believe they're
there, you do, you're air: you're in an open space in Iran you just
got off a plane centuries ago, there's no one there. A mirage is a
challenge to anyone who looks at it & when you're in a hurry it's
better to go on, the picture, it better go in, the picture the picture
might get too hot & burn go up in flames before my eyes: you're
in an open space in Iran you just got off a plane centuries ago, there's
no one there, you concentrate you remember: someone who stays
on the plane will meet you tomorrow at the ruins. So you check
the map it's a street map: fine grey lines on a white sheet: Unh, Sheh,
Shuh, Shah, Smer, Smei, Bher, Steh, Unh . . . what are these open
empty spaces like door ways in the whited out light low tan build-
ings white out in the sun you are calm you remember: centuries ago
I would've been afraid I ran she ran he ran & he ran, its periodicity:
you concentrate & study the map the streets, even, the frequency
of fear. "I am reading another language by instinct I locate the
ruins in an open space to the north at Unh." A reversal of the action
of the verb not moving, moving & a removal or release from the
state expressed by the noun immobility, mobility: memory the
double negative. Love anger. I walk north slowly I pass Aidh, to
burn I burn Sheh & I write & Edh, to eat & I eat I pass Bher, to bear
& I suffer & I nurse moving I pass Smei, to wonder & I wonder at
my self in the mirror & I caress myself a mirage I pass Reudh, to be
red & Steh, to cover & I protect myself I pass Smer, to remember,
I locate the ruins by moving around their periphery with my eye
on the map, open space. I'm walking north to find a hotel to spend
the night close to the ruins. I see no one I see clearly. I can see one
street in the north & from its british-english multiplicity of syllables
I can guess that this is the street I'll find a hotel on & people, a
peripatetic street. I float I drift into a hotel & through every room

& in the sleeping rooms people are sleeping I am invisible I walk
over their beds, in the dining room I hover over tables, people are
eating, I listen to the murmur of their periphrastic speech: so many
even syllables they cannot see me. A reversal of the action of the
verb a removal or release from the state expressed by the noun the
name: tomorrow you will walk east from this street to the ruins at
Unh to meet someone & this is your talisman, take it with you. (The
secret action in time of a reversal in language in memory will renovate
will navigate will clear this space for you, already clear, going back-
wards, Iran the nurse the memory, in white with fine grey lines
drawn marking off the borders of the streets to indicate the new
space of the ruins, an opening.). A mirage is moving around around
anyone who looks at it, you're in a hurry moving you better go on,
the picture might get too hot it might burn go up in flames the film
goes up in flames before your eyes before my eyes: the picture has
been still with a bright bulb intense illumination behind it for many
hours for many days a still picture & now it burns: you see the fire
on the screen it burns & this is your talisman, take it with you into
the moving car over the windshield of the huge car the eye can see
nothing I thought I just saw a light go out in my peripheral vision,
finally. 3 cups of coffee steaming up the car 3 scraps of paper left
over from the scarlet letter, we stopped at the chief taghkanic diner
just before the entrance to the taconic we had told j&k to get gas
the night before but they didnt there were people in their car & we
had to yell over them bob & terence it was embarassing to yell get
gas like talking to grandfather but how can you elaborate on what
you're blunt toward, words of one syllable, meanings hard to hear &
hard of hearing: get gas, Sssh, um, I eat, I'm full, there's a dog. We
had sweetheart cups & a $10 fine for littering, no we're already on
the highway ed is waiting in the car I wonder at his image how tired
is he & you have to walk so far to get the coffee always moving up
& down toward the argentine pampas this time but not that early
in the morning but maybe & here's the proof the first gas station on
the taconic, we had made kathleen eggs at her house & the sun's up
now as we go down but it's on the same side usually when we go up
it's going down on the left on the right whatever it is: we get as far
as ossining for a while I put my moccasins on the front windshield
to dry the road widens would I have time to have a child? Hawthorne
circle is a big mud puddle it's a river, thief, we move: that was the

day of the argentine pampas because now at the circle we encounter
a flag man in straw hat with orange vest on to see him I guess his flag
is orange too & he is foreign in it in some way & I say to ed there's
the pampas all right & he agrees but is too tired to & thinks that
man could have braids or a pony tail: everything is under construc-
tion, arrows orange men down the west side highway two views of
twin towers & we're about to get off at 18th street I guess k's going
to sleep & on the road down seventh what a mess. There exists a
law office george a. mango attorney next to a shoe store closed for
a whole month on vacation june 7th to sept 7th that's 3 months
exist across the street from r's house but we were just passing by no
ed dropped me off here no I dropped him off & took the car, yes
this is the day we cleaned out ridgewood & I had the car: those
strange tops of houses in ridgewood that reflect myself: the house
I was looking out is me, it isnt there, here, it's invisible, it hovers:
those strange tops of houses that look like soldiers grown out of
ground they look crooked but are so straight & I hate them: across
the street from our old house & out the window nothing except
they've taken the broken glass off the top of the one-story garage
next door, they used to put it up there all around the edge an edge
of green glass so that people wouldnt go up I mean kids us kids
wouldnt go up after balls they would go up there balls that would
get lost, homers, hoping I guess in the meantime to keep us from
playing ball against the garage I dont know I cant remember why
it had no windows at all: the gate & down on it looks cheerful
(where's the chief & where are the drums that play in the morning
when everyone comes out for breakfast to share their dreams &
strike at the one who met them, unfair, no the violence is all in-
doors) not the house next door old people used to live there neat
pins now someone else there's still a tree & iron gate with lots of
room to play in, your space, garbage cans inside hooks on the gates
if you want to keep them open, your private space, paint the gates
lead orange & black over that paint the gates lead orange every time
the others do, red lead, can I come in? What a messed up day & I
was singing real loud summer fall & so on to get away from thinking
about what I was doing what it was that I was doing which was
throwing everything away in the house: our gate less cheerful but
friendly as if old & no not much I wish I had a whole band here to
play & drums in the morning opening up, like, open up the spaces

of the backyards for good & the houses across the street, mildred or muriel used to live there as a matter of fact she owned one of them & my uncle was interested in her & never seriously he was a bachelor in the single life of blessedness because he always said she was a woman of means & she worked as well & could support him & I guess he felt disarmed by the fancy cornices she owned well-owned the gargoyles like any kid there's some asshole kid in the backyard next door & a whole row of neatly hung wash identical pants of colors hang together, free the people one by one take down the pants, shirt, then one sheet then towels then larger shirts, the man of the house, piece now pick up the gun, this sucks flower patches enclosed with little ellipses of white stones like quarters seen from the proper perspectives I'm a black man down on a whole line row of wash lines most of them empty cause it wasnt wash day & a tv aerial cannibal sky: I used to always wonder why we couldnt make one long park out of the whole thing behind people's houses so we could run in it instead of just being able to squat peer & make mudpies, find corners you never knew about & ride horses fast down the lane almost completely surrounded & all it would mean is taking the fences down & agreeing not to cultivate rosebushes & lawns those jerks. We found a snapping turtle in the backyard once. Fuck this. The yard on the other side: Did he bite you? No. Just a big lawn with flowers & other stuff on the outside & one clump in the middle the same white-painted stones things glistening in the sun but who gives a shit I picked up ed at arnold's & paul got in the car impressed with me in my cadillac who had gone to the hospital too & we dropped paul off at a dirty movie I took his picture going in but you cant see him it's adultry, that's how they put it. We parked on some street in the east fifties & dropped off some film or picked it up the sky was clear I guess it was a beautiful day all day but fuck it & started uptown on our way back through the pampas to massachusetts in one day but first stop off at ed's parents house well they werent letting anybody on the highway because a fire in the penn central yards had made part of it collapse fall down so we went on & on up different up streets riverside drive upper broadway we stopped we had a coke we changed hot drivers the car didnt break down in the middle of it but alot of other people's did & it was a real pollution fantasy haze were sick & dizzy & I took a picture I thought would look like the end of the world end to end but

didnt there was nobody going the other way south just our way
just everyone going our way north & alot of people thought alot of
people were crazy & I looked in the rear view mirror & saw a down-
hill hill of cars just cars & manic sunset so I told ed take a picture
of that behind you hurry so he did down the hill but the pink & pur-
ple insanity of it couldnt register on film it was the sun's fault &
there's some old crushed cigarette packs on the dashboard & reflected
in the windshield of the car reflecting some giant riverdale apartment
building & a view down 231st street with the setting sun much
brighter than I remembered it stopped for a light & then we had some
dinner & stayed a long time in riverdale left way after dark for the
trip up speeding repeating ourselves each of us could only drive about
half hour at a time stopped at j's in the country then when & when
then finally went home I guess I wrote this I read to you: tungsten
wednesday 18 minutes to nine on our way to ny had to switch to
am morning mist & shaft light comes through in the pictures at 50
mph we're going 55 we're going 60 careful due to cops who rob
skiers of their dope & what if my notebook were confiscated with
all the fingerprints on it the prints on it now it's 14 before already
it's that time it's mist cold freezing drive you forget to k's with the
top down in the dawn calm cows nearer to city my god eggs at k's
set alarm for F and j separately, ed in j's sunglasses again cool driving
blue flowers by side of road bill macy is 48 the dead animals of the
night before, bryant pond road that way state police that way we
go neither way rolling rolling rolling thru the usa california? texaco
& you can trust your car to the man who was a star K says I looked
pretty last night & I say I'll have to see later & my pretty red feet are
on the dashboard with their separate shoes gas station blue towel
tissues coffee double stamp day was there water there a body of it
next to the picture of the highway taken just before hawthorne ny
hawthorne circle & south to argentina from massachusetts down to
ny to downtown to uptown to back down to ridgewood to elmhurst
back to ed uptown north to massachusetts, one day: south to argen-
tina from mass down to ny to downtown 2 uptown to back down
to r-wood to e-hurst back to e uptown north to mass 1 day: hot
car city strange stage remember slide projector lens tissue sunglasses
spaced out light no registration for this car, again the notebook is
confiscated I'm pulled up in front of he's pulled up double exposures
by mistake a ticket confiscated as evidence evidence against me see

more: port authority 100 feet above us gives them the authority to
go round & round in circles in games buses round around, one is
ektachrome one is kodachrome a $20 a puerto rican guy sitting
hands folded by building dante's inferno books in the back of the
car & GP temperature 101°, buses going round in circles 101 feet
in the air see paul paul goes to the avon the avon on the hudson
theater to see some kind of trip this car & that guy's jeep adultry
sultry saw it twice the number on the house ridgewood to e-hurst
another week in the hospital mrs. sampson K & L for the test roll
& paul says we both look fine & we're wiped out & everytime you
get sick you look fine five dollars worth of gas in the car we set up
the nurse's room in the house K chews styrofoam a piece on the
floor of the drivers' seat she's here nyc today we're back country
today paul will cut the negative people who know me what a re-
lief not like queens full of limping men. So you run to not be afraid
of when your heart beats fast: laudanum paradise hashish azure
jasmine scarlet lemon & lime: bakshish bashaw bazaar bulbul
caravansary carboy dervish divan durbar firman giaour houri
Lascar mogul mohur nargileh nylghau Parsee pasha pashaw bashaw
peri roc sash sepoy serai shah shawl sirdar: orange from French
from Italian from Turkish from Persian, burns brightly brightly burns,
shah shah

July 22
To burn to be sharp to drive to nourish to choke to breathe, last
week in 1850, to bind to increase to bend to cover to vault over to
shine to seize to take hold of, last week in 1850, to cut to hide to
shut to lean, last week in 1850, to hold to run to turn round to
cultivate to cook to give to show to tame to lead to eat to live to
exist to put to place to speak, last week in 1850, to bear to trust to
knead to mould to support to burn to support to protect to break
to enjoy to bend to pour to produce to join to sleep, last week in
1850, to collect to wash to leave to shine to remain to remember
to wonder at to think to measure to grind to melt to project to rub
to bite to die to beget to destroy to know to get to know to appor-
tion to see to smell to fasten to feed to spread out to fare to fly to
fill to ask to seize to purify to stink to rule, last week in 1850, to be
red to tear to seize to cut to sit to follow to exist to sound to stand

to strew, to touch to cover to stretch to bore to cut out to endure to
be dry to thrust to swell to beat to be wet to go to carry to give to
go to come to become to clothe to carry to see to wake to live to
wind to turn to roll to speak to cry out, last week in 1850 the first
thing I see is a tree I saw when I was parked at the radio station on
the road between barrington & stockbridge still looking for old black
magic & then ed had gone somewhere or maybe he was with me I
went up route 7 to stockbridge to arrive in time to pick up grace
coming on the bus I am speaking to monument mountain what
was that it was the result of a director's viewfinder in two dimen-
sions instead of three: images of the field of view of the microscope
will annoy the observer for hours after an unusually long sitting at
the instrument. A thread tied around the finger, an unusual con-
striction in the clothing, will feel as if they're still there long after
they've been removed. I had been to zayre's that morning bought
stolen sunglasses pick up grace see lenny who is looking for
another grace & bought pens went home & ate an omelette G lying
in the hammock, M was there by then ed took his shirt off: we had
coffee & canadian oat bread also ed & the light behind him had I
bought the good coffee one of those days in the city yet, an un-
usually long sitting at the instrument: ed gets in the car to go some-
where in jack donohue's baseball camp shirt his hair was wet he
made a face drove off in stages we stayed home the trees grow on
the stairway now: I went outside to watch ed leave I went back
inside sat on the stairs no lay on the floor I went back outside &
stood on the cut down tree into logs I went back in again & upstairs
I went out on the upstairs balcony perhaps to show grace, looked
inside the door to the room was part way open the light was on the
sun was beginning to set. Like eating a lobster you dip it in butter
eat one part of the meal at a time one meal a day as three meals a
river of butter I showed grace the automatically revolving tv antenna
the lights reflecting to infinity on both sides of the room in eight
diamond windows & more did M come home: I went down in the
basement to work maybe put the stuff there: the basement ceiling
the light there spiderwebs & the spiders who run them grace went
up on the balcony picked a place for herself, we had bats in the house
all this month I guess grace took a bath her back was were her toe-
nails painted: no the water was yellow the light was yellow the light
on the water the water yellow we fixed spaghetti the smoke of

grace's cigarette went up into the exhaust on the stove she had a
green blouse on, maureen o'hara we watched tv someone says I
always feel like maureen o'hara when I wear green we watch some
mystery about a vase a piece of porcelain janet leigh her hands
clasped resting demure on the table in evening dress I suppose she's
watching jack webb play the trumpet & further on in space some in-
teresting shots of morning & through the trees in a movie favoring
the french royalists underground you were supposed to be on their
side with tony curtis or tyrone power & tony curtis dies & jacques
dies too in favor of someone weaker dying it's easier to dream
someone who could go on forever dies to die in place of a very old
man & that house now seems boring grace's bed in place she had
brought her new tape recorder with her & played for me some
haitian i think dances cause to begin with it's thursday & the men
are out at the moviola pictures from the evening before expose
themselves in the morning you forced yourself to sleep I forced my-
self to sleep & forget dreams whatever they were like jacques dies,
I made GP he's night & fog a map in my sleep for ed I sleep in the
yellow room with st. george sleeping in the other & someone says
you do have to come & I say I quit to be with to be alone to take
trips trips like pieces of information what you see is what you get
the bastian blessing co. chicago illinois nejaimes soda foundation
fountain all dry soda fountains patent pending parmesan cheddar
eds eggs canned milk bread & corn: recovering today from being
under long something somewhere where part of the west side high-
way fell down, perry mason is on tv powder is on the floor, incredible
cars on all the uptown streets fires in the penn central railroad yards
july 22 today thursday only eight more days it's nine & I've moved
to the cellar in squeaking rocking stuffed chair & yesterday after we
made it uptown stopped to see ed's summer parents, code, they'll
come up the 13th grace is going to new mexico the 10th we'd like
to go to california in september can visit halifax in september or
october & we did & I fainted e's father big E suggests arcadia na-
tional park in nova scotia for camping tom seems still to be living
there dont know we see big e's new car in the garage across the
street he sees our 1964 cadillac drive north insane I'm in the cellar
when I'm not driving I'm thinking: some memories qualify where
the present endures not for a minute or an hour or a day but for
weeks & months & years: GP & the other old men looking like

movies of a concentration camp & gp what can we do for him & the
old picture of my grandmother today, catalogue them: I know this
state of mind now after it has already dropped once from conscious-
ness, this chair chased some spiders away north dark top down
talked alot about the brights to stay awake got to j's him in some
other world our struggle to get up there I went outside cause to
caught my fingers in the front door then in the car door cried trans-
ferred everything from one car to the other crying had dropped
cigarettes in my lap on the way up went upstairs to the yellow room
to sleep & slept in the morning forced sleep & on & one & grace
came on the 4:05 bus in front of nejaimes hot sun orange soda
mailers to kodak & zayre's for a frying pan & sunglasses stopped at
berkshire broadcasting no black magic. Tom's going to some kind
of wedding this weekend & paul & B will be here no beds & E one
two three four & e's out the door at the shaggy dog recording sound
studio & leaving on the next plane 7 am for ny again & the house
is here grace is in the loft a red brace of a sister & she's making tea
she fixes tea & all the stuff from r-wood is down in the cellar &
itches & burnt bitten & switch over to #2 & J liked the films but
he died no he didnt die & H is encouraged not to come to the play
& someone says does she want her money back for nudity vile lan-
guage & omelettes creamed corn & brown bread & one two three
four tomorrows friday the queen is here the ice is here & everything's
fixed & ready & I quit quit & the soldiers quit & times have changed
& the actors quit & the movie camera's quit & silence is quit & grace
is watching me & the sailors quit & the engine quit & the milk quit
& I'm imitating myself & money quit & myself quit & color has
quit & music quit & the end quit & the door it quit & for a third of
a second I look at exposure charts for color film & then shroud my-
self in complete darkness shroud the eyes & it was as if I saw the
scene in a strange light through a dark screen & I can read off details
in it which were unnoticed while my eyes were open: this is the
primary positive after-image: according to Helmholtz one third of a
second is the most favorable length of exposure to the light for pro-
ducing it, what, a book two potatoes parmesan cheddar eggs canned
milk bread & corn & tea a map of july from the 22nd to the 31st
credit card #122-2222-030A mr. charles #212-2655279 kershem-
heimer's #6349578 ballou's #1-4584248 the nurses #1778859 &
5626255: we moved into the barn on july 8 & on 22 start living

132

there cause I quit after two weeks nobody notices but I quit, need
tire for car: jack webb & anais nin in a movie about firestone he
says no thanks & in the bath I'm reading letters from 1416 york
avenue to florida massachusetts ed's in these & advertising & left-
overs of st. saviors especially to florida cynicism & everying's all
right seems summer a dull day I'm too amazed from & by the
time ed got to lenox I seemed more real yesterday to see day today
as form a triangle I couldnt take pictures & pete kelly says act sober
& sing & someone says she's gonna sing & you're gonna listen in
pete kelly's blues where the big bottom swerve of the J. of her
name forms an interlocking circle round Leigh & the two circles
of the J contain a shared space so that if one were A & the other
B would the shared space be labelled would it be called AB, B
the lightest letter & tony curtiz comes up again in the purple mask
where they want your sympathy for the heroic french royalists,
cut off their heads, their heads were cut off & there is no black
magic so who wants to be my brother, later, so you can increase
the speed of this film to any of a variety of film speeds & to process
the film to these speeds write Kodak in Rochester for pamphlet
#1-E-2: photographing the unusual with high speed films & she's
gonna sing & you're gonna listen: there is no black magic & some-
body says that anybody saying we lack guts doesnt know what he's
talking about, no way it's true & who says we dont have guts or
some guys have given up & arent hustling cause I'd like to know
cause there is no black magic in the bright bright sun in the hazy
sun cause there is no black magic in the cloudy bright air (no sha-
dows) cause there is no black magic in the heavy overcast cause
there is no black magic in the open shade cause there is no black
magic in a large area of sky cause there is no black magic in brilliant
scenes cause there is no black magic in the skyline ten minutes after
sunset cause there is no black magic in interiors with bright fluores-
cent light cause there is no black magic in spotlighted acts (carbon
arc) cause there is no black magic in downtown street scenes at night
cause there is no black magic in brightly lighted niteclubs in theaters
at night in las vegas or times square in store window displays at night
cause there is no black magic in neon & lighted signs at night cause
there is no black magic in floodlighted buildings in fountains in
monuments cause there is no black magic in christmas lighting in
trees indoor & outdoor cause there is no black magic in fairs in

amusement parks at night cause there is no black magic in night
football in baseball in racetracks cause there is no black magic in
the shade or from airplanes cause there is no black magic in home
interiors at night in areas with bright light in areas with average
light in candlelighted close-ups cause there is no black magic in a
distant view of city skyline at night cause there is no black magic
in fireworks in displays on the ground in night football in basketball
in hockey in bowling in boxing in wrestling cause there is no black
magic in stage shows with average lighting with bright lighting in
circuses in floodlighted acts in ice shows the same cause there is no
black magic in school on stages in auditoriums cause there is no
black magic in an indoor swimming pool with tungsten lights above
the water cause there is no black magic in churches tungsten lights,
so who wants to be my brother, later, & do all those things to me

July 23
And do all those things to me that begin in the etymological dictionary
with the Indo-germanic roots so you might as well remember you
might as well do it you would remember every day of your life, it
must have endured for a certain length of time, if you had something
to remind you of it, take pictures for a week, say, then put them away
dont even show them around for a year & see what you remember & a
week's diary too: call kathleen & ed at noon stay at paul's cause H
might not be home, it's friday, villa lobos gas record teletype ma-
chine: this is the specious present in my memory presents my memory
as it might be styled as the knowledge of an event or fact or state of
mind which in the meantime I have not been thinking of but with the
additional consciousness that I've sure thought of it before I've ex-
perienced it before, all of it: 5:15 am woke up thought it was late
woke everybody up & then down told them to go back to sleep
thought it was 6:15 am coffee, sunrise from the meadow a heavy
wet mist all over now it's haze a white grey day greens out a green-
out as usual here except in yellow sun glasses where suddenly it's
bright rays & clouds in rays, some color, golden sun through haze
& the airport by one minute to seven the plane the haze white sun:
no memory is involved in the mere fact of recurrence there's a de-
lay: & that's a funny picture to be first was I up at dawn: yes to
get ed to the airport I woke up an hour too early & went out to the

field there's a delay to watch dawn come up, cant see much from
our house up at five struggle to get everybody out of the house on
time a beaut. dawn comp. w. mist on the field something in total
darkness the airport I think we got there we get there at 1 minute
to 7. This is not just a date in the past this is dated in my past that
begins in the etymological dictionary & this is myself at dawn we're
still home I have a jacket on & a red & white striped tv shirt the shirt
a ten-year-old boy gave me, not one of the magician's children, boys
give me shirts I make them do it: I look full the mist rises I should
overexpose them more but ed makes it do we remember the way
to the airport except I miss the turn at first & should've taken rte.
183 & almost ran out of gas getting there & someone says put some
gas in the gas can & call kathy & since I got this gas can for the night
dirt road the guy at the station says you gonna run a tractor & ed
has a bag & his script & his ticket executive airlines cutive lines #201E
so grace yells & ed turns around there's still a heavy fog no smoking
the man wheels the luggage cart away the propellers begin to spin
it's a de havilland twin otter he taxies away you cant see a thing in
this fog & I ask the man if it's safe. We go to see the owl & the owl
he was crazy yelling & screaming still early morning there was nobody
round the audubon society grounds, & taft farms some melons some
plants from san francisco california a cat by a crate of those melons
I was on the right track: the glass of the windshield on one of the
views & G in my sweater my shades in the cemetery half a poem. The
valley close up & far away means something to me but not if you saw
it in a newspaper, you know why cause the sky's a pale purple & the
green's got blue in it & you people who wanna see green, take a pic-
ture & come clean, I was on the right track over the glass of the
windshield, then grace makes half a poem. "Do your christ pose,"
she leaves her hands open. Old cemetery we looked for a place to
swim I showed grace the insane gazebo with wooden horse & car-
riage pecan blossoms on the pecan trees sticky get caught in a
trap get caught in spider web on the door of the barn sticky we
pick one a red pecan fluorescent a fucking truck: erving motor trans
from erving mass #34 why did we stop for it to look at it the door's
open there's purple more purple in the sky of this film is kodachrome
it loves red & blue there's purple in the sky in the pond or alford
brook that looked too muddy to swim in I tell grace all the Indo-
germanic roots of the dictionary's story at an overgrown picnic

table we float & all float with barrels white flowers I think they were
blue so grace reminds me of someone & it aint her fault I cut her
short white flowers were blue the projector lamp dims with the
refrigerator in gear & down that stream lily ponds picture the alford
brook club in the serenity of the afternoon & the alford afternoon
brook looking like georgia & listen why're they clapping cause he
finally sang that song well listen: she's gonna sing & you're gonna
listen & georgia all perfect reflections we located relations the
abandoned silver birch camp but on our way or on our way back
stopped at a gravel pit a one-man operation he needed two women
he must've seen no one all day just sand chain-gang-style with only
tire tracks & mounds of kinds of gravel a machine that poured it
out with water, many scoops & mud puddles terraced areas a moving
scoop stirs up dust, if any: grace is under exposed in her green shirt
more dust he gives us the peace sign we follow a hay truck home we
pass it by the time we get to home the truck caught up with us it
passes us by by the house a man driving a tractor pulling two loads
of hay his son mounted on the side headband over long long hair
falls down the tv's on but nothing's on it the tv equipment's on, you
know video, we made a tape of the exercise of a hay truck is like
a tv, just tilt it. The beginning of a word, Br & 7 hours go by what
was I going to write & I guess brought, what I brought was brought
by me & the context for that was this that a while ago: "& told
me to write this poem: to take a round of / to take a ride of / you
take a round of / you take a ride of / and I brought (what I
brought was brought by me) / shortly will for will / but, fast moons
/ he can gather them from the air." Who told me it was design &
then I began to leave which I'll explain later, like my brother, I had
just quit I was on vacation on a dark still night a thousand tiny gnats
at the window & was that a bee trying to get in trying to write &
felt awful 4 3 days in the midst of grace cooking dinner potatoes
on coals & M is reading he is finishing a separate reality & I think
this, that we all know so much is understood that we're here in the
time that it is & we talked about subway attacks on women &
mafioso & an italian cab driver tells me if you take drugs took drugs
in the thirties if your best friend turned you on well from then on
you were taboo, condemned ignored maybe even contracted for,
you were excluded rejected repudiated exiled secluded locked out
ostracized prohibited separated segregated eliminated expelled, you

were barred left out shut out blackballed laid aside put aside set
apart segregated stricken off struck out neglected, you were
banished. & M is still reading we speak in front of him he is re-
moved. For me there's the airport the owl the red lion inn nejaimes
abdallas for mushrooms & 2 kinds of cheese & roads look 4 a place
2 swim: explore papers, maps, here see M he leaves 4 rehearsal yoga
tape tired jacques the phone drink & I drink familia cookies here
pick up bidu sayao the studio nejaimes 4 vanilla milk shake cheese-
burger home roads the silver birch camp the gravel pit here sleep
sweat the berkshire eagle the tornado in west stockbridge flattens
the truck stop on the state line bear sightings before that the dump
the theater dump john perreault in the berkshire eagle did I dream
cold sweat turned light on & M comes home so there's peas wine &
downstairs there's talk peas wine 49THST hookers omelettes corn
potatoes in the oven wooden train guineas muscatel M singing in
the shower E back tom. that's short 4 tomorrow this kind of
writing makes it impossible to think straight G washed her hair
Anne marie Diurio Benedict Pond Beartown State Forest Windsor
State Forest October Mountain accidents in the eagle have to get
up do something I re-record the teletype machine we listen to the
supermarket G says there's no musak in supermarkets, time is
spent in massachusetts. Pussy comes in it's after midnight where
are the bats & where, are, the bats & M like John corry so does he
need more privacy & this is prison & like jeremy's brother jonathan,
flowers in the Folger's coffee can, somebody's murdered womens
liberation regular grind mountain grown gnats like silver fish wierd
cats yoga tape great great six of the actors are scorpios including
M K & B, that's bobby so listen bobby: the wooden train a 1903
train still runs where I grew up cause the steel train's too heavy
for the el except at rush hour

July 24
Time is running out, so, you know everything, the whole of it.
Which is why I deny autobiography or that the life of a man matters
more or less & someone says we are all one man & later I'll say I
count the failure of these jews as proof of their election & later I'll
say they are divine because they all die screaming like the first uni-
versal jew the gentiles will tell you had some special deal & later I'll

tell who wants to be my brother, my brother's black & I'm leaving
& that'll go on for a while & last night I fell asleep to a howard duff
movie, he is a money-hungry reporter while M is singing downstairs
on another lazy day duff wanted cash I sleep with the light on
chandelier on & grace comes in this morning so we were both bred
& both forcing sleep & when I remember my dreams I seem to say
to myself I have dreamt this same dream for a week & there's no use
in remembering it cause it's always the same it repeats itself it's how
to, maybe, make a play, but I am not dreaming the same dream all
this time or am I I I dont know, I know this one thing: my picture
was "guileless" & that is my dream, old friends. M was born in el
paso, texas, muffled talking out in the field & banging & walking
downstairs M drives off on his unlicensed vehicle motorcycle I light
my cigarette but with one of the matches that strikes, burns black &
then suddenly & by this time you've put it down, it bursts into
flame, I will illustrate this for you I will draw you a picture a film.
I've already brushed my teeth & put cold water on my face brush
hair yoga looks for the kids, it's 11:12 in the morning & birds sing
shirr carr weekend car M scared J will do the newscaster blue pillow
yellow one white one with green border pink comforter gold & red
spread white sheet & golden sun glasses brush pliers postcards from
bermuda strike anywheres I'm smoking a cigarette The Traitor's
Purse Account Unsettled still have read no books alarm The Year
of the Whale tv & tv equipment I'm leaving I'm off I'm going away,
red & black chair the blue pen top the heat grate ashtray film can
antenna box a door slams, screwdrivers & needle-nose pliers a match-
book top narcotics paraphernalia, moccasins two coffee cups the
camera newspapers: Thomas, Duane, bottle of gold coast california
wine a check envelope roach another white pillow with a great de-
sire to read, two blue work shirts hanging a black sash & a chandelier,
last night M tells us this story: he leaves home el paso, texas, comes
back after being in europe, travels all over, his mother's italian he
tells her I'm coming back so have a good meal ready, she does. He
realizes he hates her food now, asparagus pasta it's all fixed fried &
greasy, but his father's arabic & that food says M syrian food is still
good: but I say the food of the mother is better than the food of the
fatter father. Now that is all of that story. There's another motor-
cycle sounding at the furmans, this privacy their privacy Weekend
Weekend out on the balcony, shots, see what it's like out it's hot

it's been hot for a week for two weeks I'm leaving feel my con-
sciousness changed changing from the play from my life disrupted
or changing anyway and so yesterday I'm unable to talk cannot
speak & today there are images hidden in my shirt making phrases
like the ones I write down, no one understands them, phrases like
"the whole of it" that's all I can say & at the end of the tape grace
& I looked like two strawberries trees rustling in the background
noses, breasts, martians we make a wierd science fiction movie
where people shot at angles are still & are still for a long enough
time to alter your perspective & consciousness and so you begin to
believe they are in the proper perspective as not-people, the movie
can be all talk: suddenly remembered dreaming flying saying "you
get me started then I can hover" in front of a group of people may-
be J & also the book is out it's flying around loose its energy is
loose I'm going away then thunder & lightning a dream cant be too
corny I'm in the shower downstairs then flowers leaves fears of bees
& an orange & black butterfly I have no close-up lens, these flies,
M's orange nail brush another hazy day another cup of coffee &
another cup of tea another trip to great barrington to barrington
the car has reeds stuck beneath it so leave your rugs out upside
down on the morning dew or snow then dry them & bring them in
thought there is no dew or snow in the city though & a bee here
spins a web around me a clattering leaf on the road a car with 2
ladies, he cant find the flowers the weeds, today I am falling apart
in my shoes white pants I have hardly anything on where is end
where is everyone & the motorcycle starts up again it's a japanese
snowmobile & someone has nothing to do: there's cold milk there's
a fat blonde woman who worked here two years ago, rexall's in
great barrington I eat a million cheeseburgers I eat seven thinking
about the woman who serves up the food in the drugstore in town
thinking what do they do when they get up in the morning could
there be a regimen? I drink cold milk it says peach ice cream &
someone says i was so tired i thought i was going to lay down & i'm
leaving i'm departing i'm taking my departure i'm going i'm going
away i'm going off i'm getting away i'm going my way i'm getting
along i'm going on i'm shoving off i'm trotting along i'm staggering
along i'm moseying along i'm buzzing off i'm moving off i'm march-
ing away i'm pulling out i'm leaving home i'm going from home i'm
exiting i'm breaking away i'm o i'm setting forth i'm retiring i'm

going down to the sea i'm removing i'm ceasing to be i'm disappear-
ing i'm vanishing from sight i'm doing the vanishing act i'm flying
i'm going i'll be gone i'm passing away i'm passing out of sight i'm
passing out of the picture she's passing out of the picture i'm going
beyond the tree i'm retiring from sight i'm becoming lost to sight
i'm drowning i'm losing sight of myself i'm perishing i'm dying i'm
dying out i'm fading i'm doing a fade-out i'm sinking away i'm dis-
solving i'm melting i'm melting away i'm evaporating i'm evanescing
i'm vanishing into thin air i'm going up in smoke i'm dispersing i'm
dissipating i'm floating i'm ceasing to be i'm leaving no trace i'm
leaving many branches behind i'm leaving not a branch behind & some-
one says i was so tired i thought i was going to lay down & die &
leaving m & j & e & I begin to play feudal & I get worse & worse
headache & it goes to K comes home pleased at everything like P,
who's P? & bob is in rehearsal's oratory with J calm rain beings again
it's the storm that destroyed syracuse the tornado that flattened the
truck stop at state line new york massachusetts, sleep says this: going
to feeling forget-worst, like, the pay-backables. The whole of it you
knew everything. I put the colored leaves on the apple tree in the
backyard of the shower more daisies & weeds clap & someone says
you're not supposed to have anything to eat or drink & I finally
found out what eli siegel was advertising all those years in the village
voice, there's red on the bottom green on top & another hay truck
or some piece of farm equipment on its way it's the same guy, that
dead stump of a tree was making the roof of the garage collapse just
by being next to it on such a dark day a day where a thin black band
crosses the sky it's the same storm, it's easier to be a woman than a
dwarf but a woman's life is dull & so I went to rexall's for a cheese-
burger. Give. Her memory's a double negative. They had nebbishes
up near the ceiling that same guy who wrote the play the scene
from the car department barrington always looks like california &
it's san diego to be exact to me. No defense. The cards light up con-
tinental chocolates angle parking a fan for sale two fans where is
mallarme: roses hoarse to live & all the vain in interim print with
calyx blank to prompt breath in rime to give, but that the stroke
in battle saves profound, the stuff of it, shock in awe, frigid in melt-
ing, cold in thaw, in laugh in flower in waves & casting the sky by
piecing detail here so alike in fantail You are better than a phial:
nothing closed in emery scent to lose or defile, something come

from emery, eventail. Some long furry red tail hangs down from some other department of the store, everything changes. I bought a bright orange scarf 49¢ & something changes darkened up for the outside light & now it looks like massachusetts again, clear autumn, a giraffe: the monterey police picnic-dance saturday july 31 1971 a buffet & music by ambrosia vacation values & nebbishes are now called according to the sign in the window sillisculpts, the cards light up stuffed animals cross the street at the hardware store lawnmowers to remind me of two years ago an ad for summer of '42 at the mahaiwe & something changes a boy & a girl walk by leading with different feet she has a watch on he has a leather bracelet with different feet sneakers sandals & shorts, a tree an awning glass is worth it is complicated an awning that was above the glass & a woman going into the hardware store stands next to a pail and a red wheelbarrow, brand new, they cheer & she looks black on top, her face & arms, but her legs are pure white & from the waist down she looks like a man but its clear she has breasts though her back's to me what the fuck's the moon. There's a change in the whole of it, everybody's beauty. What the fuck were we doing at the red lion inn swimming pool. Paul & barbara arrive there's a piece of toast on a book there's a change: were they there when we got back & they bring ed with them paul had helped ed cut the negative now everyone's eating hermits not toast, barbara in dark blue, they went to norway they're in norway now & grace purses her lips & leans down she's wearing kathy dillon's shirt & getting out of the car I pulled up next to paul's car barbara's car excited they were back, ed, I broke the side view mirror copper color shows through where the glass fell off I cracked it with my hip I ran right into it & is this the same day: we go to rehearsals leave everyone at the house & that's right they were pissed off later. Ed sat in a chair & I looked at the sky, some green plastic leaves above a red lantern sink I went back inside ed was drinking coffee still in the chair: his hand holding up his chin one finger in his mouth at his mouth the other holding a cup of coffee he looked over at me I think he was bored just then he drank more coffee he drinks more coffee the light of the room on ed yellows his face golden & his hands together on his lap a brown shirt on behind the sky & trees everyone else is stirring around having a discussion, kate is standing up leaning over & later M E & J play feudal, K had invited m over for some grass I think & J went to terence's house

for a while to work so when he got back they started playing & I
went to sleep, M was traveling with us his m-cycle broken down no
gas no I played for a while too two teams of us on the blue board
the wasps vs. the jews & arabs & my head aches for days: when we
got home a mattress for us was on the floor P&B slept on springs &
early in the morning then ed in the black fur hat that showed up on
the doorstep like animals appear except & ed took his shirt off paul
looking amazing in a black t-shirt leica in one hand shines a flash-
light with the other into my eyes & M is out on deck studying his
script in a snakeskin shirt & sandals & he turns around, a hood, some-
one is reading a book in the hammock I miss them it's grace reading
carlos castaneda the book makes a shadow on her face prolonging
memory & it was one of those days the country provokes many
people no one gets together no one speaks alone no one gets to
speak no privacy: paul & barbara keep saying they are leaving
finally they do right after I watch them leaning & sitting against
barbara's car: paul sits on the car, his watch on. Barbara leans back
against his lap. He puts his hands on her chest she smiles puts her
hands over his, they stay in that position. Barbara leans back fur-
ther her head against paul's chest, she reaches her arms up to paul's
shoulders still balancing against his lap he puts his hands under her
shortsleeved shirt through the arm holes she looks up. Barbara gets
up starts to sit on the car she rests one hand on paul's knee she has
one foot on the ground she sits on the car one knee bent with the
foot up on the car one leg just hanging paul puts his arms around
her waist her back against his chest she holds his two hands clasped
at her waist with one of hers. Paul looks at me Barbara looks away.
So you know everything, everybody's beauty, the whole of it &
something changes: GP, a screen, dies & sleep says this: I would
never set this up again. Paul looks at me Barbara looks away

July 25
I would never do this again, said in the house as a kind of warning.
& as I write all this stuff down I know it comes out of nowhere goes
nowhere & remains, nothing leaves. It's almost a truth. I set myself
up. July 25th though it's already begun begins again with ed without
a shirt sitting in the car & flowers arranged in a large folger's coffee
can on a yellow pillow outside that's decadence in daylight in decay

that's an idea that follows itself meaning nothing meaning nothing
leaves & paul and barbara must've left by now taking grace with them
but tight-assed they wouldnt drop her in manhattan she had to take
the train. Also, there are things you study, usually accepted as sciences,
which specifically deal with man & not with the external world which
is contrasted with him, like psychology & anthropology for example;
how are they consistent with the view that science is characteristically
non-human? Ed's working I think he was I begin to think about reflec-
tions: car window the chrome both sides two car doors windows you
can see through we're working on the car everything's open I open my
orange which is almost red scarf & tuck it under one of the windshield
wipers I put potatoes a tomato two ferns & a coke on the car gasoline
the air hole taped closed but the can leaks anyway massachusetts san
francisco sky over anyway I went down the road coke in the grass 8
oz. the beginning of a puddle a series around it telephone poles a series
no sun I looked in the puddle telephone pole no sun, Ed went upstairs
I followed him he took his clothes off we put the bed back together I
took my clothes off we took a bath we went to the theater to the barn:
they cut these trees down for eating into the barn building there's one
long low branch leaning I went to the lenox arts center to see ira & john's
performance with balloons, beverly was there taking pictures so I
asked her for an exposure she gave me a good one ira & noun blew up
balloons they mounted up caught the light, I went back to their
room there was a terrible yellow lamp on the table & we had a few
swallows out of a bottle of something & went to the red lion inn
I took ira in my car john made remarks about fucking then mostly
about emily dickinson & joan didion & got very drunk. Back at
kathleen's I was waiting to meet ed there while he & J were working
she was practicing her cello & this may have been the night that
paul the cellist came by & E&J were very late at the sound studio I
got very stoned K holds out her bow the cello case stands up by it-
self, made for corners I forget the rest & later dawning ed gets into
the car with his script & a station wagon dawns on us, no, but it's
clean cars parked & car windows on them in stockbridge clean town
while a guy goes into the berkshire bank & trust co. the one that was
robbed & he looks down the street & ed walks out of the bank onto
the astroturf you spit on flounced by white roman pillars & the sky
falls then over an airstream jet trailer that day this day from ohio or
somewhere white somewhere else white as ed pushed me into it &

a guy in a hat unloading he's about to unload a schaeffer beer truck
it looks blue all around the boston globe is there apollo 15 is ready
to go for 12-day moon trip the herald the traveller the telegraph
something is happening in brooklyn a man dreams at night & works
during the day he swears susquehanna at liberty bell sorority cursed
the victor frank robinson's on the cover of sporting news it must be
monday now balloons or balls in a box come together in front of
abdallah's but that was yesterday when: with the help of harry new-
ton, huey mother face newton, baby face newton, we part: he gets
in the cave with the others, breasts are the solution. Blue(y) newton
that was dream this was: last night this book gets rained on, rain
heavy rain all night through to day bright day I look at pictures of
July 2 shots of construction projects now sitting in bathtub after
spending the morning with no attention, just car & sound, sound &
car, ready 4 6 o'clock at the shaggy dog sound studios with 16
separate tracks on 2-inch tape while paul barbara & grace reluctantly
leave b&p to rockville center, grace to get home from there by the
long island railroad M studying & reading all day in leopard like under-
shirt, snakelike I mean scorpio. No time to read feel raped of country
information. Tom M & grace have read a separate reality before me
now grace takes it back to the city. GP no better as E heard from
R maybe worse. E brings me a can of magnolia condensed milk from
the city, no, he left it at R's, today, last night I cried at the distance
between us — work, hate. Berkshire week, where to eat. We cant be
this busy for no reason at all & last night saw milt & cliff & warren,
jeff outlaw & tigger at fred lords barn, w in bright red vest, cliff &
milt looking sparkling & clean, did we? Go to the farmer, say to-
bacco, do you have any tobacco, we're out of cigarettes, have eaten
too many cheeseburgers, put milt back in the book, some place to
be, this place is one place that place another place, where I was,
where do your spirits rise higher, where do mine, where do my dogs
cats his hers their lovers lower, many towels in the bathroom many,
two, wide windows behind them trees you can become part of me
do what I do, I wish my robe were red, yours is, follow it, follow
she she follows free follows later today I make it, over the rough
dirt road into, where, ever, I want it to be, into it, with wine, you
arent there, you are a curse, like the weather sending coal through
my veins, hot coal, I sink into you, listen, its through you, something
started once on some trip, & something fell, fell, & one night, forgot,

144

& in the meantime with another person some things began to happen & before the end of it, no defined as a reversal of the action going on, as a removal or release from the state that exists, & before the end of it, it was morning when something new defined something edgy & all this has to do with yesterday too, young & old & older, sometimes through that we are set back, very set back, & stony, like rocks & stone, & stones run through our veins like the weather, the storm comes here that destroyed syracuse & at 6 o'clock we will have moved these stones in a pile, heap, coals, moans, driving, south, then north of here & when one part of your body seems hanging hanging loosely from the rest do you judge, do not judge for yourself but do not accept from someone else their remarks as a judgment, someone knows. White walls, pink dresser, pink orange & grey towels like the weather which sends, some, sun, rise, to our meeting, 6 o'clock, we'll be there but e's gone to europe & M has no car or motorcycle & jeff & t live in washington & j has a listed number & R has a can of condensed milk meant for me & a sports car passes by & waves, not, still, in the bathtub & a hand, e's, rests on my knee for a while, & I have no pictures of fucking & g, p & b are in b's car somewhere & b told me it drives p crazy not to have any money, hurts his pride she said & I couldnt believe that but wondered why p hangs around with such fucked up friends & v must have come back from toronto by now & k loves the cello she says, residue, & k & g never met yet & neither did p meet k & t we havent seen or talked to & the pink paint, roughly there, extends onto the unpainted part of the two drawers & j talked about beckett & molloy & likes them too & actors are very strange & money grows on trees & ed's reading big phils kid & m's reading something like another roadside tomorrow or attraction by somebody named robbins & anais nin's about the house & h is probably in woodstock fuck her she wouldnt let k live in our house & so on, residue, also, the rest of the story goes: we go into town in about half an hour we take M to his bike go to see chris & john baker get cigarettes: speed makes ed depressed the next day which was yesterday & there's a sleeping man interfering with my pen & then we'll eat go to j's to pick him up for sound sessions & I'll try to call R & then we'll go to the s.d.sound studio 4 at least 4 or 5 hours they'll do the sound mixing & so on I'll take pictures & notes & note nothing wrong with being an observer is there as I am that was the end of that page, these precious little

words, written small, are not meant to come on too strong but just
to lull you like the whirr of a car or an airplane interior or like the
sound of birds clinking glasses together at tea, glasses of tea, to lull
you then into now being for a while into being me, can you feel it,
becoming part of the rest of the story goes: I hear them talking, I
speak to them, it sounds like russian, a sleeping man's heavy head
on my shoulder my muscle aching, not from holding the head or the
book but from writing writing pictures of, the head the heavy head
shifts, of paul & barbara, murray, then a new roll, movement more
movement there, pictures of ed's back, the car, the vegetables & the
car, the coke the bottle, the rooms up stairs — all instruments of
wrath or of fucking — autoerotic scenes, & later the sound studio
where you alone can blast yourself into another, space, now, a
sleeping man's rubbing my cunt with his little finger, I have no
pictures, please go on, I am not anxious to leave this off again &
stop hurt & everything goes by, it's one or the other wasnt it, &
then, & the mirror smashed later where my hip bone hit it squarely
as I ran & a man in the village restaurant says I've been reading
about you in the papers & I've just left ed off blue car took 4.4
gallons of gas a dollar eighty, I have the director's viewfinder on
my stomach. The studio wasnt ready so e&j went for ice cream,
afterwards, the balloons of john & ira where beverly took pictures
& I review pantaloons panel noons the cellist Tom the devils blow
christ beverly & anne poetry of the lenox arts center lives next to
jacques the red lion, sherry, a red mink coat it's 10 to 2 there's 10
to go the boys not home I'm wasting time I go through lines:
pantaloons panel noons pantaloons panel noons john ira howard
anne & hemingway or hem g.stein e.dickinson john eat your salad
someone says & someone says he's nostalgic & someone says you
drink too much like books by women by joan didion & someone
says time & again is a good book & someone says & that's the dif-
ference between me & ira & ira says I havent been away from john
in so long while we drive in my car & john says did you fuck so I
review I go through lines: virgil cane is my name & I served on the
denver train & how about over is how I got over, M's not home he
stays in town no motorcycle & K says she'll read this review:
christophe lee michael paul & someone says you can sleep here &
someone answers you can sleep here & all the people were singing,
look at slides there's darkness, the director's viewfinder finds ed

exhausted in pictures, the night they drove, cellos belong they were made for corners, I went back to the house for the slide projector & drove here through the fog I had some wine with me & since that time I always drive with wine, you put a beer between your legs, there's a truck there's a tractor at the big farm driving down the road with bright red lights & I'm scared so paul gets lost winds up on mohawk trail road, whatever that is, we dont know the names of the roads we travel, dirt roads, with names, paul lives in dalton & we will probably never know, die: I go through k's fantasies driving by GE, it's a concentration camp, nowhere, nowhere, private, the private charge of general electric's barbed wire, the private parts of their government contracts, the titles they give their weaponry, the naval surge site the site for beneficent missile launching the barbed wire fence enclosing the heap of iron filings that went up in flame engulfing the assistant prime minister as he fell into a pot of boiling pitch, it has something to do with iron, making molten weapons for the employment of ethnic groups that hang around, they have good beer in the neighborhood, they're launching sections of apollo XOX & my father used to work for the company that made the cameras for the moon & oh they warned me & she's in the bathtub again reading lines & someone remembers composing a line for a play when we were little & the line was gosh I'd die & I'm tired of lines so when will the play be over or when will the play be spoken in real time: we have to move out, do the laundry, tom hasnt moved out yet & it's hard to talk to have to talk to & someone says barraged & I am, we ate grinders & drank beer, saw a man we knew sitting at the red snake skin alligator table cover again, singing for the actors feeding them lines for the actors the scorpios & someone says john hates actors & john's teaching at fordham where the priests signal actors to get dressed & there's 10 to go a race a laugh a nap simple safe something cripple dormitory dreams dormitory room a picture of a cello on the ship we're on & beverly was pushing it to 1600 & she says how sweet of him to remember & john got drunk with her & someone said he loved her & someone said if I ever did see one, talked to R could barely hear her they wouldnt let her into the hospital today I'm tired of telling about the play the end of the day I'm almost tired of telling this is not the end of the play a book to get inside of me & a scene was, changed &, my side hurts, fear

July 26
Already started. It's monday I bought Amontillado pumpkin pie
small salts & sweetheart dish detergent a mrs. anna myers strawberry
preserves a canadian oat bread that had wheat flour water sugar shor-
tening nonfat dry milk wheat germ yeast salt bran soy flour malt
yeast nutrient emulsifier in it & ten giant mowhawk busybugs &
tonic water club soda a carton of pall malls & make notes for plastic
bags, when does the play close the laundry check the slides salt &
salt yoghurts cherry vanilla strawberry apricot half gallon crystal
milk perri italian brand sausage two dozen eggs & wild horses, these
were bought at the supermarket, seized 8 oz pure maple syrup &
make a design for the rig & took note of a design for the rig drawn
up on july 8th & more notes: big caps bloom. Something about
shopping bags a splicing block white leader more wild horses go to
lafayette, airplane, earphone, fifties movie magazines, pictures of
james dean, marlboro poster, plastic eggs, the natural foods cook-
book, radio changing stations, the new york city list, old black
magic again, pick up letters, flash powder, capital, paramount,
theatrical supply, slide projector, bring t's check for nyc night
now, the man that was used up by, Poe, the narrative begins: al-
ready started the fear to finish: I know we've been to the theater
& maybe I'm doing the wash now or something in stockbridge or
just hanging around like a power fixture, mice like bread I cant
seem to get off on these days I wish I had some delicate sauces to
eat, freshpak all purpose grind coffee what if I had to finish? For
the irate women in the audience, someone says, we intended tonight
to deal with male homosexuality, perhaps we'll get around to the
other some other time & the mouse is taking over the house, this is
the view from the laundromat, yes I was doing the laundry & was I
also addressing books or writing to holly or both & now I'm smoking
butts & waiting for the coffee to settle: please no more than 1/3
cup of soap & fill only to the line with clothes & then what, it was
the giant machine no one was using it chrome on display it was
broken that's why, a woman's legs laundromat legs in pale blue
slippers from down the street a ways they had a change machine
it looks like the moon in the window of the big machine all systems
go & some station's signing off, the backs of the leaves were being
blown up, I left ed off at the theater did the laundry & walked back
without it, left it in the dryer, we picked it up later, the backs of

the leaves which means its gonna rain & when's it gonna rain &
something about this scene looked funny to me - 2 cars & a pickup
like a pickup or crime a great crime a small crime done by great
criminals the two cars one a panel truck back to back a blue &
white panel truck & a 64 ford & one big black thing & they're play-
ing the national anthem for all the criminals so I was enjoying my-
self now, orange berries the same one light then dark over the land
of the free & home of brave, I beat the melody of the rockets in
air & steal syrup, more leaf backs, looks black & the shell station
with little flowers all over decorating so they laughed at me out of
shame I guess the studs in there who cant change a tire & another
shiny station wagon parked on the lawn, some ad, fuck the car
chris gets a phone call he looks like a woman from behind, ed's not
back. I walked down to the theater saw steven sitting on a rock his
head on his knees he didnt see me or look up they had the sprinklers
on they're nuts, ed shows up we had a talk on the stairs with nick
& gar, nick in a red & blue or black striped t-shirt, russiyan, smoked,
ed smoked blue with a blue script so we pick up the laundry, ed gets
two sodas without labels on, one red one green we go to the super-
market to record more sound & buy more food, it was adams & we
give each other rides on the cart it's practically empty we stop at
the lunch counter for a snack at least they dont have fluorescent
lights & ed wheels the groceries out to the flying car: we'd just
cashed a check another sky over zayre's, close down. We went home.
I went out, saw the yellow light through the window & igor's pussy,
a new day's not there but here's a new day in the middle of the day,
I take out the margins & go on going crazy it's monday at one end &
the drilling's started again at the other so for dinner we had white
wine with prosciutto & melon pizza rustica bread & pastries it was
good but the noise from the men outside drives us nuts & I left off
on the white pussy who was orange & we saw glen & randa, met
donna on the street little moths mosquitoes & fruit flies & I'm only
adding to the noise of our ears are not our own amnesia stores, I
feel delicate, as, sick & the pussy looking right at the camera he
kills chipmunks with his bare hands & he'd kill for that pussy & I
killed a little moth flying around my desk I'm alone, went out back
of the house in the field the field backwards white flowers & little
light the giant footprint or hole with a white piece of paper in it,
message from them, next to it a broken cinder block I often thought

of using it for something & it's dark we went upstairs: the unfinished
wiring in the ceiling & a weird hole or trap as though they built the
house without doors & had to have a way to slip out while they were
working, a bare bulb, looks like cary grant & somebody else on the
tv myself in the mirror yellow orange: fear already started as a finish
to memory, what's rote: having pumpkin pie & sassafras tea & it's
still monday the 26th of the month there's still plenty of pink light
out so it must be about 8pm & scary sitting here alone, I took some
of the sassafras out of the tea while the bird who only sings half
the song he did last year sings half the song but when I try to re-
member what half is I cant: it's four clear notes in a high-pitched
range followed by four clear notes sounding low, but that's the
whole song. I took a picture of everything I saw today on the way
to the theater, making space dramas & courtroom scenes: there's
golden light inside it will take pictures of my thought I thought I
heard someone knocking & I hope this isnt going to be fear, sure
the knocking was a dog barking in the distance, it's myself tonight
& looks like rain again hot for days, all men shirts off & pictures
are becoming either too difficult or really easy to remember take
this it's the first time I ever sat down in this house & read, I am not
reading: the rehearsal of blue. There's some committment to memory,
it's already started a finish to fear. A's letter she says I sound like a
real writer, missed j&i's movies tonight & a car passes by, singing,
where would I run from here, so obsessed with objects like always
up here, looked at different kinds of paper today & leaves, some-
thing's still missing & later minus parch dinghy nipple cupid like
cord I write while m & susan or someone are fucking outside, or
yesterday, dryly altar excise tackle cards & M says grace is deter-
mined, naked autumn, a flight of mallards gets me up so early, three
shots in a glass, coffee strong coffee piano music & he says I love
this it's like watching a girl undress, star star a star & now I'm so re-
moved compared to P or e or g & it goes on I'm so removed that I
say it's like watching a boy undress, star star a star: Springfield
Center to be purple: Springfield's battle of the bricks ended
abruptly last week when mayor frank freedman told the officials
concerned to stop squabbling: A Springfield Redevelopment Authority
official had threatened Monday to bring legal action against civic
center officials if they proceeded to use purple-colored bricks on
the $10 million center, after the urban renewal agency had approved

bricks of a red color: Freedman met with both parties & told them,
"I'm sick & tired of hearing about bricks & having two agencies
squabbling over an immaterial thing such as the color of a brick. If
it were a ghoulish color, then this issue would be different.": The
two agencies then agreed to use the delivered purple bricks. The sky
is always a spectacle Anne is on the islands. We ride the carts to
adams Ed puts a ham in the cart. We have to pay the rent Ed gets
chocolates. Someone says you attach alot of importance to your
independence dont you I say I attack alot of importance to my
independence yes but only by mistake. So stars: simone signoret is
a traveling tutor & racing car driver, at the rehearsal of blue we saw
the business of bill, the water pitcher was stage front before &
there's too much stuff on the table, rita moreno embraces everyone,
I'm pasting things up & an old mother is thinking she's like the tutor
of the starlight movie from hartford, triangle triangle a triangle a sur-
prise: home, red custard & e races off I'm here alone, who's paul
sage? M & S I'm taken while cooking mushrooms potatoes & carrots,
eating bread & tomatoes, aback I want my alone dinners, trees, to
be alone, so is my life over now, they go dancing in the corner, why
dont I want people to know that I eat? I dont want people to know
that I eat, I am made of sand I am made of pebbles, if I eat I can be
eaten or eaten out of house & home, triangle how bravely triangle
triangle: how bravely m & s lie downstairs, the M train to Ridgewood
the SS train in rush hours & I dont feel like A's real writer or my
grandfather dying, he dies. Arrow arrow a turning arrow: meaning
is a physiognomy what's the name of the greatest artist who ever
lived? it's raining out, marcel bump, triangle: ed's not home yet at
almost it must be two giant bugs & moths banging at the screens over-
taking the house & little gnats covering the glass of the windows
creeping in through the cracks, I am a power fissure & as I get foggy
the bugs seem to be more inside than out & after reading all the
letters I wrote to ed, the rest, there's more, to ed in florida &
massachusetts to ed from prison I must make myself known I think
maybe my idea of continuing like perfection is to have a person at a
distance to direct my flow of words at & it isnt even words I am
speaking about can speak about & bang! there's a person who doesnt
answer, ed never answers letters & maybe that is the trouble with
breaking through being really there, power to make myself known,
a pressure, so that when I'm there we're there together, I must creep

in through these little cracks I remembered from before cracks in
the finely made windows. Ed is remote sometimes. Like the pressure
power fissure that I am setting myself up to be. & then I used the
typewriter to write fast, saw the words differently & I still need to
race-write but better going from one page to the next by hand than
by insertion & wait for the slow explosions, I'll go race to the
printers tomorrow & I said three years ago no question marks, lots
of questions but no question marks & is ed like my mother & he
looks as beautiful? you watch him while he sleeps & I look? for a
father ted & on & a brother warren & tom & on & a son the same
the freudian analysts are meeting in vienna, they didnt want to
choose vienna the town had been so unkind to freud but now a freud
museum is set up there so some things, sentences, stick in your
mind, I call them sentences that stand out & one is some old people
try to live on one can of soup a day. Dear g.s., when I think of you
I think I am you but not so harsh you were right o.k. to be harsh
like t.v. but you were rich, you & dash & me, you were busy when
you were busy, so go on, i'm here I like massachusetts, it's tea, tea
is striking I could sell it for myself, the public ora aura, an orbital
circus, I mentioned, I'll repeat it, circus & on, in a note, broken in
a note, for tea to drink & hashish, with it I've lost it, comes hashish,
you can see it, turn over, it goes on, you never mentioned your note-
book or other process, is that something we got from marcel bump
& his friends, do you know him, how wasnt p (icasso) a bore? you
swore, something else, a friend, you see that through to the end, &
begin again. Star falls, the end, troy, a dawning, a mix-up, the play,
curtain, design, design of the curtain, fighting the curtain, I see the
play, I see the sun rise too, most of them saw it, at the end of the
day & close to what was happening, all cross the globe, we saw it,
what are they doing?, near it, a buzzing, a cloth on the door, the
dent in the car, who made it, not sure of it, closely one at a time,
banging, banging on glass, crusader, marauder, a catholic, sink into
mine, mine are pillows, the floor, stretch across a wider plain to
pain, to pain drift & think about someone with fear, & think about
memory with fear, too much time went into the windows, we saw
it, so stretch down, a new sign, save it, it's needed, use it, it's
thrown, throw it & so on, safer at distances, come over here, where
were worrying where were time. Yours else be. The calendar year
1971 July & August in Massachusetts: reason, the reason the pic-

tures of night light are so green, the reason photoflood without a
filter makes night light turn turquoise, the reason fluorescents need
blue, the reason you saw something & wrote "sight", you found a
letter from tom in 1967 with a poem in it he was 19 I was 22 & I'm
thinking about e's parents staying in this room when they visit,
sleeping here, for some reason, it's not tomorrow yet ed's still not
home, it's always at the end, I'm itchy, there are moans from down-
stairs, catching cold while memory started a finish to fear of myself
in the mirror shrieking yellow orange & the light on the right side
of my face my right eye staring, I turn my head to the right & it
was my left eye & look two eyes facing the light by eyes looking
at the camera at myself, cave, the glare, was ed asleep & I was de-
termined to catch up with myself by as before looking in the mirror
eight times ten times looking at light, yours mine, the light dimmed
on the directors viewfinder whited out over red pants & a white silk
shirt the cossack's pajamas & a glass of amontillado, the bricks the
pressure the haze on the mirror in a streak of light the bone of my
hip & the vein of my forearm fall the way the light from below on
my face makes a triangle, diamond-shaped, with my nose at the bot-
tom eyes white & surrounded in my reflection bulging out in shadow
now the light turns on my left eye & the left side of my face I am
too close to it I strike the pose of the first day housed in the pink
rimmed mirror camera resting on my knee, foot up on the counter,
my ring catches the light & eyes two black dots with white light
in them infinity behind me I'm smoking & come closer, I rest more
I resist more there's a haze then & two eyes just eyes open wide
this one's a joke or else the climax, light inches warmth away from
my left eye, I look at you I play I'm exhausted

July 27
I did I went I: Ed saw this in the circus: a guy is raised up by ropes
in chains, they burn his ropes as he escapes. Pole high-wire day.
I went down the road I was thinking about I was looking at tele-
phone poles I stopped at the fence on the dirt road I pulled over to
the side of the road to take a picture of rocks, I was on my way to
Williamstown, I sat there a while I picked up 100 copies of my book
from the printer I stopped at the top of the hill to read it but couldnt
concentrate, instead of reading I looked over to the left, I was thinking

about telephone poles more & more I drove back the same way I came I pulled up at a restaurant, things were looking small they still are, I look for ed to show him the book, I looked up I finally looked right at it, I went back I went back to the barn I remember the sky I couldnt believe what I looked like in tom's black belt I knelt down one knee down one knee up I looked at that late afternoon I tried to make objects fly I went out in the field & I went down the road I was thinking about the green & yellow in the dark & a strange kind of light I was thinking if I walk just a little further it'll be worth it I'll be able to see the whole valley I saw poles: when we say that a body is a magnet we are again asserting an invariable association of properties, the body will deflect a compass needle & it will generate an electric current in a coil of wire rotated rapidly in its neighborhood. The statement that there are magnets is a law asserting that these properties are invariably associated. I'm not the only one who's scared or angry. Last night I stepped in a cup of coffee next to the bed & now I broke my neck trying to get a picture of a bird against the sky, what sky. The yellow birds are out & a black one just flew by me close & out into the field with a crumb a white crumb which he dropped in the morning field I get pictures of birds against the sky against its wishes, these golden yellow sunglasses are too much there's a fly on the camera & someone says it wasnt very good for our health, they must mean the sea & the denseness in my head this morning's gone, triangle: running around but very little running around just games & swim, lie, run, sun, jewish star: followed a bird with the camera he lighted on the top of the tallest tree at the far end of the field he's still there & a butterfly banging against the window black brown & orange it's 5:30 whatever that means & little buzzing & few birds & where's some bird flying home, there's a bee up here he went back down very still then a roar of bee I went to williamstown to see the second proofs to get the book & now the stars will be crooked but I cant think, there's a problem it's still it's gotten cool at last & I'm in white with a big black belt wearing the color contrast spectra viewing glass from photo research corp burbank calif so yellow bird flew off, ed's napping ed's sleeping, bought late quartets blue leader, no good, lunch at friendly's steel food & aluminum ice cream no rust aluminum eat out eat oil & bugs going crazy in the midnight hour flying ones what can you

do in a month while every moment gp is lying in hospital & what's
in his mind, I'll draw tonight purple matches & a big pink ink spot
on my pants there's a special on pain on channel three & something
about this house makes me think people are going to play tricks on
us, the hat on the doorstep the branch on the other door & polter-
geists voodoo dolls trolls igor I wish I had a gun walked down the
road at sundown the road took me too far took last pictures of a
motorcycle that kept passing me back & forth, looking, dogs fucked
up my picture of a cow down at the first red farm & in syracuse the
temperature's 56 degrees: you get the weather forecast in the middle
of the spectrum high in the eighties low humidity you die in the
nineties sunny thursday more humid this is the travelers weather
service, how is your grandfather? my grandfather is a woman sitting
in a yellow light at a secretary, I can see her through a perfect
window in a perfect setting & know she will live forever, another
hay truck waving, another motorcycle going fast & a new moon
the mountain above it the darkening sky an aura of light light be-
ginning of last night's movie & all the movies I've ever seen & to-
night's black trees & telephone poles against the sky auras of light
not feeling completely light yet but lighter what's on the starlight
movie tonight, it's brides of dracula: that was the end of a long series
of very bad days, this is my pole high-wire act where I do a turn in
air again, & of those days there's a feeling of horror to recount
them & disconnection & every time I associate myself with them
it's the 20th of september which is odd which is a dissociation from
the world & everything around me which is science but the noise
may be the cause of it, so I drew the green patches of the canals of
Mars & I drew the day up as a series, as a moment in the present,
sept. 20, & as an action: I did I went I: as a series there's a grey pole
fence by the side of the road next to a telephone pole & now I got
my hair caught in the fan the hair stopped the fan & I did this I
went down the road I was thinking about telephone poles I was
looking at poles & then rocks these rocks on the side of the dirt
road & now I light a cigarette, I had stopped on the dirt road for
once I stopped by the fence a different fence & then I saw the
rocks on rte. 7 & a car comes by station wagon & now I drink &
smoke, I had pulled over to the side of the road to take a picture
of rocks, I was on my way to williamstown, a blue pick-up passes &
I sat there a while, simultaneous, at the top of a hill near adams,

more telephone poles & the sky, now I get music from the tv & noise,
anger, I would strangle them susannah, am I a gnome & I picked up
my book from the printer, 100 copies & I stopped at the top of this
hill to read it but couldnt concentrate I couldnt even decide whether
to turn the car off & to the left a mountain maybe greylock & so on
& white post & mechanisms of all kinds & now none, I wish I had some
& I looked over to the left instead of reading, I had picked up a
hitchiker on my way way up & he said I wish I were going to wil-
liamstown today I often go there but I have friends in new ashford &
I must see them, he wanted to buy the car, & there were telephone
poles with five wires in a white sky & now I wish somebody would
come by every day to read this & talk & drink beer & then, it's true,
I was thinking about telephone poles, the pole became the frame of
a long picture, mountains, like a dish of something & now ed runs
out to the bathroom, sleeping & says I want to hear that typing
louder than that other stuff & the other stuff is noise from drilling
or noise from the tv & I say I can turn it up want me to turn it up
& he says yeah & I say how's that & he says turn it down & I was
thinking about the poles more & more & then the dark blue cap-
tain's cabin surrounded by telephone poles & now nothing, it must've
been a big lunch place, there were alot of cars & I had seen it on
my way up but didnt stop to look around, I got closer to it the
color of its blue was disappointing from the point of view of a pole
or including a pole & now something should've been wilder & move
more out of focus & I had pulled up cause things were looking too
small that day, they still are & then the top of the barn for re-
hearsals with the sun coming over, fucking con artists & I had looked
for ed to show him the book & then writing in the sky, a trail of it,
or just one of those long dispersed clouds, the fibers, see mnemonists
& I had looked up & now nothing & then the strange heap of hay
tied up outside the barn with something on top of it & now I am
out of control & I was out of control then & I had finally looked
right at it & then out the paned window on green & it's inside with
no poles but wires & what were we doing in friendly's near rte. 20,
something about pictures, what a downer & then ed read the menu,
strangely distorted & green his lips are red & he's wearing the tye-
died shirt & its telephone poles & this was when we vowed never to
eat there again & it looks like the one in great barrington & then out
the window a darker tree trunk & it looked like a picture we ate &

then a sun way sun telephone wire closed down viewfinder some
tree something moving very fast & we went back & now there's a
slot of people talking on tv, it's a crowd scene in person & then a
green tree & more wire & did I want to call someone & tell them
about something, by wire & then a greener tree & we went back to
the barn & then the other side of it with sky, it's alford pole & I
remember the sky & then, shit, their telephone pole & a contorted
accumulation of trees, the pole's bent & then a wisp sky & myself
in white in braids in the window with wood blue sky wisp & green
barefoot at hip, I'm a pole an Indian & what kind of strange person
am I I can hear the voice of george sanders in my ear & the barn in
alford later on I couldnt believe what I looked like in tom's black
belt & then in the same reflection I'm kneeling straight as an arrow,
braids are poles & I knelt down one knee down one knee up, knee
kneel, & then pink & orange pens & smokes & two yellow pillows a
notebook shades & sandals on the deck & I looked at that in the
late afternoon: telephone poles: I wasnt kidding, I put my shades
up on a pole so they could be in the sky or so that the public could
see through them as I could what the sky looked like in three di-
mensions of cloud: they couldnt but, so the idea of the poles wasnt
that they were telephone: to reach someone & the young mr. pitt
directed by sir carol reed costumes by cecil beaton & all original
speeches, you can see it every september 20th, it wasnt to reach
someone but just poles for the sake of poles so that in most cases
analogies probably dont hold just poles & of course they reach in
or up & the sky's as much a part of things & so on & then the glasses
fly, the pole, the light stand & I had tried to make them fly, pilot's
shades, & poles & fly & then the back of ed in his shirt & he can
fly, it's dark long hair & ed looked shortened this day, a back like
a girl's he said or just this one & then the red & black chair with a
lapse of yellow pillow over it, it's in the grass & no it wasnt in the
grass but on the deck cut off to look like it's high in the grass, an
elevated chair & fly are there any more elevations & maybe it was
the deck that did it & then a darker green than there is in the field
& I was high so why did I keep taking it & then still darker & forest
white flowers & I went out in the field & I went down the road &
then the silver moon was up & high the black trees against the eve-
ning light, a dead black tree & then telephone pole silhouette & get a
job & trees dead & silver moon exposed among them & I was taking

an evening walk too far down the road to get back before dark &
then a view of sunset but with still more wires in it, I was scared
& finally a hill in different shades, moon over it & I was thinking
the green & yellow in the dark makes a strange kind of light & then
the sunset sea, you've seen it the famous one, it's from above look-
ing down on a valley & I know if I go a little further it'll be worth
it & then it's dark & in the end two dark trees in a clear pink light
topped by just blue & a telephone pole: so I drew the canals of
Mars: I drew an all of the colors drawing it looks like a map of the
u.s. turned on its side brown on the eastern coast the red of the
desert the green of california mexico begins the gulf green & yellow
gold stream currents up in blue against black outline of eastern
shore northern borders on canadian blue & violet a streak of
lightning in the canadian part, that lightning enlarged & africa below
a halo an aura of cells, the spectra all the visible spectra plus a
planet & saturn the rings we are looking at head on this year

July 28
After pole high-wire game, what? Roseanna, it's getting late: switched
from white ed wine to red wine, still with a cube, I want some wine
white wine, ed said, I'll get you some & there isnt enough is there,
there's enough, I'll have to get you an ice cube, enough to whet your
appetite & wh wh whi whe what does, did, moving having to do
with poles, the poles. & the next day we left early in the morning
for the city with kathleen, to pick up the projectors? I dont know.
Marlboros on the dashboard of the cadillac, a reflection, a bright
sign, we went off early, it's amoco the only one certified lead-free &
a red car passes by blue flowers in the field, we went off early we
stopped at the chief taghkanic for breakfast sandwiches & coffee
heard something about a murder a beating of kids hippies listening
to tapes at a pond nearby & blue & white flowers passing from the
center & pink ones, were they blue now they're blue, K & E were
in the diner & the sign of the chief taghkanic diner, blue sky &
telephone pole, the head of an Indian chief, fluorescents off, I
waited for the big trucks to go by, one oil, one empty, they didnt
collide, & the side of the diner reflecting chrome, chrome stale
curtains palefaces a metal awning in reflection I went around to the
side of the diner happy we were wasting time & maybe this was the

158

day ed got the ticket & the side of the sign same sign with spots, a
blue car passing, is now, then right, in the middle of a telephone
pole the pole makes a, or rather the wires running from it at right
angles make a, perfect perspective, it's confused, let's go back over
it: you wake up at dawn blue black dawn, ed not home, lights on,
clothes on, take plates downstairs, change into nightgown cold get
back into cold bed, eat a piece of pumpkin pie sleep wake up worry
then begin to computerize the possible on logs on sleepers, you eat
them out of ideas one by one & put them on the used pile, you're
building a railroad: what happened to E, still working of course,
kathleen comes by to pick me up, pick up ed go to the city black
coffee, sign arrow, fat suntanned woman in pale turquoise dress
waiting to cross the road from the car, the national beauty award
highway 1969, in the winter of 69 we lived here, blue flowers by
the side of the road purple flowers here's the story of bell pond
listen: some guys were listening to music at dawn, they were beaten
up, dying, near the chief taghkanic diner: dudes: dudes in the diner
their shirts say Pigs Is Beautiful & all drawings are like maps &
someone says you sure you didnt take mescaline last night & fear
& caffeine & schenectady 71 degrees ed's reading in the back of
the car & a truck with a turquoise thing a trailer back in it crosses
the road, iroquois, two people in a sports car a neat compact close
fast-moving unit, good thing ours is in the smithsonian, finished
emma goldman last night I had a liverwurst sandwich & that reminds
me dont I digest this food & how fast can it happen, I use it up, I
need it & someone says you know about your metabolism & I can
see K a good actress & can she see me a good something, hot sun
everybody wants to be a something too, watch closely, another gas
station, another beatles song, we took off k's jacket & they just
happen to be, the people in this book, we. B. Now a 16th century
air, over, thunder in the car, we've come from afar. The the the
king is air, is here, we must be, almost there, B. pink pen, & lighter
there, W-A-B-C too too B-B, little darling, double You, A-C/D-C,
bum dee, A-B-C baby, waddee waddee, B-C-C, A.B.Dick, cha cha,
cola B.B., Bible, AWOL, wac, choc full, cab, the BeeGees, R-R,
R'n'R, R'n'B, COP, wa wa, mojo, lake secor, C.C., A is for, W.W.II,
U get an A 4 effort, double U double U two, saucy susan sauce with
franks, N-Y, B.Castro, hamburgs, I.Reed, GP, R, Ear, 2 A.D., 2 B.C.,
Bless You, 10 to 1, Eddie Lake, maybe baby, baby blue business,

Cane & Abel, Abel Gance, Gimme a 'A', Gimme B a 'B', a 'C',
Chappaqua Rd., M-E-N, men, it goes on: where are we, where are
the landau jewelers 2061 what street? & who is this girl in purple
passing by, sandals, some kind of kerchief, a great girl, she looks
like she's got a dog with her until you see it's one of those fireplugs
sticking out of a building, the building of the landau jewelers, yes
this is where we got the ticket I wanted to take a picture of the cop
but he was two spanish cops, very nice, they revoked ed's license, a
man comes out of 2061 to stare at the big scene with so many police,
you see we had no registration & we explained, putnam valley & so
on & a woman in yellow with a green hem passes, she wears white
stockings, white shoes like a nurse, a red bag with a white handle,
no the other way around, her arm bent to carry it & a light colored
band in her hair, she's crazy & behind her a woman in white white
dress gloves shoes bag a wide-brimmed white hat-type hat, the man
stares, he thinks to himself they've been stopped, what else could
he have thought. My real feelings at this time were a third or fourth
woman passes by, also wearing a wide-brimmed white hat & carrying
a white bag but she's got white sandals on, an extra bag, a dark shirt
& a tropical pink & orange blouse on, she looks into the hole out of
which the man stares, he's gone, back into the audio language school:
we get away. & then the 1st street gallery on the bowery, it's red
light & we go down to home & then the blue fish of the fish store in
a blue sea: baccala everyday & I went shopping with R & rich wooden
church doors, they look good to me & I went uptown & out the
window of the car a taxi with passenger window reflecting highrise
apartment building, taxi backed by garbage, no, packed extras, those
carts, what do you call them, bales of clean garbage, strings & left-
overs, pieces of fabric, we drove somewhere, we went to florio's
for calzone, this is a lost day, the ship a sailing one in florio's win-
dow & behind it, a backwards schlitz sign & a few men in a boat,
fluorescent & all the light of florio's fluorescent, it's like being
blind, inside & out, reflected & read & it's dusk about 8 or 9 o'clock
& a guy comes up to the counter, one of those police trainees in
grey from the station, from central headquarters down the street &
in the foreground an old woman sits in a booth & the waiter is
coming at us so I finally get a picture of him & mrs. florio in the
back, focus, in flowered house dress, she's tony's mother, the batboy
for the yankees & so on & the waiter wears glasses & talks to us

about breasts & bras & yeah, he says, but he likes to take them off a
girl, or woman, if she doesnt wear one then & table service thank you
& little balls of dough for calzone & one big one for pizza & I looked
over my shoulder yelling waiter, water & then the yellow light of
j&k's house & what were we doing here & I dont know I'm getting
pissed off, it's that yellow light, we went over there, it's ed shaving,
I feel like a fool, ed had to shave we had no razor with us, traitor I
mean & K had shaving cream & did we have cocaine maybe & rod
mckuen's on tv we saw rod mckuen on tv looking rare or medium &
an embarrassing conversation with kathleen & K makes up her finger
to her eye but where was she going I dont know & there's a recessed
red light, what's there, it must've been there & the sink at our own
house, clean dishes, an upsidedown coffee pot, clean jars, we went
home, toys on the floor, I've made a mess of things especially mo-
tions emotions, like a film, all the toys, see the devils, spilled out to
look for an egg a plastic egg, & H thought they were part of a robbery,
a staged robbery especially after ed rampaged through the house
looking for a blank check & couldnt find it strewing papers around,
there was nothing to steal & the light in the white room looks much
like itself, all the lights, bulbs hidden from your view & white foam
blocks glued to folding cardboard, part of the packing that comes
around a machine, pack me, next to my desk on the floor no where
the stereo used to be & I went around the house looking & ed was
in bed face down, was he dressed, was he sleeping was he posing, no
pillow cases but pillows english garden red & ed's ass, just asleep or
going there, the sheets come, about halfway up his legs, the dark
loft lightens, once it gets light, it can be light as & why keep it down,
many books & taken by surprise, it's sideways, windows open, a
ladder in the window, two shirts on the bed, one died & army, news-
papers all, light, the address of the magic store is here, I'm numb with
lemonade, GP's better home friday & the devils collapse with that,
between black & white is blue, it's all light

July 29
We've lost we've won we havent used our checkbook. I'm going
crazy, the bulbs, I keep trapping cockroaches buried live maybe
it comes out for them like a vacation & they turn over on their backs
legs up & in the air & then when you lift up the trap a few days later

they turn over & walk away, not very fast. Coffee & a pizza rustica the 29th: forgot to drink milk it's raining again, why I'm not a scientist: thursday: get caps an egg flash powder splicer leader & a present for jacques' birthday, then dialogue: this is a jacques for the summer bought a 1964 cadillac I said & she said oh great & convertible oh good & I said we took it to the city alot because we always had to pick up things & our car was too small & that's ed's body of the body of that car, ed's torso in the cadillac & she said those are good colors & I said this is like the 29th of july & she asked were you were you glad when you finished when you came close to finishing the gathering material part or were you & she trailed off, well funny thing was like the reason I wanted to look at these pictures was they really pick up towards the end of the month in a funny way they all get clearer & more vivid & more interesting but just to me somehow I said & she said do you think it's because they & do you think they are & well lemme see what I think I mean I wanna see if I think the pictures are or if they seem that way to you because they are new now & I said what & then well I mean the reasons for it are so complicated or they could be so complicated I have no idea what you mean or what I mean but I might be wrong yes it's true we'll see & she said yes I mean I wonder if as you got into them & what you were doing you were actually taking better pictures or whether something in your mind was becoming similar to something in the air & I answered yeah & it seems though I dont know what I mean but it seems also that maybe more was happening more things were happening & well alot of things were happening all the time all summer but I mean just things it wasnt that well what I mean is we were bored alot of the time but we had to do work I mean that kind of work & that much of it is always sort of boring, always boring but there was alot of moving around, we were always moving around alot & gradually more began to happen I mean really happen I think because of the moving & she said well I meant like in the days that you showed me before there were alot of things that were indistinct because they were indistinct happenings, things that you did with no reference, no referential nature but maybe with the same people & about the same time there wouldnt be that much difference, it's only a month going by but you probably were having a feeling of deja vu in the city when you were sitting in some restaurant about this time

ordering a cheeseburger, same one that you probably got in the
others & saw pictures of it in your mind whereas here, I dont know
& I said yeah I guess so, I was only intending to concentrate a little
bit & this is 23rd street I think, no it's somewhere else it's uptown
on the west side or something oh I know where it was we were pick-
ing up flash powder from the magic store, there's an exploding
bouquet in the play & we were picking up & this is that same street
the new yorker hotel is on & she said oh that's around times square
& I said I think so a horrible day & she said I was on my roof today
& I said oh yeah & she continued it was incredible I was looking at
the world trade buildings they're so close & have you seem em from
down here & I said well you cant miss em from the west side high-
way & I have alot of pictures of them & she said our roof is fan-
tastic it's really just amazing even from our living room it's too bad
that that area is so horrible from our living room windows you can
look at the statue of liberty & the harbor & the verrazano bridge
& all of manhattan it's really too bad it's such a horrible place to
live because it has very good windows & I said somebody threw
these papers all over the floor I mean the street on west something
street 42nd I guess they're probably still there & me at the hotdog
stand & she said you look as though you're & I interrupted dont I
look exhausted & she went on you look as though you're really
making a decision about what you're going to get there & I said I
think I was waiting for a hotdog yeah & she said that's pretty
strange a station wagon but what are those things on top & I ex-
plained yeah it's one of the airline, one of those airline, those
limousine things, limousines, very shiney though & she said what is
that there & I said this is on 47THST I think & she said what is that
below that something or other & I explained oh it's a box that con-
tained a new razor sort of a space age razor that ed got, yeah that's
47THST, alot of people were yelling at me that day because I had a
I was waiting for Ed & I had this huge car double parked it
eventually rained I remember that day it was a horrible day,
bergers delicatessen, fuck & she said the light is strange in that
picture & I said that blue is like the blue of the tinted windshield
& she said no that's not what I mean there's alot of green in the
buildings & in the cabs & maybe that's, anyway there's alot of
colors & I said well it always gets green uptown when it's going
to rain & she said yeah it does what time was it & I said I think it

was probably about four & she said yeah it must be late but the sky
there doesnt look all that much like rain but its light is queer, I guess
it does look like rain I guess there's sort of sun in the light & it's
grey & I said I eventually pulled up & parked in that space where the
gas truck is & there's the sky, now this is on 23RDST where we were
picking up grace who was coming to the country with us, there was
a fruit truck & I guess cops either chased them away or something it
was one of those illegal fruit peddlers alot of people buying fruit &
this is grace's hallway, west side highway & she said yup, looks as
though you're going south, nope north I said we're going this way &
she said are you that's north but that car looks as though it's going
south & I said yeah but that's the other side of the highway & she
said oh i see it now & I said the south side is closer to the river &
she said yeah sort of a nice picture but the colors are too something
& I said that's new york & the haze & the palisades & she said that's
good & I said this must be further up the taconic & now that, if
you look closely, is a bat & she said jesus were there bats in your
house & I said yeah & now let's see if we can, there it is, I had grace
shine a flashlight on him that bat so I could take a picture of it &
you cant believe the nerve it took to get that close to it & she said
oh yeah a bat & I said we had three in the house, flying too & she
said yeah & I said I'm glad that picture came out, can you see it's
red eyes & she said no I cant see but at least you could see the bat
& I said yes & there was another bat but the flashlight was off,
cant see & she said in a way that's even worse & I said yeah they're
horrible looking, arent they, have you seen them before & she said
not real bats, there was a bat at trinity once in one of those in one
of the dormitories but I didnt go near it & I said this is the bathroom
those are some drawings I made in my notebook & she said is that
a sherry bottle & I said yeah amontillado & she said oh I noticed
those towels here I noted them because, those colors yeah, those
nice colors & I said yeah somebody gave them to us to use in the
country in the house & we never returned alot of them & she said
you know I've never seen that kind of color before, let the um out-
door light change the color of the towels, you let it change alot
yeah, the bathroom sink, your clothes, with a pair of white pants
in it, rusting paint sets, it's a nice sink & I laugh it's one of those
lights & she laughs that light is too strange coming out on top & I
said yeah that's like from the tensor light, makes that beautiful halo

& she said you could make a picture like that with the halo around
someone's head & what's that & I said that's the light that's on the
rheostat from the bottom though & she said jesus beautiful isnt it
amazing it's not quite centered right & I'd like it better I think if it
was, wonderful colors, I really like that raspberry, yeah, another one
further down, it looks as though it's growing there & I said yeah
doesnt it & if I could've stood on the ceiling I could've really made
it look that way & she asked how did you take that what did you
lie on the floor or & I said yeah & she said it's hypnotizing isnt it
it's like an eye that does something or other, yeah, hmm & two of
them & that moves too I cant decide if that looks like some sort
of growth, it's from somewhere, sort of shaped like a rod a protozoa
or something, I wonder what, looks like something organic doesnt
it & there's your hammock & I said yeah that's like the whole house
you see, we brought the hammock up & we moved the bed upstairs
& that's like everything but the upstairs part of the house & she
said yeah the main um room & I said yeah & she said the hammock
really looks nice in that tree um house & I said yeah that's grace's
ah cousin ah niece who came up to visit with grace & she said I
thought that was a pile of books she's wearing a striped shirt I
didnt realize there was a child there until you said that it's really
a wonderful house & I said yeah it was I took pictures of everybody
everybody was writing everybody in the whole house was writing
that night & she said that's a nice picture of grace & I said yeah that's
all we went to bed then, she boxed the bed down. Why I'm not a
scientist: ed's torso in the cadillac, jack donohue shirt patched jeans
the burnt ones & we threw them away no we didnt, he's at the
wheel: I'm imagining things the magic store we must've run errands,
not the projectors the magic store on 42NDST: flash powder above
the irish house bar restaurant people passing & a whole store of
magic shown in private, a man balding glasses tan clothes crosses
the street with a striped sports car down the street from the new
yorker hotel like I said before we've parked down the street & a
haze on the empire state building builds up well what do you ex-
pect: red light I'm waiting I waited no fog no traffic in our direc-
tion, all other: that's the light & somebody had strewn pink papers
& white papers saying something all over, black people's legs walk-
ing & me in an army shirt, ed had changed his to a log, did I switch
into his old one & waiting for a hotdog at the hotdog stand. The

stand's painted red, we're out in front of some red brick buildings
painted pink in the dark light with the bottom windows closed up.
I'm panic sticken. I can see the cadillac parked top down down the
street. We saw this guy from a distance. One of us pulled up. Which
of us said you know what I'd like, or, in a hurry, hotdog, repeat it:
silver objets d'art & antique engagement rings you get married in in
the next one which is taken over by one of those airline limousines
like I said before cutting off people's heads on the other side of the
street, only thing is there's no driver so it must be parked the head-
less hollow: looks like 47THST again, fuck cant be, this, window:
luggage rack empty & yes it's 47THST again U.S. cultured peal co.
& the hog hong kong inn for cocktails close enough to the tallest
building in the world for attack for cocktails, not me: u.s. mail
truck we're double parked by the place where del pezzo's spinach
omelettes used to be: do we devote alot of attention to this or just
struggle? & behind me fisher & somebody packing division probably
body & the u.s. mail: he had a number, dent: the cockroach trapped
over the drain under a glass got out & could they be that smart &
could he have crawled through the hole hatching eggs all along the
way trapping him & up & out another & a thousand new ones with
em: berger's across the street by the opportunity shop a jewish man
in a blue sports jacket with a black attache case hurries by followed
by a black woman carrying a shopping bag. 47THST: we get our
film equipment here in a place above the gotham book mart, arnold
eagle's studio & that is why we are always waiting: even negatives can
be cut upstairs & films screened in a hurry about art. Magic & jewels?
jerry samuels china silverware crystal & so on we buy yellow taxis
big traffic jam so I pulled back u.s. mail pulls up, gas truck pulls in
taxi parks across the street tells me to move I tell him to go to hell
he's the one blocking traffic he says he can park wherever he wants
the whole world's a taxi stand I get pissed off I pull up anyway, cop
comes by tells him to move there's a fight there's another cadillac
& people abuse the car I'm in: another lofty sky aloft & bent build-
ings into the frame, we're through with that & on to 14THST where
fruit vender attracts alot of attention like I said before, outside
grace's house where we picked her up to take with us & freya her
niece, the vender & cop car before the casa moneo where's the
magic & jewels? this day? with k, g, f, & e: well magic & money
moneo anyway or jewels & money or total depression in the car,

leave that in, viva la sangre de salvador allende la via del tren social-
ismo es pelligrosa & in the car k asks g all about dieting & exercise &
is she serious of course she was & storms in stormville soon as we
hit stormville though you cant see them yet or ever & the electric
electric window got stuck down on us in blankets & the girl hitch-
hiking soaking wet to poughkeepsie where it seems alot of crazy
people live poughkeepsie again & again, a tough town: grace's door-
way & a black woman goes by is she moving is she still she looks
still: at first I went in the wrong door, peel, arson, on the west side
highway I must've must musnt've been too down yet one giant
palisades building & still some trees blurred green & yellow separating
two cars on the greener highway just before the storm storm so
great the guy at the station wouldnt put gas in cars he says let them
wait in his slicker they were all in slickers, let them wait and, and a
long interruption for depression, ed lets us off & goes off, takes k
back & stays later, was he afraid, we had bats the first bats, more
bats, bats let me let go of my anguish: while g pointed a flashlight
at one on the wall of m's room where we thought we had him trapped,
m didnt come home that night, I took a picture he looks down he
cant see flash flat as a bat he arches like a cat, it was magic & jewels
& a little money too, could use some now, I shot the insane drawings
& drew some darker ones & someone says again were you on
mescaline & the one that came out like a map & one like lightning
the color wheel, like the light I took pictures of lying on the floor
no style no nerves the bottle of amontillado smokes tampax strike
anywheres newspapers & towels a long bath film can ashtray &
matchpack up closer blurred who cares? a spiral binding for the
earth. The world: saucers, earth, jupiter, saturn uranus neptune,
no: saturn with her rings seen from the side or in two dimensions, the
earth with mountains, green & color wheel, sun I guess with rays
sort of & all the same things including pink pen, when hung up the
towels dry towels ann dries them by the wood stove fast so they
dont smell like mildew like grass she never washes them: signs of
the zodiac: prepared for recognition: I know you, towels blurred
get closer to things, the white pants in the sink against close to the
end, powder toothpaste salt the ribbon stuck a glass, razor, soap
ivory & strawberry magic & jewels faucets shaving cream, mirror
rimmed pink pink & grey towel & fab, tom's shaving case. The
lights of the bathroom jewels but not magic I thought they were

spiderwebs hanging infinity magic but concentration, put something
in too much it must continue on, pain. I washed my hair & some-
one says something about the water, it's difficult to remember pain,
g washes her hair here & did I take this picture of the light of the
tensor light making a haze on myself & was it the night it thunder-
stormed & we lay on the floor telling what we saw & did we all
sleep in our room for fear of the bat, not this night, prisms from
the light so look at it, right at it, what? jewels: for sure, the light
from the bottom, how many jewels in its dimmer purple it was off
center, a gold rim, a strange ring makes perspective it glows it
hangs from one side of a sloping pointed ceiling, makes two stand
still looking at one then moves then you move then stand still again
looking at the same one, you have two with a connection in be-
tween as wide as the thing of it, amoeba like I said before, make a
greater distance now between the same one, cant hold still for the
real one real jewel is in focus, or, to make two again jewels multiply
they tend to divide where's mallarme here: freya's writing in the
hammock: dear s, please dont be angry because I havent written
in such a long time. I really cant say much because there's nothing
happening. When I get to Vermont I'll write a real long letter telling
you all the details on what happens there. So for now I miss you &
I miss you again, love, & grace is writing in the nook, red-orange,
red apple three red tomatoes one green apple a bunch of green grapes
the festering pecan blossom pots dishes & spoons: sink the doors to
the closet: room, we slept there later another haze from a light haze
makes bats or do they & a few crevices for them a crevices day from
the fissures left of power, where, check on that, behind & if it rains
enough they wont be able to work tomorrow & g's bed in another
nook, a bat's roost next to f's sleeping bags, pillows & cases & a tiny
baby sheet a tiny bat sheet & the light with tape near it, the tape
from g's last visit, the shade from the light she couldnt turn off the
switch was at the other end of the loft, poking the bat. Ed went
into the magic store like I said before silhouettes on the shades
from down on the streets. You cant hear in the house cant hear in the
streets you're on the wrong block. The manhattan center one
thousand men on the steps, it's cloudy bright & heavy over awful
new york day, grey, views of 47THST 6, 7, 8, 9, 10, 11, 12 views
of 47THST: fanfare, presents, slides, chirps, beeps & someone says
anything a matter with you guys & two start talking at once & some-

one says maybe you should get into each other, so, it's dirty,
how'll it look on film, practically everybody on the street works
for somebody & tina says I wish I were doing something like
that & she'd like to work, work for somebody too, a scene on the
streets: pissed off to describe it anger, he threatens me with a cop
& someone says move that shit car & crying on the streets why don't
more people do it & how can they stand it, they hang in there &
I'm freaked about the car it's raining so he gets a ticket for blocking
traffic: space-trip in a spaceship the worst ever, can I tell from the
times before like I was saying before & is there anything in that: now
I'm in the bathtub it's not over yet a million possibilities are mount-
ing, amontillado, a million bricks closing in on me or someone on
someone around me close to me & the bat helped a car passes by,
what am I thinking, we played joe cocker to scare the bat, scared
him into m's room taped the curtains closed & opening the door, we
talked to the bat, we said for at dusk you who dont understand
amontillado & we dont get a chance to finish, the bat's little white
teeth are bared, long black legs, white sitting like an indian & the
house become a belfry allright I'm sweating, blind as a bat: radar:
is there blood all around us, blood in the space-ship, blood on the
space trip a nightmare out of age 13, I stay in the car, maybe be-
cause of freya but she's so relaxed maybe that's why I wanted to
make a scene on the highway, space, now I'm sweating I feel like
brigid now pearl, where's the dope I run through the things, space,
what, why am I hurrying & was I pretending to be dead, like unlike
GP is this whole way of expression clear unclear like logic like
worst of all applied logic to death & came out with, sweating, I'll
leave my hair alone I'll leave my hair dirty I'll just die like that, un-
washed like child, more nerve I need to sweat & sweat more & K
says to E you're such a mess & G gives K this recipe: 1 cup shredded
carrots 1 cup shredded spinach the same celery ½ cup shredded
parsley in a quart of water low heat cook 25 minutes bubbling at
least add cup tomato juice & vegetable salt cook five minutes strain
out vegetables & drink & K says to G you're a gold mine of infor-
mation so, am I ignoring them am I here have I left, left out or just
imaging as ed says it & how would I support myself with a hot bath,
amontillado, M hasnt been here since we left, years, how did the
bat get in, pearl, the worst is feeling the conspiracy bite between
e & k, total, the beautiful people on one side & ragamuffins on the

other, line em up next to the cadillac, the window doesnt work: cant get over that & storms stormville one two three four I know e's thinking about being somewhere else, that's the function of magic & jewels & the city too or maybe it's me just drifting away how can we ever tell together, in a meeting? where is he? sweating in the car: e's parents are not mine I should hate them: picture GP: the old man, the bumb K thought was handsome: why has dash life dash dash this & why am I waiting for an accident I hope for one is the blood between me & GP real, I feel like I know him, can see looks on his face, defend his states of consciousness, no one else does, force it, desparate disparate & now right now a thousand, that, what I'm worst at, I called today a, b, or c, disgusting, I didnt come clear I couldnt finish a sentence, the whole of it & about the bat & someone says this is the most exciting thing that's hap-pened all wrong: exciting deliberate & sweat, identity floats some-where between a review of masterplots in the dictionary & the word girlfriend, she is a woman, I cant stand it this notebook's just some step away & what about my friends I sure dont care about filling up pages for a moment, defend the states of consciousness, write about them maybe: this notebook's just some step away from a fear & that fear has to do with communication & as a finish to memory I learn one thing, that the fear's already started, it's the same one, already begun, always back to where we both began no matter how far back & it's sincere it's boring for words & it's also anger, I just threw that in, dont let the anger have an effectiveness, drain it, use it, store it, whatever you do with it, never take advice like from a mountain running down & as far as it's almost truth it isnt worth syllables, the syllables break up to make a mask to make logs like the sleepers you build a rail road from like I said before & I repeat you get harder tougher or sleepier; you sleep: alternatives, fuck & spending the night alone I see that this is one idea, a block with a long handle on it like a sliver like a splinter of a log & from a pile of sleepers I extract them one by one & I eat out the ideas the possibilities, alternatives, you masturbate, extract them & then throw them on the used pile one by one if you're spending the night alone & to know more to write faster or slower to be sure to see julie m. today, shit I still have the momentum to make every-thing seem great until it stops & not to figure it out to run it down, to make a scene my scene scene in a play, fuck that sunrise & I'm

170

lifeless ashes & blood is what I create at least, what were you think-
ing about, the ike & tina turner review: it's jacques birthday got
him a cake from miss grumbles or grimbles same as last year at $6.50
butter cake & last year it was larger more butter loomed larger but
H was not in the hospital yet, review: oooaruuew, ouew, do you
like good music, review: thursday july 29 cant figure this one out:
I live with ed should I try to work with him should I try to live
alone am I giving up or just beginning to have the fear to see it
right: sit back, be immobile & leave it alone, what's leave it alone
& whole hands are you in am I in: do what I can, that's shit & may-
be it's just the syllables that make the words, try others: milk
preacher love each match mother silk matchstick anus penis
penultimate bat butt cigarette search built message batter bulk
much butter milk toast master muster bitter earth friend search
missed passed cup cat car mulch milt which? weather wealth mrs.
cadillac try toaster met still when? wet blood mix tool mind
sinecure section easel pest sink & now amontillado in the bathtub
the bathtub, bat, & someone says what is this menu for & someone
says save us a piece of cake & someone says if jacques doesnt eat it
all all the cream all the butter, lucked out: caucus serious must musty
respect boop sweat & smell sweat & mulch bottom dogs regis debray
salvador allende it's almost friday, call r call pat & ted & sink a ship,
no reminders, cross those out, sink a ship, sink it, respect, worry
again, disaster, each car that goes by sinking, expect disaster, respect
the word, sink it, I'm not the captain, repeat it, sink it, murder it,
hate it, the pictures of girls naked, I looked at the sunday morning,
I came home to find my father dead, later, my period, I looked at
my book to see if two days would do it, deplete it, experience a
phial: experienced at a title experience a vial a file a daughter a
title: daughter & color: you write like a child. How? in pink? It's
purplish so, there, you, are, in a moment, subservient, in a position,
defiled, foliage, filial, deflate, destitute, dethroned, the youngest
daughter, a fantasy, never princess, never printed: recess, rested,
play, with words, sink them, a ship, store them, restore & when I'm
far away now, pearl, smoke them a rule, be dirty not clean, but
clean not dirty, opposites a ruse, to write, down, down, yes I got,
pause & sink it, the ship, the sink, a ship in the characters, chinese
characters, the organ, milks, every, last word rite, pause pause, it
will be good to be in pink for a white, & everyone will think, with

the orange, I'm losing my mind, low swing my mind, freedoms just
another word calm secrets, soul, weather, I never leave this, I never
have

July 30

When you are a woman you make a great record & a daughter, whose
daughter, the doors & the bust armor plate of a woman and curls,
black bats, impending disaster impending doom unending impending
a reorganization of the employment of faculties a pigeon flies by
the window the subject frames, see, just, so, much who are you? how
did I come by you? I'm anger my anger is sense drills into you I am
set in this piece this is a move you little man doll fall down little
woman doll moves closer, is wounded, you get up again a miracle,
we mate, like two watch faces on the same wrist band, water-proof i
hope. Set them. Set them back a few hours to noon. Back a few
hours to noon. Inked, your move, in a certain number of hours
moves hours. Like you mentioned before as a reorganization of
the one who was mentioned before, to the one my presence here
speaks to, I shoot the moon men all at once & then I've got all this
time left to twiddle my thumbs. I've got to get a watch face & start
needing it. There's no two ways about it it's like pissing on the most
analytical version of all the stars, it's like breathing, breathe the
smoke of your own fucking brand. So I smoke yours. You renegade,
why not admit it & set me free. I hate chess sets. I hate all power
fixes except the power I have to show you something. I resign, so
you cant move. There are some motherfuckers I would like to show
the stars to stars climbing up in the sky, not you, i dont mean you.
Stars climbing up, what a trick, for a trick you get money, see the
ones in front of the sun, of course you can lunatic, for a trick you
get money, for a match you gotta win, I want evens & who am I
speaking to the market place. No deferrals, we do not cash checks,
what a lioness she's tempting to be bitter what a lion is are you
that is hungry. Eat meat. Pay at the store. Only thing is you cant
walk out, my legs wont hold you. Better transactions go on in the
south, at the pole, at random. You wanna know why? the pole at
the north, it cant be seen from there, it cant even be dreamed of.
Opposites attract a couple hard lines of defense stinks money. Child
loves patterns of any kind. Where am I going, I'm going out I'm

172

mad I'm playing feinting fainting mad I'm always playing I'm going
out to play, I'll play with a few hims & hers, I'll say to one of them
I'll find a chance a good smelly reason & i'll say you stink you stink
& then I'll laugh, you feel so bad you want me to devour you? then?
sure o.k. whatever you say you say goes what a mess a great mess
stinking again, I'm no princess to end the day with a start sweet-
heart, wanna roller skate I'm faster than you wanna race my time
is race I'm no sinking ship noble captains of which are covered with
shit. My infections a rage at the hospital, the doctors are covered
with blood, honor would spit, I just chew naturally a full count,
higher than ever what a bloody tundra on the pitchers mound. I
curve a fast knuckle spit one & spew it all round the bend to the
monkey moon far fucking out what a gas explosion that was, the
crowd's still steaming all energy is loose & a little gnu says new sys-
tems can be found on any field or fields. It's unreal, scared shitless
who is. Fuck. What a spot. A few of the hers & I will mosey down
to mexico to suck cock, dribble the cream on our blouses, prostrate
at the nunnery invested into the order without oil on our heads
bare heads new order of the all of the saints cocksuckers all stars
south of the border, no time for a snooze it's the rising sun so pay
attention, I forgot to include the fee in this prospectus coincident
with the new day, you dont pay, we levitate, like elevators sentient
beings glow with the auras of saints their very cells amazing blue
light, about two fade away you'll never see us again, mother-
fuckers, you a new race of blacks & us a visitation on your absence
of color. We are close we got this image from the church that made
us angels in the red, a vicious lay. Sex slain is sex slayer. Now that
we know this we make the relic institution pay, shell out through
its fucking teeth & eyes & nose & asshole, the well-hung robbers of
our sex ingest themselves before our eyes as we get up to go, we
go over the preceding was a play. Now lets eat dinner, watch the
tube, love, design. I want to leave this place

July 31
Exactly as it happened like Jack Webb, the files of the D.A. of L.A.
county I'm counting on you with no patience for something not
finished that takes long, or, you might say, a frenzy a web a review:
so I dream I'm in the play & we have to go through long tiny tunnels

to get from place to place from palace to palace, bats & wombats a
dinner with relatives, cigars, jacques hugging me: I ask for black cof-
fee & aunt E is there, we rehearse lines & dash in a red cloak is at
the door, a girl, another man & is dash an aristocrat? she quotes his
french she quotes his german she quotes & so on, someone casts a
doubt doubt on his car & then two men & a woman get into a little
yellow box that fits into a big black camera. It's to be washed, also,
culture with necessity for claustrophobia, astronauts, shorthand, the
woman emerges suffused with golden light, the men clean except
one man puts tape on his ass, she remarks "& when I ask how's
your ass . . .?" & In the same dream we are selling the tv equipment
& the three sit on top of the camera with sun with philosophy, re-
hearsals & school, turn over, rehearsals in the barn, rehearsals in the
hatch, a flat tire, last night the window on j's car wont go down &
someone says dont sit on that desk while E eats yoghurt while the
tire's being changed at the stud shell station there's a dead bird in
front of the house, the garbage ransacked I need new shoes need
new grass shoes brakes adjusted already have souls & cylinders need
new drums & someone asks where do the furmans live, back for the
script, GP is home, nurse not there yet, R sounds hassled, pictures
of the barn, camera on B all morning & the camera will go to new
mexico sunday at five thirty east of eden & pictures of james dean
go over big bob trying to recite his list & m is contagious back
tomorrow how did the bat get in tom gorman ben delight mellow &
t. sitting in the grass at a great distance & b says the hippies are
here, the purple restaurant, the bowling alley, the truck on top of
the gas station all over-exposed, camera loose, many gas stations,
too old to be out & blah blah blah should we go do the supermarket
just one more time & the carts are here tornadoes flooding rains
are here, thank you very much, the explosion & on account of bats
I'll be unable to sleep here tonight & on account of bats a driving
rain & a half moon & more morelles, the bats here, I couldnt finish
a roll of film on account of the light dimming every few seconds
when the water pump turns on & sudden rains when it was supposed
to clear & ten north frederick street & harder & harder rain & itchi-
ness & now the doors are closed but bat still flying here crazy to-
night last night we locked him in m's room, taped the curtains &
the windows closed the door opened the door to the outside this
morning he seemed to be gone & tonight when I went over about

three am to turn off the front lights the bat flying nearly hit me
square in the face: and what broke & what broke through the plastic
so violent to get to the garbage & the dead bird across the street,
cats & bats earlier we eat coffee & cherry pie with vanilla ice cream
at the village restaurant & talked about our little dogs identities &
the play from boston university a great play the mexican american's
chorus line, I'll write in the dark, home eat tomatoes & potatoes a
constant dripping flat tire, I wrote about that the message ends,
bat got your tongue & insults freckles pennies beer amontillado
magic words to dispel a bat the peoples home encyclopedia mystic
mysteries of the valley of tom ball mountain: squeaking noises at
night noise in the bedroom as if someone is coming nearer & nearer
& up the stars, ed's poking me with his elbow, g is reading, f is
asleep i think to make a mystery of it to murder a bird a crow to
kill a bat leave the doors open at dusk when you write there's
nothing to feel nothing to feel but smoke in front of the slide
projector rain and prisms prisms and rain we have no identity do
you need you one or two or more or would you rather go right
out the door, at dusk, and on to something new, and you? two-
two to wit ha ha, hoo hoo, hoot, who whit, whoo, who what how
hoo shoo boo moo light flicker too for you moo land animal too,
custom guilt, orang utang & slang, & bang a gang of clang, beep
roar growwl hoot, honk ducks wild geese & fleece, mallards in the
lining of my lying down position posture my new coast & coat &
swift hen, the hen I bought, when I was new, a review, a bat a hat
on my head I hope, not slides of july one and five kodachrome photo-
flood & mother earth purples gentle tones of slick movie magazines
& someone says five minutes miss badney & did k drink from the
bottle of crisco oil & someone says do you watch rehearsals every
day & g stirs, the rain seems to be dripping all over but isnt the
sky is dry as a bone as a peach as a plum the sky is done over, ed
moans freya is quiet we are camping in the nest in the woods care-
less nest bat nest who's dreaming of bats who's promising them
things? Suzy parker falls in love with the late gary cooper & diane
varsi his daughter approves, I'm itchy I've lost my memory I've lost
my money in a minute lost it in a card game, dont, come, on, too,
strong, he said, the other itchy man on the poolside table top
dancing like a poor ragged crow, not scared, where is everyone &
where is ice & where is ferns for delivery, tv & car where is mescaline

light & tight where is furniture & furnace, furman & furnmenace
furn ice & ferry growth, hippopotamus & lost toy grimace & colonial
kernel & cool southern dopes their drops of icy crinoline & milk &
mulch & so it's raining harder & harder on the night it was supposed
to clear, try to get g & e to be serious together with me watching,
real, play the trumpet, steal, skate, couple of skaters & a couple of
thieves, houses, what people live in, a crackling crunching noise in
the forest, like bears breaking bottles near but not visible & some-
one says not a garbanzo bean like grandma browns baked beans
faint but not sticky, not sticky & almost white, they are tan as the
whites of grace's eyes, but beans, beady yes, shouldnt be tan, should
be brown as the ace of spades with red in them, red eyes in the face
of the moon, red eyes sinking in a half-face before the sun has really
set, face all day, the other way, the other side of the page, with a
back to it, is redder, fuller, a red car, at least six of them, fast as
typewriters, go at 70 mph, speed up to leaving the light or the tv
on all night needing someone to stand guard duty, taking shifts to
sweat out the bat or bats in the belfry, wondering how if they sleep
all day there could be so much to write down in such large letters
to add to address, strangely, I couldnt understand it, to no one,
keeping the narrative going, & now has grace gone to sleep & will
I have to turn out the light in chronological order, the 1st to the
31st and vice versa, I mean backwards & things straight & a certain
heavy rain beating down now thicker and thicker, thumb & fore-
finger & head even or maybe starting with head & coming to some
kind of climax circus & thinning out & coming to it again, reach
here higher in the crooked the slanted belfry, where lights, after
lights, artificial ones, tungsten shine, how? into infinity widening
the depth of field to account for reflections with everyone sleeping
how but the book & the pictures in a book & lights flashing trees
moving, cut down, the house moving, the walls the lights pinned to
the walls crunching in on me, a discussion: the lights on for no rea-
son & search & suddenly g & e both awake & why dont we all start
fucking to upset this night so determined to crunch down through
the trees over this house & this curtain in alford coming down off
the mountain, cupped over, I wish it under, feathers in the ground
an aching a fire a reach for effect come sinister crackling & pounding
& beating, high growing secret & frowning & seven sets & series all
secret, certain wonder, sex, ceiling, cylinders brakes souls & elevators,

176

satchels of coming over, how i got there & over, heat, niche, cave,
batman & robin, robin hood & hood milk, it's all the same, sinking
dressing the stars, some sun, sunday now & such & this: I see pink
I see pink ink, a shaft of light a kernel of corn in the garbage, drops,
rains a bursting cloud ears hurt & at right angles to this: sac a sexy
lunch of & sac a sexy lunch love month drunks & month drunks or
ducks and mom'll drink vodka & tv'll drink it oo and eec sec dry
mad money & sex & sec dry mad mommy & tilt on desert eye op
now new & kilton stewart & kilton's vest his eye op now, new & on
gray stamen-money the vestry grows & beat the om's eye out for
tryin it, my heart my eyes serve out the cannibal status-seeker status-
seeker at the cannibal status-seeker at lay over in pittsburgh on the
country searchway where thule match ultima, struck a thicket on
the chest struck a thicket on incest as an intro, strike the thicket's
thickest intro, curbway long purple legs of strike that case right
thru & strike that, can like, can try, safest lifeless poison & the
safest lifeless position is the safest lifeless platoon, a fool, aloof is
in & a fool aloof is in the lifeless pink pillow with the lifeless blue
stain the stain it was a web, a web still making dolls I'm getting ex-
cited I'm getting over I'm continuing on, on coffee: webs that's
jack read flaubert, no you, me: the spider webs of the barn, the
spider webs over the barn, read flaubert no you, me, b., over the
spider webs of the barn over closer the spider web of the white barn
over the trees whited out just a little green in the right hand corner
over lines over a dog upside down the dog that was drooling so much
with his tongue out, they mounted the last two rolls upside down or
was it the camera, over & a triple of cars all over the place a truck
traveling on a building a gas station over jacobs pillow and a crooked
well, I went hitched to pick up the car or with somebody's wife,
over, over now, it's over, I've righted it, over webs get alot of ex-
posure over a very straight gas station, they took master charge over
so much I cant see it, white, over the sky a corner of something in
the sky over I've realized it, it's me frowning over at myself in the
picked up car, I got an estimate, over two hundred dollars two bills
slightly over two bills, little bit over purple restaurant & bowling
alley over cocktails over cock over tails & two plain cars parked,
detectives cars over detectives dead bodies, detectives over cock-
tails, to make something of something: it's over, to make something
of anything: & done with, alot of the past was under, over is joy,

over e & m in a headband making explosives over into the dark side
of the human mind & over e the army light over jeans, over me dark
under snakeskin & white pants, turn over, over he looks over he holds
a piece of the explosive in one hand & m looking over too, one arm
bent over e & nick light the explosive near a haystack outside the
barn, it's over they both bend over: ties, poles, magic, over: double
exposure double explosion over little terence's head he's sitting in
the grass & there are three, one over the other: barn, car, hand, flare,
pencil: I watch it, over the light through the barn windows, vines
growing over, telephone wires hanging over the hill & a swimming
pool an umbrella over the mountain over my shoulders & dust in
the light catches my eye, lights my side & any umbrella over the
mountains looks up over: I'm on top of the mountain, sun through
tree moves over now further over than it was: I made it over over
evening light on field: five trees & two rows mountains parched hay
& hay season over apple tree in hay: magic & fever spread over pool
blue by red white barn, look through birdhouse, space intrude
space over garage over make a space over make a light & over in-
trude over sun walks in on eye, intrude over sun make spectacle
blue & a spot, eye like cloud, a harsh one, over birdhouse in sky
like pole up a tree five holes for birds come in over see through
barn light up to a certain point & through to green light, came over
to the other side where terence is still in the grass, a finger over a
path own a path light light green, I went back up the hill I went
over where I'd been before the pool dips expands over flows over
it's rained over sky been before same sky thin clouds cover pervade
thin layer no holes in it: we went home over puddle on the deck I
went over the field once more, a review: more light it's gone over
the sky enough of it & ed's back from close-up I'm behind a back
against green, it calms down here but I'm closer come closer to
grace red hair makes a face blue shirt freya & g at the phone booth
over in town, striped shirts reflections, grace on the phone freya
stares hates pictures, a girl in a florid shirt gets out of a car a wo-
man sits on a bench grace goes over to the phone & calls new hamp-
shire: the reflections guide my own arm it's gone & it's extending
over an open newspaper covered with trees & the reflections guide
my own arm so I dont remember this at all at all & nothing is com-
posed, extending over, two breasts, that brains should give rise to a
knowing consciousness at all, this is the one mystery which returns,

no matter what sort the consciousness is & what kind the knowledge
may be: sensations, aware of mere qualities, involve the mystery as
much as thoughts, aware of complex systems, involve it: and a day is
over another one begins exactly as it happened so lets pool all our
mysteries into one great mystery and I dont remember this at all
at all, it's bright sun for a minute & raining all morning the furmans
pull out, it's quarter to one or quarter to two on saturday again on
saturday all over, the mystery that brain processes occasion knowledge
at all: I'm lost so lost how lost can you be when everywhere you go
it's morning & the sun's coming up over a map, lost & I am losing
someone or something how lost can you be when kodachrome II
& some double exposures show, we must go. Ed decides not to come
with us & we creep go to town, I take the rest of the pictures, come
out, go about, we make ourselves richer we explore. G & freya make
calls to bus depot & middlebury, we weep, hot sun, crowded in the
town hippies crowd in front of the library I creep, I weep scour I
wish I could scout I scour, ignore the story build a cemetery: eat
seltzer & grilled cheese in nejaimes buy bacon milk half & half
blueberry yoghurt packet of smokes we return, astronauts on tv
astronaut of dust son of tv: tension ed goes takes slide projector
goes I weep creep about scout put shirts in the basin clean up gar-
bage outside upstairs: collect luck collect glasses sweep upstairs
& downstairs counter, find checkbook have iced coffee freya weeps
grace creeps outside the store the ancient the old: do checkbook a
mess no money money here there write postcards to calvin, r, rII,
v&k, rIII, worn out & light I meant tight, pictures a boy an exclama-
tion means finally. Earlier two people a french man with a camera,
a girl in red pants come by sky its saturday all over again from blue-
berry hill, ed wanted to be on his own today or at least not bothered
by the details of the memory of the presence of other people, all
around, I give the girl a match through the top of the dutch doors
I throw the dead bird away, M will be back tonight we must open
the doors at dusk is now to try to get rid of the bat, bats: I thought
dusk was morning I thought the esophagus was the glottis, dusk &
dawn calm & I killed a wasp, how? high school we're all on speed &
sex & sink & more sky a pie & I stop rhyming today it's the last day,
rhyming its the day stop today last dead, am I lucky or dead? Blue-
berry hill, talking, cars: amazing grace? days? place? dead? animal?
bat? curse? igor & vampire, gut & bird, wing? I picked him up by

the wing, bugs, & then washed my hands glands? dirt? sand & snow,
back & light, close & up, ant & frantic wasp, gut & Now, pebbles &
stones, fill me up, birds & the byrds, we almost saw & lights dim-
ming with the water heater & I feel heavy I scout, grace feels
heavy & I think ed feels heavy, triangle changes in the weather now,
we do the tape about high school: 1½ houses 1½ hours: I have a
very poor memory because I was never systematically made to learn
poetry at school: my love is like a red red rose that's newly sprung
in june, attention: a process fills its old bed in a different way from
that in which it makes a new bed, so, ed walks up the stairs, we
walk down the road the bats not here yet, take pictures see cows
bulls & car breaks down a little nervous sitting here in the hammock
where bats fly across generally I'm afraid I'm filled with fear it's
always different & g has read a book, sear, jackson maclow: there's
something to it & something against it, how's this, I cant write our
house down right now how house I feel about sex or about one
time, we fuck like tonight even though I have thousands of thoughts
lying in a new bed even though it takes me over making up the old
bed it would be good maybe to be sick today like it's good maybe to
sweat today & something heavy the half moon & some holding back,
musk, left from the air & lift from the air & something heavy &
relaxed maybe & now thinking I'll get trychinosis from the pork or
from the air or from an r & something heavy & now relaxed maybe
tomorrow will come from the air I'm full of & pooling our mysteries
we fall into one great mystery & tomorrow will come from the air I'm
full of boccaccio 70's on tv & we ate beside the sausage home fries
& corn & next time we have a house in the country, as if I'm closing
as if this is an end, let's not invite anyone to come & alot of people
will come & look at us as if we split & is this an ongoing operation
that brain processes occasion knowledge at all or not? can you stop
2 test? to rest? at all? make noise make sounds the hoot of the owl
howt bool ghoul & crush crunch & black back bracken slime blick
click whose click a click like ink ant sluck & tick tac toe with a dot
& what looks like some Indian pipe, a white fungus. I dont wanna
finish. Might as well use the ruler for this, might as well be exact as
a calendar like remembering a calendar scares the shit out of you in
the bright lights big city & baby I will violate your rights some day:
extending over: an open newspaper covered with trees is me it isnt
mounted, turn towards me now turn around & there's always enough

smoke, for what? & can you see me well I could go down & get
some & I could become how become become what for the end no
end just float just a float that can turn into anything by using color
& design: & this idea of my having had those ideas is a very compli-
cated idea, including the idea of myself of the present moment re-
membering & that of myself of the past moment conceiving & the
whole series of the states of consciousness which intervened between
myself remembering & myself conceiving clouds make a wall, stop,
light grass over what's on the deck & antenna juts just too neat for
clouds jesus a blue so grey & dark freya in the rain & dark yellow
garage dark road I'm waiting for what will happen & it's grey it's
not clear the telephone pole the best bent & darker freya her breasts
the darker road & this material always presents its denseness cause
it's impossible, poetry & memory: I am married 6½ years. My wife
worked when we were first married for about 1½ years. Instead of
things getting better the firm I was with showed signs of failing &
my wife went to work again. Shortly after that my firm failed & I
was practically unemployed for a year. During this time I attended
a radio-television course in the evenings. I could not obtain satis-
factory employment at that time in the radio field. After that period
I obtained employment in original line which was upholstery fabric
line. February of last year I obtained my present position with the
western electric company testing communications equipment. This
position enabled my wife to leave her employment. The point I am
trying to bring out is that my wife only worked because of condi-
tions. February 27 of this year my wife gave birth to a baby girl &
being a nursing mother she will not be able to work for at least a
year. As you will note I had 1¼ years training in radio theory &
practice & have been employed for the past year using this training.
I feel I am doing more for the war effort where I am than I would
in the service as I am 35 years old & probably would not hold up
too well in the rigors of life in the service. & was I going back &
forth cant concentrate on ends the middle bellows out grows over
first & last: freya's my sister, that's good. There's a small light a
car coming, we walked down the road the 3 of us or the 6 or 8 of
us, f, g & l eye, there's some gift being given here, repeat it till you
get it right & car closer best car at night some mystery ends with
mystery beginning headlights & is that white after all this dark all
yellow-orange parking lights, tungsten light explosure table, basic

daylight exposure & daylight daylight daylight exposure in bright or hazy
sun in cloudy bright in heavy overcast in open shade, existing light
pictures & daylight exposure table for kodachrome II film with
shutter speeds & f-stops, given, my wife due to the attention re-
quired by the baby will not be able to work & being in an essential
industry I will be more useful to the war effort by staying where I
am & they are having a difficult time getting my replacement & my
name & a darker road I panic no light, a still darker road it looks
like the backs of my friends, the ones who were with me, I dont
know cant see the sun made spectacles for me & I was complaining
of no light & shakespeare, I'm here, with the telephone poles, kill
the king quite a sky, more of it changed the rest in heaven so we
thought it was corny but it isnt & that, over, blue that over blue
could be so real like a set & more, for instance, I drove through
Paris a day or two ago & though I saw plainly some sixty or eighty
new faces I cant now recall any one of them. Some extraordinary
circumstances, a fit of delirium or the excitement of hashish would
be necessary to give them a chance of revival, and, so, lose control,
if you want, stirring up dust, if any, the end of the play sun set sets
not the end of the day but when someone puts a fire there, I will,
I made it glow still burning & we move down religious sets on fire
burn religion down, saint bernadette was made a saint by devil's
advocate a process fills its old bed there's nothing black there's
nothing clear there's no nathaniel hawthorne here there's nothing
black I cant believe this & that car must've killed us, hatch & sear:
in all part in point in singing part in mountains, part in point, the
store the ancient the old always have intermissions, part of this is
too bold, but owning a part of the old may turn into science, part
of the bold, that's the ending. In quiet parts of the old: now, after,
always, a light, we silence not ours but the enemy's toward an ef-
ficiency wanting an end. The end. We make ourselves richer, we
start what's untold, in papers, turned into words not marks, that's
red & design which is racial absorbed, where are elements, man, to
raise, he's happy, nothing in detroit the hall of fantasy excludes,
why not: plumber, a mass, a nude, & so on to alternates & aver-
ages, averages & tombs, two spaces told spaces, deny it again, sold.
Question in pleat, the unanimous fold now in rites then in bells,
execute: ignore the story build a cemetery. An abstraction, the end,
the owl, where in point, language of country, exhort, so to end the

expelling of exploit the untelling of dams putting in these reminders
of death, that's purple: toward denying to continue to the end, here
by continuing the end of & done we expel them for social the kind
of space of the actual, import of breath & with it the space for space
of the rest as a joke for retelling cannot persist in unpeeling all the
world's explorations, we rise to get up at the stroke of, found what
was lost in the heat of, white battle & waves & found in rough the
gut of it, having in melting how, the rest in awe, still how in awe,
flower in laugh, in flower in waves & singing & entering & awe again
& this time it's awe of the reverse, that's green, of returning to scream
without thinking, the end, in thinner, of thick & simpler of trees in
parrot to lisp, sea anemone, closed. Apology in rest: research isnt fes-
tive, looking for names, burning down piers & papers & scoring the
time I'm translated to shore on the back of a whale & to see like a
mirror turned on the port, so for saying injection as far as it goes in
the arm, truth, of black symbols, will adopt parents that cannot
grow: anthem, emblem, knife, a knife for the course that ends like
this not like that & they'll all come to orbit, arbit, exhibit in the
courts by force, we'll make the exchange & to count, continue, to
embrace, forgetting parts important to 'in concurrence', that's
grey. We'll fissure the end & cleave in parting by statements by
surgery by force, cerebral from parent, dim from latin, everything's
in half, we do it by force, by the time & this is the final please let
me ending in dive in ring proposing in answer the positions for:
silence, growing, minerals, closed sky another & how to prepare:
rhyme to give, phial in waves, blank to prompt in ending amend,
that's brown & that car must've killed us, it will this way but I leave
in that dark sloping hill & nothing & nothing but one long line on a
horizon plane & two lights another car another are & some fire
like a candle glow, two cars in a row one more golden, you can
make this out in other days that brains should give rise to a knowing
consciousness at all & this is the one mystery which returns no matter
what kind of consciousness it is & what kind of knowledge it may
be & sensations, aware of just qualities, mere qualities, involve the
mystery as much as thoughts, aware of complex systems, what other
days? The pile of film on the floor black & blue & exposed green &
that puddle country sideways hole that runs off shaped like a man
reflecting trees the bib of a dress for ground into green & wire, over,
dont know the end extending over into light, over there to the left,

over above upon beside beyond & like the branch hung over the
house & they boarded over the window & we'll discuss it over din-
ner & she spread the frosting over the cake & he cast a spell over our
group & he will preside over the meeting & I flew over the lake &
the city's over the border & we went over the states of consciousness
& the dictionary was in production over a period of several years &
it cost over five dollars & stay over easter & he went over the
precipice by design & they were gone three hours or over & the
wound healed over & he took out his money & counted it over &
the tree fell over & they turned the plank over & we went back &
did it over & over in England they did too & the party's new policy
won him over but it did him no good cause they murdered him any-
way & you make your property over to her & the game is over &
how I got over & he is three hours over for the week & that shot
hit over & that bomb explodes over & we were over against them
from end to end & besides there's more than that because over &
over & over again it's all over it's all over it's all over with, there's
nothing can be done with it, like light, up from the field on a house
on glass, tired question impatient question a fog question shows
nothing, wont receive, the impregnable house like past door closed
old white flowers older dried weeds get darker & where's light
shown, it's cool. Time running on its own all backwards & you can
run but you sure cant hide, there are no secrets here, there's a part
of my memory's a picture show & then I think what do I do next:
next to memory running with memory motion information & design
design a motion design forward motion design style let me save you
the trouble, let me repeat: I could design style conceals, let me add
simply add & you accumulate cause you come close like the dreams
& pictures all over the walls & floor: the best branches blow back-
wards but one left: look closer, over again, no conclusion, please
grey please it, look up pleasure, what's his pleasure what's the
matter, it's sense a safe return & one great tree on an orchestra,
cant speak question stump question & it spoke, not me, I carried
it around for weeks: bats & bats inside the house & at the windows,
giant moth, a dead bird on the doorstep, nothing leaves & a worm
with two antennae like a crooked brown bean, a pollynose, noise,
on the cellar floor, four spiders under the table & their debris,
we found the bat nest & do they have nests there's a raccoon at the
door & that was last year someone told me about a field near here

where in the evening the field is filled with deer, the owl in pleasant valley & the silver fox, porcupine & crow, they're in cages, the yellow bird completely gone except for his wings, black wings, many crows, the worm is crawling curling coming closer he's in the shadow of the table, the man across the street loves his red cat so much he tried to poison b's dog, she owns this house & the house: the house changes its size: when the doors are open at dusk to give the bats a chance to leave, I feel I should leave the house but unless someone else is home, the strange man who lives across the street who peers makes me stay very close to the house when I leave, he's supposed to be a russian prince who lives with his mother & a princess, there's a house on ice glen road where another princess is supposed to live & her house is stone & so hard to keep warm that nobody lives there & fred lord has put his whole house & farm up as collateral for the black panthers & blueberry hill where you cant see the house from the road is the house of some french diplomats, a car full of french people & once we met the son of the guy who owns the lenox photo shop on a street in new york city & french people stop here for directions to blueberry hill & the last time we lived up here we lived in a house that was connected to another smaller house where a doctor of psychology lived with his wife & seven pistols, one shot gun, & when we left they were about to move to a bigger house down the road & right now I'm in the cellar & in front of the fire now & at the window now at dawn & upstairs, the room where we sleep, that room is like a tree house, the floor slants up & out towards the field & towards a row of long narrow windows, on each side of the room, each side of the room has a large diamond shaped window, through these windows you can see trees, a little below one of them is another long narrow window, this one shows you the rest of the house & lying in bed I can look through this window & further on through one of the downstairs windows & out to the parallel trees & Gail: I had met gail before but today I found out her name, she comes from west stockbridge, her grandmother until she died owned the card lake hotel there, we used to go there for beers & cheeseburgers, one night tina who lived on main street took me over to the hotel very late to get a pack of cigarettes & I met gail's grandmother. When she died she left gail & her sister some money, about $14,000. Gail took the money, bought a car & went to florida to sleep on the beach. When gail told me she had inherited the money,

I thought her parents were dead, that's the way I had inherited about
the same amount of money. The hotel has been bought by a man
from connecticut. When we got to my house gail told me that the
next house down the road, a white one, is owned by the parents of
a boy she was in love with, he's in california & just getting back into
heroin. Gail went to school with Sprague, tina & I had invaded
sprague's house one night when we took mescaline, that's when I
met him, he's playing now at the silver city bar, we go there alot,
with jacuqes, for beers & cheeseburgers & where's the light question
you look too good too professional conducting those trees by that
tree, there's the light & that blue dot is new for the end, none: wires
across & wing clouds make a great gigantic bird thin as one feather
for point in some direction where was the eye: my hand in this was
that, that tree by the telephone pole was a space I'm in. Here the
phone wires slope in gentle they're loose from the pole or as if so,
weeds & trees stand up & into the air: in a system every fact is con-
nected with every other by some thought-relation & the consequence
is that every fact is retained by the combined suggestive power of all
the other facts in the system & forgetting is almost impossible &
into the air & a white towel flies onto the deck, coffee cups notes
leaves a leaf a bag & right into it again, an edge of grass & a picture
of me I cant solve the mystery I'm crooked & full my mouth tom's
arm, dont look up it's only a piece, matter how veins & a cut hand
flat on the space of the deck, storms, it's pictures all over the walls
& floor & he leans against the machine a fortune in tom's shirt &
who do you love I mean who do you love just come away with me
& we are an image speed we are an image sound & some song sung
being sun & call me call me any old time, ed rests in bed, they've
turned the people working into rest & they've turned the people
working into rest & you can run but you sure cant hide, hurricane
erica attica station prison & that view again because the story goes:
I'll wheel the colors you like to your new location but I'm lost so
lost how lost can you be when everywhere you go it's morning &
the sun's coming up over a map & mountains in merica zoom no
moon, that's silver & gold case you didnt know you fucker & my
hunger creates a food that everybody needs: matter how veins &
a cut hand flat on the deck in my tye-dyed shirt I want to leave
this place I want to get out of here I want to move into an eternal
space the right space I want to design it have you freed me to addict

myself to take that risk, escape no longer draws me in, just kill the
pain, take my wrists in your hands, I cant find anything on the floor,
we have no regular plan, no drama, in the dark everything's a mess,
there's no end to it in a space as big as this no walls & I hate my-
self for keeping on going as if the production of something out of
nothing out of here where there is nothing were worthwhile. Pre-
serve my sainthood. You help to preserve it, perpetrating the finest
evil that was ever devised, a false glamor on the surface of simple
veins bulging, their blood bursts back into the needle, & then flows
through back through the veins, southeast asia, axis, infusion, in-
jection, replacement maze there was a fog all through the city be-
fore my eyes, I was sweating what's the verdict of sleep: I cant find
out: observe me as I trance myself beyond death: write it down a
written record dead poet flying crows & a trace, a stronger texture
impossible to tear, I still imitate I still review, the fog goes on there's
a name for it: the surface of the eyes pervert senses, & double:
crumpled up & we threw in the towel a white towel half rewound
and the end of a joint half sky, those trees expect to connect: the
other half of those trees is around but days lead on: there was an
almost blind pennsylvania farmer who could remember the day of
the week on which any date had fallen for forty-two years past &
also the kind of weather it was & what he was doing on each of more
than fifteen thousand days & points point more directions than you
give away without an end so I stopped remembering days & made a
new thing haze, but a set & an end but then, something more, day,
now fit that in, what will who do next: when I stopped remember-
ing days & made a new thing & so on to day & you are eating & the
idea that I would do anything for him has become a joke, tomorrow
the joke's perverted & I mean it again. what is it? that he would do
anything for me is clearer, is accepted, is loved. Sure the love is in-
herent in murder & the closeness designs a wish for death, the death
of someone is the death of all. Reminded. Can you still see? A small
dark & trembling tree is able to reassemble the qualities of wind
within its leaves, by means of them. The tree, its image is a trick,
come out of nowhere, committed, Committed to an institution,
you must stay there, committed to a man or woman, you must
leave them free, committed a sin a crime, you must commit
another & maybe commit another person to your crime. You can-
not be alone, you cannot escape. Bulbous images in dark balloons

lustrous growths of them emerge from under your arms from your
groin from whatever's beneath your feet, I cant imagine. Insects
bite you bite your feet, lay eggs on them, hatch & grow even larger
than the haze of your eyes can conceal. You are eating, a day is
over another one begins exactly as it happened: the mystery stated
up to two cars coming at us then light on other days & nothing seems
to be happening then but that mystery, maybe felt, not then but
now, ties in the pole high-wire act to moving, moving & a trip: I
had to go get, watch it, stop, & pool all our mysteries into one
great mystery & back to magic, left jewels there & bats brought out
the light over, about space, about face & sun, set, mystery at me,
finale by the tree: ones, ones & days. A process fills its old bed &
then it makes a new bed: to you past structure is backwards, you
forget, you remember the past backwards & forget.

Dreaming

Cause memory & the process of remembering of seeing what's in
sight, what's data, what comes in for a while for a month & a
month's a good time for an experiment memory stifles dream it
shuts dream up. What's in sight, it was there, it's over, dream makes
memory present, hidden memory the secret dream, it's not allowed,
forbidden, dont come out the door, there's an assassin at it or a
lion, wild Indian, a boar, a little bear upside down in the dream, so,
memory creates an explosion of dream in August & I no longer
rest I dont rest anymore I dont resist anymore & there's a haze
then & two eyes my eyes just eyes wide open & this is the climax
the reversal, light inches warmth toward the eye in dream & I look
at you I play I'm exhausted: cause fear had already started as a
finish to memory & memory as an opening onto a finish for fear.
And dream's an analogy to reprocessing in process, so rewrite it it's
changed but a memory according to how you record it now & as it
could go on forever, this could, dream's a memory kept in process
kept in present by whose consciousness by whose design, so,
memory creates an explosion of dream in August & let me narrate
for you & listen, let me violate the rights you got let me tell you that
I dream let me design it: August 4: Grace & I are in a movie directed
by Jacques-in-charge. & first the men in the movie & I try to
make it, a reversal a withdrawal an October Sunday & a man wears
a cape, he leaves his rich mother early in the morning without sleep,
he walks down the road & I follow, lose him, there's no more man
in the house & we're on our own now, who are the girls? & we are
trying to hitchhike on the road but there's a giant evergreen stretch-
ing out in the way & October Sunday traffic & a man wears a cape,
he leaves the house early in the morning, he leaves his rich mother,
I follow but lose him. We wind up in church, a liberal service, Dan
Graham is conducting something in the aisles & he says this wont
hurt a bit we are conducting a test & Grace & I have no shirts on:
a white machine is put against our shoulders, then a long needle
shot through, through the right shoulder, a dull sharp pain & I ask
them to stop & I say Grace & I have already made love as the end
of the movie & now we laugh at Jacques-in-charge for not predicting
that·Grace & another woman will begin to make love, are making
love, the director's a fool & Jacques-in-charge says I just wish you
girls wouldnt always be wearing those leather jerkins or smocks or

jodphers or whatever-they-are & I insist they are dresses & Jacques-in-charge says even though we are improvising the movie we at least have to have a really good designer, for costumes I guess, but the movie's over, we're in church, we're going backwards, it's the end, I have my feet wrapped, I have wrapped up my feet & unwrapped them, then you wrap your feet & unwrap them to make them so small so small you cant walk: I was afraid to go out alone, she was afraid to go out to them alone. Ed & I leave to pick up film, to pick up heavy radiation containers in a drug store, radiation containers for each roll of film & we laugh in the church, yes you get to make love in exchange for every treatment, no you get love in exchange for every treatment, yes every treatment is evolving now into sex is making love & we laugh in the church, I try to put a white blouse on, it's part of the costume design that's over & it's too small but the blouse is really too big, big as someone's wedding dress & you say does this hurt? You bet it does, so I wear black in the morning & I dream, a white market: as I seem to dream her dreams as I seem to walk her steps & what's the pleasure it's the pleasure of ice & removal & taking nothing taking no one, as if, you speak, you are planning the imminence of your own death & only have a moment to lose, close to loss of consciousness, on the edge of loss of consciousness, at any time, a desertion the man leaves his rich mother, any moment, an intention - to lose & I accuse Marie of planning & I am trying to understand something, a narrative, you wrap up your feet & then you make your feet too small to walk but her steps, someone else's steps, they get mixed up & will a white market fit in at all, white slavery, sold, I'm too sold on this I dont trust it like I didnt trust her I accused her of planning death as her own pleasure & she says it's at my pleasure at my leisure & it took years & Marie look at this it's what I say & I say at my anger, at my anger is a place for your invasion of my seduction, so, you planned the disappearance of my desire: August 5: Night, I am in stockbridge & stockbridge is a white town, Indians on the school board, a liberal reservation, I am in stockbridge I think to meet Ed who is away. Justine Freya & I climb up on a high chair at least a hundred feet in the air, I say it's to watch something & we get scared, dizzy, I put my head in Freya's lap, she's full of patience or something, it turns me on I have a long quiet orgasm coming down the bannister, the saint's pole, the isolation tank, the light,

the absence of light, or are we still up there, I cant tell & do people
notice my legs in a spasm as Rosemary falls down the stairs. We
drive to main street white main street & I realize Ed will not be
here at least until tomorrow & I wonder what we're doing here. I
suggest we go across the bridge to the stocks in the sticks, still
punished still unpunished to Ridgewood, while, Graham & Bob are
bending over backwards, Bobby drive-ass in the front seat & black
Graham brown in the back, to kiss each other & it seems real strong
& I wonder why I dont approve of it & it's cause there are still no
men, it's a withdrawal & I dont touch Bob. I am attached to a tele-
phone pole, hello Marie how come you never call me & I'm attached
to a telephone pole like the trucks driving away with the pay phones
you're trying to make a call on in em & before all this I've carried
Justine over a lake, she stood in the water, it was over her head like
it was over my head like it was over your head when you watched
everybody make love, grown, ups, & I picked her up. The lake was
full of people. & I picked her up. Over the bridge in Ridgewood we
are & has there been an accident, we're in front of my house the
house I grew up in & suddenly everybody starts making noise, alot
of noise. & I've brought alot of people with me, groups, on foot in
cars & at the moment I see this I see Vito standing inside the gate.
There's a hammock hung in the courtyard & is Vito in the hammock,
no. Still no men. But he detains me, by name. & at this same mo-
ment again my car is on the sidewalk & people begin to file out of
the house I was born in, files of butlers files of clowns, they're but-
lers or clowns, it's a gauntlet, all the houses, especially my house &
butlers & clowns line the courtyard & women with faces made-up
down the street lean out their wondows yelling about the noise &
who is it under the sheet being carried out, it's no one, nevermind
& the, a, woman, D. downstairs comes out & I hide in the hammock
calmly covering my face with elbow & arm, like sleep. But I'm
panicking I'm full of fear & I say she'll call the police, she's running
to call the police, it's because of the noise I make it's because of the
noises I make returning, running to the scene of the crime so quick
over the bridge from Stockbridge to Ridgewood, why what's my
crime what's my mistake we must make our escape, I get into the
car & someone a girl has shown me that the gearshaft or shift &
some other pole pole of the car have come loose, she puts them
back but the car doesnt start & I lock the gear pole in place, it starts,

I am driving on the opposite sidewalk, I am driving away, my body
shifts for the gears, I must move in a certain way, with the car &
there's confusion & rain & now Vito sees me & says "It's Bernadette."
I am walking with him in front of my car, he's an old man made up
for the stage, grey spots, bygones, on his face & I ask him what he
was doing there in the first place & he says mamma your mamma is
leaving there she's leaving them & I'm amazed & I think of it. I say
oh. So who's gonna run the gauntlet me or her? & I think we should
hurry, get back in the car but Vito & two friends who are with
him pulled out on motorcycles & I cant work it out, I cant stop
stop talking to him he detains me & he cant come in my car & leave
his motorcycle & we cant seem to arrange to meet in stockbridge &
by the time we've decided something & I'm about to get into the
car & we've still made no progress up the street, I see a hazy dark
police car in the street in the night, it's parallel to my car & the
top's down, they can see me they can make me out & I think we're
caught & I think I wake up heart beating & I try to fall asleep again
because I want to get away, make the escape, I cant make it so I
guess it's me who's gonna run the gauntlet for them, run through
the butlers the clowns the funeral service, the crime, the war. &
something drew me in, like a place you might get into, a foxhole,
for one. August 6: Ed can turn into a mother & Ed can turn into
a moth & fly. He was a rooster until I told him there was one down-
stairs, he was a rooster till I told him there was a rooster downstairs
& he cleans the wings of another moth, he is acting like a moth &
four of Holly's bodies have been left in our barn & care, he is will-
ing to do it & four of her bodies left in our barn, who is the fourth,
where a stream-swamp flows through & I am disguised on a boat
trip, disguised as an animal, I cant remember, I look for masks in
the museum, body masks & who do you pretend to be or watch or
watch for, visions, I find a mask with zippered nose & eyes, then it
sees me & two young lawyers come, I must be suing her, I wont
take credit for the crime this time cause this time it's murder & I
know I didnt do it, she sees me, full moon. August 7: You
planned the disappearance of my desire. Ed is giving me medical
tests. It's an art show & the show is the kiss: we kiss you you kiss
us, the whiskers deal. & we're driving, little bears. & Ed takes one
acupuncture needle & heads it towards me, he says with this one I
touch the liver kidney & gall bladder & on & on & someone's father

is on stage for the kiss: you planned the disappearance of my desire
& to be simple of her you have to be him but who could you,
recognize, be & in dream & I dream a blond boy who does the pro-
jections pretends he doesnt know me, we go up the stairways of
different apartments & finally to Jacques, his heavy steam-bath
house, damp corridors with a round bed around stone couches &
the bed is stone too. August 10: Many people come to the house.
I am asleep in the bed past the two long windows, so I must be
sleeping outside. There's a curtain round the bed, drawn on one
side. Jacques is there & many middle-aged couples come & people
fade in & out of the background, there's a meal cooking. & Jacques
says to me Jimmy was here, he asked if Bernadette was home & I
say I'm too old for that & Jacques laughs, agrees & says Parnell was
here he didnt ask for Bernadette. I roll around on the bed, I sleep,
pretend to sleep in my sleep. Dinner is ready so everyone has to
leave & one of the couples wonders if the maid, what maid?, made
arrangements to take the kids out to dinner cause the kids are nuts
I mean disturbed about being thrown out & they say then I guess
we really dont have to call before we come & someone wants
cigarettes but they're too 'cracked' & we find a whole drawerful of
different brands & now it's J's house again & we give the guy some
cigars, they're not so cracking. I'm up now as everyone's leaving,
they all leave through the hallway, I've been stretching around the
bed, in hiding, in cracking that's how you make gasoline, I've also
cracked the case & now I'm crawling I'm sliding on the floor I
meet someone's legs, we talk, the legs are Michael Brandman's
legs & I put my knee in his crotch, they had old grand-dad in the
drawer with the cigars, it was only four years old & I wake up turn
over & dream I am outside in the field, only, the way it is now, it's
half a field, in the dream it's a full field a full circle with a path
around & I say I think I see a turkey, I see wings flapping in the
distance, it comes comes closer very quickly, grey wings moved up
like a zoom & I see a small face sticking out like a man in a bunny
suit & when it's close it's a group a whole ensemble: a woman in a
turkey costume being pulled by a sled on which are the three ages
of disease: a little child, someone else & a large grown naked sexless
hairless man. They begin to do their act. The turkey moves up &
embraces the child, the child gets into position with the 'someone
else' & they all make a background for the large man who moves

around finally to show his asshole, spread his anus, for the others,
And they are begging in a way. By this time Ed has come & tries to
explain all this to me but no words come out of his mouth. He
seems familiar with it. I whisper something like, do they want
money but I know they dont. Money monkey turnkey & they havent
noticed us at all, they've pretended not to notice us except to come
right up in front of us like this & perform, perform their curing
dance, perform Iwo Jima, I think of actors & when I write this down
it turns me on. August 11: I see myself getting out of the car, I
stand around the old black car, at first I am ten or twelve years old,
I'm looking at myself, I think something like "that's not right,
move the film up now" & then I can see myself in front of the
younger self, but I look like I imagine I look & not like I look at
all: I look old as memory a hundred years old, not pretty, my face
is not defined, it's round, I painted an image of myself & it was
what I would look like in the future, over what was past, I couldnt
pin the present down & I think capture & kill sex. August 20: Blue
Earth walks in, only once, once more, he says kill them, they'll
die, you killed them, you give up, you do what you're told. He sees
the other people in the room, lined up like Indians & he whispers
you do what you're told, a person, a child, put yourself in the hands
of . . ., trails off into a hundred years old but new here & three deer
cross the road & someone says have you gotten into revealing your-
self more, nothing leaves. August 24: Dream about the theater still
& Bob shows pictures of fucking upside down to the librarian &
laugh & make-up & sleep between two, I cant see either of them,
they cant make love or plan to make love & open cars, movies
changed, flowers play upside down & lose this book & money too
& something else, I pay to get it back, we hold hands though. Labor
Day: Kaleidoscope, the fall foliage: In Massachusetts theres a yellow
fur running along the side of the road & on a field, sable, . . . &
someone is picking is harvesting the fur for fur coats & I am running
along the side of it I am running along it, no one sees it, to a barn
where there's a meeting a formal, forum, social gathering & I get
there & I'm looking for someone I'm looking for warren or ted &
the sky is full of foliage. I think it's the northern lights, it's tree
branches, colors you see, colors you never see in the sky, it changes
like a kaleidoscope turned slowly so that at some point everything
shifts like the minute hand on a school clock, you get to watch it,

you get to watch new colors new designs 4 a minute. I point this
phenomenon out to people, they dont see it. It's described on the
horizon & I'm amazed, I meet Ted in three states & he says to me
you get around & states, & this is the beginning of states of con-
sciousness & on the subway each stop is a state & I eat plenty of
bread & butter in cummington, there's no one home so I heap the
butter on the bread & lay more butter over it. Some people come,
nothing leaves, the house falls down. That's dreaming & baby what you
want baby I got it & all they are doing is wanting, seek out your
own hand writing hand writing of another one & pieced like eyes
they look together at the dream & who am I speaking of & who
am I talking to, I am talking with you I am violating you & my
length like the length of this table's body violates your separate
rights, stirring up dust, if any. Your own space & plenty of mo-
tion. Now why should you bother to be me in this way as a mix
which is final insult as ax on the head of the murderer & this is
this a public act: they get empty, thoughts fill them endlessly & all
they are doing is waiting all they are wanting is motion & beyond
that false ending on the last page on the cover of the book is a
fake a last fake a fake in a series, fake tree made into a book, re-
read what's been written etc. & beyond the space, no, the tree,
the chance to go there & baby that's what you want baby that's
what I got & energy never leaks out it runs around loose & the
tree is formless, it follows its rules around like a fake & someone
wants you to let you take them there & someone wants you to
let them take you there & you find it out, what's there, as a struggle
already dying to explore, what's there, as a piece, to mesmerize,
to suck you in to leave all out to include all, you gotta be ready
you're ready, eyes violate as I do every day, all born. Now you
tell me, can I say that